the

Mongols

The Peoples of Europe

General Editors: James Campbell and Barry Cunliffe

This series is about the European tribes and peoples from their origins in prehistory to the present day. Drawing upon a wide range of archaeological and historical evidence, each volume presents a fresh and absorbing account of a group's culture, society, and usually turbulent history.

Already published

The Etruscans
Graeme Barker and Thomas Rasmussen

The Byzantines
Averil Cameron

The Normans
Marjorie Chibnall

The Norsemen in the Viking Age
Eric Christiansen

The Lombards
Neil Christie

The Serbs
Sima Ćirković

The Basques *
Roger Collins

The English
Geoffrey Elton

The Gypsies
Second edition
Angus Fraser

The Bretons
Patrick Galliou and Michael Jones

The Goths
Peter Heather

The Franks *
Edward James

The Russians
Robin Milner-Gulland

The Mongols
Second edition
David Morgan

The Armenians
A. E. Redgate

The Britons
Christopher A. Snyder

The Huns
E. A. Thompson

The Early Germans
Second edition
Malcolm Todd

The Illyrians
John Wilkes

In preparation

The Sicilians
David Abulafia

The Irish
Francis John Byrne and Michael Herity

The Spanish
Roger Collins

The Scots
Colin Kidd and Dauvit Broun

The Picts
Charles Thomas

The Angles and Saxons
Helena Hamerow

*Denotes title now out of print

the
Mongols

Second Edition

David Morgan

Blackwell
Publishing

© 1986, 1990, 2007 by David Morgan

BLACKWELL PUBLISHING
350 Main Street, Malden, MA 02148-5020, USA
9600 Garsington Road, Oxford OX4 2DQ, UK
550 Swanston Street, Carlton, Victoria 3053, Australia

First edition published 1986
Paperback edition published 1990
Second edition published 2007 by Blackwell Publishing Ltd

10   2016

Library of Congress Cataloging-in-Publication Data

Morgan, David, 1945–
   The Mongols / David Morgan.—2d ed.
      p. cm.—(The people of Asia)
   Includes bibliographical references and index.
   ISBN 978-1-4051-3539-9 (pbk.)

   1. Mongols—History. I. Title

DS19.M67   2007
950'.2—dc22

2006050495

A catalogue record for this title is available from the British Library.

Set in 10 on 12.5 pt Sabon
by SNP Best-set Typesetter Ltd, Hong Kong
Printed and bound in Singapore
by Markono Print Media Pte Ltd

For further information on
Blackwell Publishing, visit our website:
www.blackwellpublishing.com

Contents

List of Maps and Plates

Maps

Plates

x   Illustrations

Preface to the Second Edition

Though a number of friends have been kind enough, since this book was first published in 1986, to suggest that I ought to prepare a second, revised, edition, I have until now always resisted the idea. This is for two reasons. First, my own preference, if I am to write a book, is for writing one I have not already written. Secondly, I think that this book is something of a period piece. It represents, or it attempts to represent, where the subject was at the point at which I finished it, in 1985. I did not think that it was a book that could easily be tinkered with. It would need to be rewritten completely; and that I was disinclined to embark on. On the other hand, the book has gone through twenty-two printings, which suggests that readers have found it useful; and I have over the years become increasingly uneasy at the extent to which it has, inevitably, become badly out of date and hence misleading at a number of points.

I owe a number of debts to Professor Peter Brown, the historian (almost the inventor) of Late Antiquity, among them the fact that, during long conversations in Tehran in 1974, he put into my head the idea that resulted in my first published article ('Cassiodorus and Rashīd al-Dīn . . .' – see the Bibliography: the article, improbably, was reprinted in 2005: see the Supplementary Bibliography under 'Hawting'). And now I have stolen another idea from him. In 2000 he published a second edition of his celebrated 1967 biography, *Augustine of Hippo*. He left the original text untouched, but added two chapters, one on new evidence, the other on new directions. It seemed to me that something on these lines might be a way of making *The Mongols* continue to be of use without my having to rewrite the entire book. For the Mongols, we have not, since 1985, acquired a sufficient quantity of new evidence for it to justify its own chapter, though there is no shortage of new directions. So I have merged Brown's two subjects into one chapter, chapter 9, 'The Mongol Empire since 1985'.

As I hope that chapter demonstrates, the past twenty years have been extraordinarily productive, so far as Mongol Empire studies are concerned. Significant new publications continue to appear. For example, after I had completed and definitively sent off the new chapter, I received in the same post two new books: Dr George Lane (among whose lesser distinctions is that of having been my last London PhD student, and who has subsequently become a prolific Mongol historian) published his *Daily Life in the Mongol Empire*, and Dr Judith Kolbas her *The Mongols in Iran. Chingiz Khan to Uljaytu 1220–1309.* So neither of these is discussed in the chapter. But one has to draw the line somewhere; and it is immensely encouraging that the rate of publication on the subject is now so much greater than it used to be.

Of scholars mentioned in the book's original Preface, I have continued to learn especially from Professors A. K. S. Lambton and Peter Jackson and Dr Igor de Rachewiltz. My friend and former tutor Professor James Campbell, joint editor of the series in which this book appears, has now been reading and listening to me on the subject of the Mongols for well over forty years: I thank him for his apparently inexhaustible patience. Both Professor Jackson and Dr Charles Melville of the University of Cambridge kindly read and commented on a draft of the new chapter. Since I moved from the School of Oriental and African Studies in 1999 I have found the University of Wisconsin-Madison a most congenial scholarly environment: I thank my colleagues there for making it so.

David Morgan
June 2006

Preface to
the Paperback Edition

This book has been through three impressions in hardback, and I am pleased that the publishers have now decided to reissue it in paperback, which I hope will introduce it to a wider circle of readers. This is a further impression, not a second edition. Some mistakes and misprints to be found in the first printing have been corrected, but I have not attempted any significant revision of the text: this, in my view, would be premature in the case of a book published as recently as 1986. I have not found it necessary to change my opinions on any matters of major importance since 1986, though there are certainly things that I would wish ultimately to modify or to add, in the light both of the comments of reviewers and readers who have written to me and of more recent research by myself and others. I intend one day to produce a thorough revision: but not yet.

The forebodings I expressed in the Introduction (pp. 3–4) have proved amply justified. Reviewers, varying in accordance with their own interests, have remarked that I did not discuss the later religious cult of Chingiz Khān (C. R. Bawden in *Bulletin of the School of Oriental and African Studies* 50/1, 1988, pp. 163–4), failed to consult an important institutional study in Mongolian (Paul D. Buell in *Middle East Studies Association Bulletin* 22, 1988, pp. 59–60), transliterated Mongolian improperly (Denis Sinor in *English Historical Review* CIV, April 1989, pp. 458–9), treated the Shaybanids inadequately (John E. Woods in *Journal of Near Eastern Studies* 47/3, 1988, pp. 231–2), and did not say enough about Mongol women's liberation (Robert Irwin in *Times Literary Supplement*, 6 March 1987). But it should be said that my reviewers, including most of those mentioned above, have been very generous, much more so than I had anticipated; I have learnt a good deal from them, and I am grateful to them for their indulgence. Only one reviewer (Gene R. Garthwaite in the [US] History Book Club fly-sheet) saw fit to comment on the Bill Tidy cartoon on p. 77; and he, to my delight, pointed out, correctly, that its inclusion was not *just* a joke. I recommend to anyone with a real interest in the subject the long critical review by John Masson Smith, Jr (*Journal of the Royal Asiatic Society* 1, 1989, pp. 158–61), a constructive discussion characterized by all its author's usual learning and courtesy – which is not to say that I am prepared to concede all the points he makes! What has pleased me most about those reactions to the book that have reached me is that many of its readers seem to have enjoyed the experience.

Among the considerable number of publications on the Mongols which have appeared since this book was completed, I would single out the following as of particular interest: T. T. Allsen, *Mongol Imperialism: the Policies of the Grand Qan Möngke in China, Russia, and the Islamic Lands, 1251–1259* (Berkeley, 1987); E. Endicott-West, *Mongolian Rule in China: Local Administration in the Yuan Dynasty* (Cambridge, MA and London, 1989); J. F. Fletcher, 'The Mongols: ecological and social perspectives', *Harvard Journal of Asiatic Studies*, 46/1 (1986), pp. 11–50; B. Forbes Manz, *The Rise and Rule of Tamerlane* (Cambridge, 1989); C. J. Halperin, *Russia and the Golden Horde: the Mongol Impact on Medieval Russian History* (Bloomington, 1985; London, 1987); A. K. S. Lambton, *Continuity and Change in Medieval Persia: Aspects of Administrative, Economic and Social History, 11th–14th Century* (New York and London, 1988); A. K. S. Lambton, 'Mongol fiscal administration in Persia', 2 parts, *Studia Islamica*, 64–5 (1986–7), pp. 79–99, 97–123; J. R. S. Phillips, *The Medieval Expansion of Europe* (Oxford, 1988); M. Rossabi, *Khubilai Khan: his Life and Times* (Berkeley, 1988).

In addition, I should mention L. N. Gumilev's highly eccentric but enjoyable *Searches for an Imaginary Kingdom: the Legend of the Kingdom of Prester John* (Cambridge, 1987), and L. de Hartog's *Genghis Khan: Conqueror of the World* (London, 1989), which until the appearance of Thomas Haining's translation of Ratchnevsky's *Cinggis-Khan* will be the most recommendable biography of Chingiz available in English.

Lastly, I should like to include a word of thanks to the staff of Basil Blackwell, and especially to John Davey, for making so pleasing an artifact out of my book.

David Morgan
September 1989

Preface to the First Edition

When I was asked at my Worcester College scholarship interview in 1963 whether I had any special historical interest, it presumably did not occur to James Campbell that he would be obliged to listen to my answer, off and on, for the next 20 years. If he has now had to read it as well, he has only himself to blame. I am grateful to him for his invitation to contribute to his and Professor Cunliffe's series, and for much else.

I have learned a great deal from many colleagues at the School of Oriental and African Studies, University of London, where there is usually someone who knows the answer to any Oriental question. My most considerable debts are to Professor A. K. S. Lambton, to whom I owe most of what I know and understand about the Islamic world in general and Persia in particular, and to my now (regrettably) former colleague Professor William Atwell, with whom I taught a London University history option on the Mongol Empire between 1980 and his return to the United States in 1984. A large part of my scant knowledge of China is derived from listening to his lectures and comments. He kindly cast a Sinological eye over a draft of chapter 5. I must also acknowledge the extent to which my ideas have in all sorts of ways been clarified by discussions with the intrepid students who chose to take our outlandish course.

I am grateful too to Dr Peter Jackson of Keele University for many Mongol conversations over a number of years. He could have written a better book than this one, but fortunately for me was not asked. Both he and Professor Lambton read and commented on the first draft of the book, and to them should be attributed the better ideas rather than the remaining mistakes, for which I must shoulder the responsibility. Of historians not known to me personally, I have learned most from the writings of Dr Igor de Rachewiltz of the Australian National University. It is a real pleasure to record my debt to these scholars, as well as something of a relief that by so doing I may with luck have prevented at least some of them from being invited to review the book.

Like most married authors I could not have written, even at such modest length, without the support and tolerance of my wife. The forbearance of my daughters in not interrupting when they could hear the typewriter should also be noted with gratitude. As well as submitting a draft of the book to expert scrutiny I also persuaded both my wife and an old friend, Richard Frost, to read it from the standpoint of that perhaps fabulous personage, the general reader. Mr Frost turned out to be my severest critic, and I am very grateful to him for the trouble he took, even if I did not always appear to be so at the time.

Last of all I must mention my parents, although they are no longer here to read these words. They unquestioningly tolerated and to a considerable extent financed what must have seemed an interminable student career. Without their encouragement of interests very remote indeed from their own, I could not have begun the studies which have ultimately led to the writing of this book. I therefore dedicate it, gratefully and affectionately, to their memory.

January 1985

Postscript   I have to thank Mr Reuven Amitai of the Hebrew University, Jerusalem, for his kindness in reading and correcting a set of proofs.

Maps

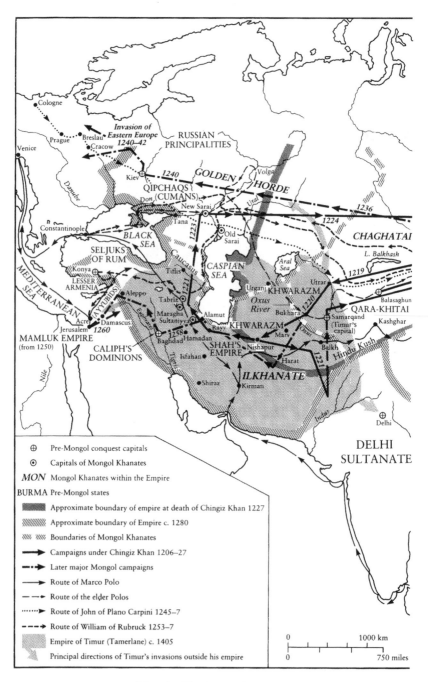

Map 1 The Mongol Empire

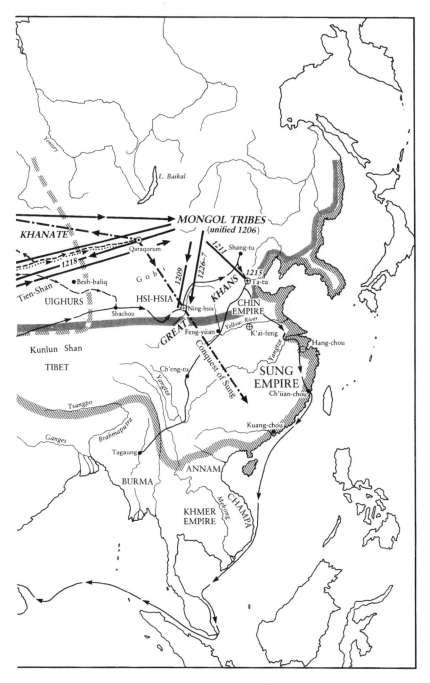

Map 1 *Continued*

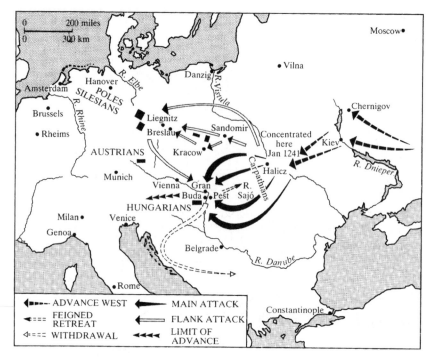

Map 2 The Mongols in Europe, 1240–1

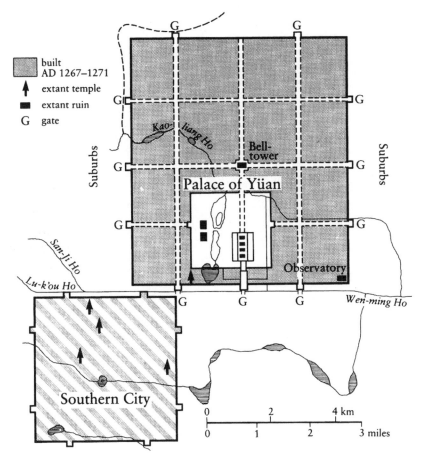

built
AD 1267–1271

↑ extant temple

■ extant ruin

G gate

Suburbs

Suburbs

Kao-liang Ho

Bell-tower

Palace of Yüan

Observatory

San-li Ho

Lu-k'ou Ho

Wen-ming Ho

Southern City

0   2   4 km
0   1   2   3 miles

Map 3   Ta-tu (Mongol Peking)

Introduction

The Mongols are not very obviously a 'people of Europe'. But they have significantly influenced the history of Europe. Their empire was so huge that although its centre was in the Far East, it constituted for a century or more Europe's most formidable and dangerous eastern neighbour. Its influence on Europe, from the point of view of politics, commerce or religion, was considerable, though nothing approaching what it would have been had the Mongol armies not withdrawn from central Europe in 1242. In a famous passage, Gibbon speculated over what might have been the result of a Muslim victory over Charles Martel in 732, and envisaged the prospect of the Qur'ān being taught in the schools of Oxford.[1] We know now that the Muslim expedition of 732 was not the advance guard of a full-scale invasion of western Christendom, and that Charles Martel's victory was of more symbolic than real importance. But the Mongols were a different matter. They may not have thought the comparison between their native steppes and the forests and mountains of central Europe one that told in Europe's favour; and they may have wondered where they were to find the grassland on which to feed their myriads of horses. But they had advanced to the borders of Germany; they had reached the Adriatic; and they were within striking distance of Vienna. There was no reason to suppose that armies which had defeated the best that China and the Islamic world could throw against them would meet their match in Europe.

It is not wholly fanciful, then, to suggest that Europe may have had a lucky escape from becoming another province of a great Eurasian empire – a fate that the European powers had done little to avert. The

---

[1] E. Gibbon, *The History of the Decline and Fall of the Roman Empire*, ed. J. B. Bury (1905–6), vol. 6, p. 15.

consequences, obviously, would have been incalculable. But one thing may be said with a degree of certainty: the study of Mongol history would not now be the concern only of a few specialists in historical exotica.

The might-have-beens of history are endlessly fascinating, but it is not usually thought proper (except by Lord Dacre of Glanton[2]) that they should distract the attention of the serious student for very long. So in this book I shall be concerned with what actually did happen. I shall try, as far as I am able, to make the extraordinary Mongol phenomenon comprehensible, and I shall place a particular emphasis on the history of the Mongol Empire as it relates to Europe. Considered from the Mongols' own point of view, this will give a lop-sided impression. For them it was the Far East that mattered above all, and a balanced history of the Mongol Empire would expend far more of its space on China than on the Middle East, Russia, or relations with Europe. In terms of the history of civilisation, Europe in the thirteenth century was still an insignificant backwater compared with China.

This book would therefore make no kind of sense if China were to be left out of the picture, and I shall devote one chapter to the Mongol Yüan dynasty there, as well as giving some account of the Mongols' military campaigns which led to the conquest of China. But my emphasis will be on the western half of the Mongol domains. This is perhaps fortunate in view of the linguistic demands, discussed in chapter 1, that face anyone who attempts to study the Mongols. The most important languages, I contend, are Persian and Chinese, in that order. The linguistic difficulties and the tendencies of academic specialisation are such that there have been very few scholars who have contrived to learn both, let alone all or most of the other relevant tongues; and I am not a member of that prodigious class. One of the Orientalists I most admire, Arthur Waley, once wrote the following daunting words: 'Despite the fact that in this book I translate from Chinese, Japanese, Ainu, Mongol and Syriac, I do not want to give the impression that I am a master of many languages. Chinese and Japanese I do know fairly well' – one of the greatest academic understatements ever made – '. . . Mongol I have been studying for some thirty years, but I am far from being a

[2]   H. R. Trevor-Roper, 'History and imagination', in H. Lloyd-Jones, V. Pearl and B. Worden (eds), *History and Imagination: Essays in Honour of H. R. Trevor-Roper* (1981), pp. 356–69.

Mongolist.'[3] This is enough to make anyone contemplate giving up the struggle. As for myself, I have some knowledge of Persian, but I know no Chinese at all, and I have been able to make use of Chinese sources only when they are available in translation. The bias of treatment in this book makes this, perhaps, a less serious deficiency than it might otherwise have been; but I am conscious that I am unlikely to have done justice to the Sinological aspects of the subject. I have, however, been able to take advantage of some of the first fruits of the recent greatly increased interest, particularly in the United States, in the formerly rather neglected history of China in the Yüan period.

This is a book, then, that reflects the character of the series in which it appears, as well as my own interests. It is a book about the Mongols and their empire rather than a history of the empire, and not everyone will agree with my selection of topics on which to concentrate, or think my sketchy treatment of other matters adequate. I have not hesitated to make free with the results of other scholars' research, of which there is now a considerable bulk – something that could not have been said until fairly recently. Within the limits of my linguistic competence, I have tried to take this research fully into account, though I am mindful of Sir Steven Runciman's all too accurate observation that 'however conscientiously he (the historian) may strive, there will always be at least one article, tucked away in some obscure periodical or some forgotten *Festschrift*, which he has missed and which his critcs will say is the most important of all'.[4]

I have not written in the first instance for my fellow specialists in medieval Asian history, though I hope they may find something to interest them. Rather, I have tried to bear in mind that this may, for some, be the only book on the Mongols that they ever look at – while trusting that this will not be the inevitable result of reading it. Indeed, if I succeed in tempting any of my readers into looking into larger-scale works by larger-scale scholars, or into glancing at some of the specialist articles to see whether there is actually any foundation for what I have said, I shall at least have achieved something.

There is no satisfactory solution to the problem of transliteration when one is dealing with words from so many languages and scripts.

[3] A. Waley, *The Secret History of the Mongols and Other Pieces* (1963), p. 8.
[4] S. Runciman, 'On the writing of history', in *The Historical Association 1906–1956* (1957), pp. 115–16.

Even Mongolists do not by any means all use the same system for Mongolian. For Mongol names I have tried to produce something that may be recognisable to a Mongolist, though I have not followed the current tendency to replace Q (as in Qubilai) with KH, as this introduces confusion when one is also transliterating words from the Islamic languages. For transliterations from the Arabic script I have used the system conventionally followed by British Orientalists, i.e. approximately that of the *Encyclopaedia of Islam*, slightly modified to exclude such oddities as Ḳ for Q and DJ for J. Persian is usually transliterated as Arabic, e.g. the letter pronounced V in Persian appears as W. Chinese is represented unashamedly in good old Wade-Giles. All in all, I cannot claim to have achieved, or really to have struggled very hard to achieve, anything approaching consistency. I take the view that as long as words and names are clearly identifiable, rigorously uniform transliteration is not a matter of major importance, at least in a general book of this kind. That is perhaps my justification for transliterating the founder of the Mongol Empire as Chingiz (which is how he is represented in Persian), rather than in a form that a Mongolist might prefer.

1

The Study of Mongol History

The Mongol Empire of the thirteenth and fourteenth centuries was the largest continuous land empire that has so far existed. At its greatest extent it stretched from Korea to Hungary, including, except for India and the south-east of the continent, most of Asia, as well as a good deal of eastern Europe. As a whole it lasted for well over a century, and parts of it survived for very much longer. It was merely one, albeit by far the most extensive, of a series of great steppe empires; and it should be seen in the context provided by its predecessors. The major difference between the Mongols and previous conquerors is that no other nomad empire had succeeded in holding both the Inner Asian steppe and the neighbouring sedentary lands simultaneously. This has a further consequence from the historian's point of view: it means that the Mongol Empire is much more fully documented than its predecessors, since writers from the sedentary civilisations were in many cases writing about the Mongols from within their empire, not discussing them as a threat that was external and therefore of limited interest and little known in detail.

The study of the Mongol Empire therefore has its difficulties. Consider the language problem. The sources available to the historian are in Mongolian, Chinese, Persian, Arabic, Turkish, Japanese, Russian, Armenian, Georgian, Latin, and other languages. No one can hope to be able to read more than a fraction of them in the original. Then there is a cultural difficulty. Even if we could read the sources in all these languages, could we be sure that we had understood them correctly? The societies of medieval China, Islam, Europe, and the steppe peoples were all different from one another; their historical writing has different assumptions and different conventions, and is underlain by quite different patterns of thought.

What is the historian to do? Two solutions have been attempted, with varying degrees of success. In the past, historians of the Mongols have most commonly been exponents of what is called *haute vulgarisation*, making little serious attempt to master the necessary languages, and producing syntheses based on secondary sources, in which they have drawn on what the specialists on China, Mongolia, the Islamic world or Europe have written. They have supplemented this with material from such original sources as those same specialists have translated into accessible languages. Used intelligently, such an approach has its virtues, and some useful books on the Mongols, notably those of René Grousset, are of this type.

Perhaps the only alternative to this approach is for a specialist in one part or other of the lands that made up the Mongol Empire to try to write a broader survey on the basis of his specialist knowledge, using the works of the experts on the other areas. He may hope that a first-hand acquaintance with at least part of the evidence will be some safeguard against ineptitude in his treatment of the rest. This is now probably the approach that is usual, and this book is an example of it. Essentially, the historian of the Mongol Empire is required to choose his end of Asia, west or east, and to base his work on the sources in one of the two major languages – Persian and Chinese. Except for a linguistic prodigy, there is no escaping the necessity for relying on translations; but it is obligatory to remember that translations can, and do, mislead.

It might be thought that a knowledge of Mongolian rather than Persian or Chinese was the first essential. This is not in fact so. Mongolian was not a written language before the time of Chingiz Khān, and the only really capital Mongolian source is the extraordinary work known as the *Secret History of the Mongols*, of which there are several translations, including two in English, by well-qualified Mongolists.[1] There are other, more fragmentary pieces of evidence in Mongolian, but the corpus as a whole does not in itself really justify the very considerable effort involved in learning Mongolian.

Persian and Chinese, though, are a very different matter. The historiographical traditions of both Persia and China were established long

---

[1]   F. W. Cleaves (tr.), *The Secret History of the Mongols* (1982) is the only complete English translation of the *Secret History* available at the time of writing. It will probably be superseded by I. de Rachewiltz, 'The Secret History of the Mongols', *Papers in Far Eastern History* (1971–1981), when finished. I give references to the paragraphs of the text and to Cleaves as it is more accessible than de Rachewiltz as well as complete. For the Chinese abridgement see A. Waley, *The Secret History of the Mongols and Other Pieces* (1963). For a useful review of Cleaves see C. R. Bawden, 'Riding with the Khans', *Times Literary Supplement*, 24 June 1983, p. 669.

before the advent of Chingiz Khān, and the wealth of material in the two languages on the history of the Mongols comprises the major part of the really important evidence. If this book places more emphasis on what Persian writers have to say than on what may be established from Chinese sources, it is partly because a book in this series, as explained in the introduction, ought to concentrate to some extent on the parts of the Mongol Empire nearer to Europe, and partly because its author happens to be able to read Persian rather than Chinese.

The sources used in this book are, for the most part, contemporary of near-contemporary chronicles. The archives of the Mongol Empire, if they ever existed, have long since vanished: for Mongol history we have no equivalent to the Vatican or the Public Record Office in London. Indeed, so far as the Islamic world is concerned, no systematic archives at all seem to have survived for any state before the Ottoman Empire. There are occasional collections of Islamic documents that have survived by chance, and a good many isolated documents are embedded in chronicles or administrative handbooks; in addition, the archives of some European states have yielded a useful harvest of letters to and from the Mongol rulers. Europe also provides some of the most acute and well-informed travellers' narratives of Mongol Asia. But chronicles are the bread and butter of the Mongol historian – a state of affairs that has ceased to obtain for some areas of medieval European history. Is this a serious handicap to our understanding of the subject?

The answer is yes – and no. To find archives relating to Persia or China in the years of Mongol rule would no doubt set the study of the subject on an entirely new foundation, once scholars had been able to sift them – in a century or two, perhaps, if work on the Ottoman archives is anything to go by. But this is no more than a pipe dream. We must make do with what we have. It is not as though we possessed only the Asian equivalent of a few monastic chronicles. For China, the major source is the official dynastic history, the *Yüan-shih* (Yüan being the dynastic name adopted by the Mongols in China). Chinese administrative practice dictated that year by year records should be kept of everything that concerned the government. No synthesised official history would be compiled from the resulting 'veritable records', however, until the dynasty fell. The Chinese bureaucracy was as eternal as the taxation system it administered, and was usually comparatively little affected by changes in dynasty. The new dynasty would mark its accession, and the definitive end of its predecessor, by instructing the appropriate bureaucrats to commence work on the official history of the fallen rulers. This was done by the new Ming government of China after the fall of the Yüan in 1368.

Persia had evolved no institutional arrangements of this kind, but it did produce its own variety of 'official' history in the period of Mongol rule. The most important of the chronicles that deal with the years after Chingiz Khān's invasion were written by Rashīd al-Dīn, Juwaynī, and Waṣṣāf – all of them high-ranking government servants, and the most authoritative of them, Rashīd al-Dīn, for 20 years the chief minister of the Ilkhanate, the Mongol kingdom in Persia and Iraq. It is incontrovertible, therefore, that all three historians had access to good sources of information, and that they understood what they were writing about. The problem is that most of these histories, even if they were not in all cases precisely official productions, were written for royal patrons and reflect to a greater or lesser extent the points of view and the preconceptions of the rulers and the official classes. It is rather as though we knew the history of the Henrician Reformation mainly through the writings of Thomas Cromwell – one sided, no doubt, but so close to the centre of events as to be invaluable to us.

It is possible to apply correctives of various kinds. Persia is fortunate in its wealth of local histories for the period; if they are taken into account we can avoid an excessive concentration on affairs in the capital. Externally, although the Mongols tried very hard to conquer the world, they did not wholly succeed, and we have the writings of historians in the unconquered states (states in rebellion, as the Mongols saw them) to compare with the internal evidence. Writings from Japan, India, Egypt and western Europe all have something to offer here.

The Secret History of the Mongols

The Mongols' illiteracy before the time of Chingiz Khān has already been mentioned. Even after his reign they were not, perhaps, strikingly literate.[2] The result is that almost all the written historical evidence available on the Mongol Empire is from the pens and brushes either of the Mongols' enemies or of the conquered and more civilised subject peoples. These are valid and valuable perspectives, but it is a pity that they have to be virtually the only ones. It is this fact that gives the *Secret*

---

[2]   See the comments of P. Anderson, *Passages from Antiquity to Feudalism* (1974), p. 222.

History of the Mongols its unique importance: it is the only substantial surviving Mongol work about the Mongol Empire, the only direct insight we possess into how the Mongols viewed things, undistorted by the spectacles of the conquered or the hostile.

The *Secret History* as we now have it survived in the Mongolian language, but not in the script which Chingiz Khān had caused to be adapted from the Uighur variety of Turkish for the writing of Mongolian. At some stage in the fourteenth century, a copy of the book was painstakingly transcribed into Chinese characters, using the phonetic value of the characters irrespective of their meaning to represent the Mongolian sounds. This worked better than one might have expected, and it is this version, together with an abridgement into the Chinese language, that has come down to us. We do not know the name of its author or compiler, and its date of composition is uncertain. The Mongols used a 12-year animal cycle for dating purposes, and we know from the *Secret History's* text that it was completed in the year of the Rat. It deals with the course of events from the mythical origins of the Chingizid house in legendary times until the latter part of the reign of Chingiz Khān's first successor, Ögedei, who died in 1241. The section on the period after Chingiz Khān's death in 1227 has the appearance of a later addition. Though later interpolations have been detected, perhaps indicating subsequent editorial work, the likely Rat years are 1228 – in which case the *Secret History* must have been a compilation made at the time of the enthronement of Ögedei – or, if the last section is part of the original work, 1240.[3] Either way it represents a Mongol view of their history and perspective on the world that is contemporary with their rise to world dominion.

Whether it also provides a reliable guide to events is another mater. Scholarly opinions on this point have varied a good deal. Arthur Waley, who translated a large part of the Chinese abridgement into English, thought the *Secret History* historically valueless, and presented it as legendary story-telling. A recent article has described it as 'a pseudo-historical novel'.[4] Most historians in this century, on the other hand, have used it as their main source for the life and career of Chingiz Khān.

---

[3]   For a discussion of the dating, see I. de Rachewiltz, 'Some remarks on the dating of the *Secret History of the Mongols*', *Monumenta Serica*, 24 (1965), 185–206.

[4]   Waley, *The Secret History*, pp. 7–8; L. Kwanten, *Imperial Nomads: a History of Central Asia, 500–1500* (1979), p. 316, n. 8.

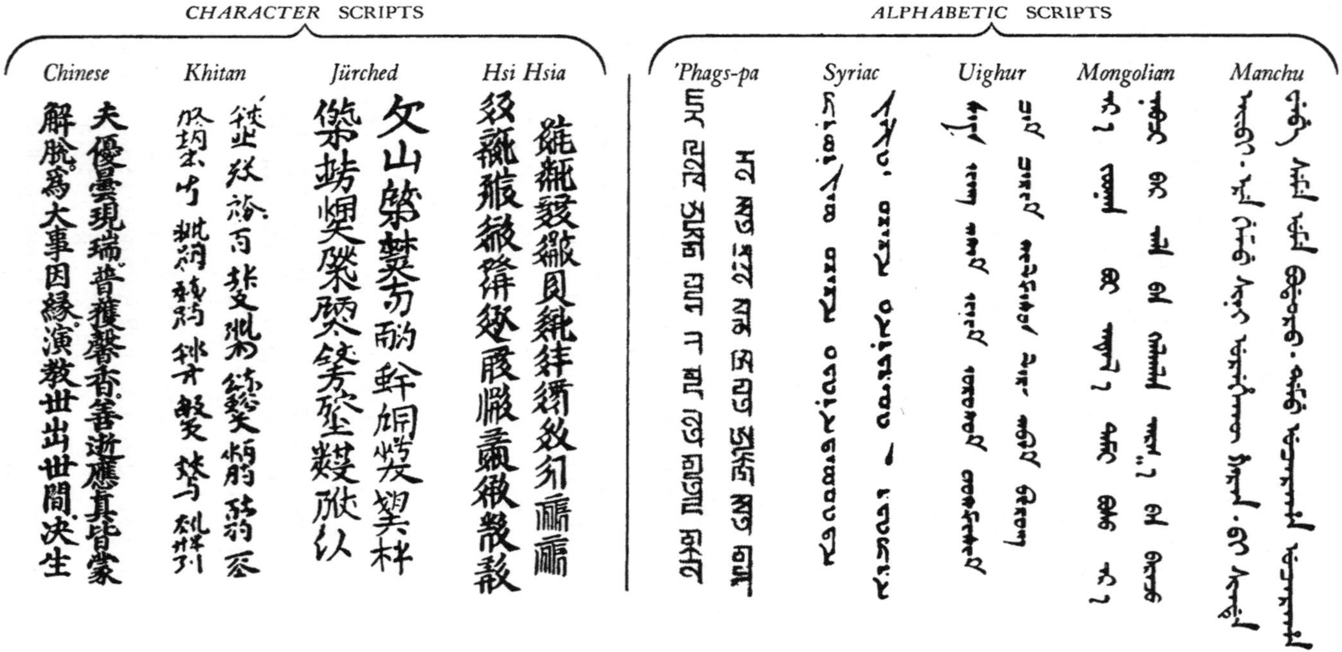

Manchu

Mongolian

Uighur

Syriac

'Phags-pa

Hsi Hsia

Jürched

Khitan

Chinese

Plate 1.1 Scripts used or created by Inner Asian peoples. John K. Fairbank, Edwin O. Reischauer and Albert M. Craig (eds.), *East Asia: Tradition and Transformation*, Allen & Unwin, London. © 1973, Houghton Mifflin, Boston

The matter is bedevilled by the *Secret History's* uniqueness. There is often no certain way of confirming or denying much of what it tells us. It might therefore be untrue. But equally, we might by rejecting it be throwing away our best and most detailed authentic information.

One check on the *Secret History's* reliability can, in a general way, be made. No other Mongolian history of the period has come down to us, but we do know that there was once an official history called the *Altan Debter*, the 'Golden Book'. This was kept at the courts of the Mongol rulers, and copies of it were taboo documents; no non-Mongol was permitted to see them. But when the Persian Rashīd al-Dīn was commissioned by the Īlkhān Ghazan to write the history of the Mongols, he clearly needed to know what was in the *Altan Debter*. Its contents were therefore conveyed to him through an intermediary. What we have in Rashīd al-Dīn's account of the early history of the Mongol Empire is, then, a version at second hand of the *Altan Debter's* material. It so happens that in China, too, a version of the *Altan Debter* was compiled, in Chinese: the *Sheng-wu ch'in-cheng lu*. So we have two versions apparently derived from the same matter, and it has been shown that a comparison between the two provides a very fair idea of the *Altan Debter's* probable original appearance.[5] How does this shed light on the question of the *Secret History's* reliability? Two points should be made: first, a reading of the *Secret History* and the *Altan Debter* material shows that they are clearly quite independent of each other; and second, though what they say is by no means identical, they do talk, broadly, about the same events and in much the same way. There seems to be no case for regarding the *Secret History* as wholly fictional unless the *Altan Debter* is to be seen as another, independent work of fiction. This would impose something of a strain on our credulity.

This is to say not that the *Secret History* is to be regarded as gospel, merely that it is to be treated seriously as historical evidence and not simply dismissed as legendary story-telling. Legend there certainly is in it: the book begins with the tribal myth of the Mongols' origins, their descent from a wolf and a doe. What substratum of truth may be lurking in the early sections is not easy to say. But when the *Secret History* reaches the twelfth century, as it soon does, we enter a known world, one overshadowed by the power of China, and one for which the Chinese sources provide a good deal of evidence. The *Secret History's*

[5]   P. Pelliot and L. Hambis, *Histoire des campagnes de Gengis Khan* (1951), vol. 1, introduction.

account of Chingiz Khān's immediate ancestors, the Mongol khāns of the twelfth century, is evidently anchored in reality, whatever its truth in matters of detail. The bulk of the book is concerned with Chingiz Khān's childhood, early exploits and rise to power in Mongolia. It reads in a saga-like way, there are lengthy passages in verse, and it is full of conversations in direct speech – though these conversations are no better justification for rejecting the book as evidence than the battlefield speeches are a reason for rejecting Thucydides. The general sequence of events, as Chingiz rises from little more than a successful bandit to supreme ruler of the steppe tribes, Mongol and Turkish, of Mongolia, is plausible enough, and the stages of this process, as represented, seem reasonable. First, individual followers are attracted by the young warrior's personal qualities; then the support of a powerful patron is gained; ultimately there is a breach with that patron, and a gradual increase of strength is maintained as the various tribes are one by one defeated and either killed, enslaved or, in most cases, simply incorporated into the new Mongol military machine.

Acceptance of the motives ascribed by the *Secret History* to Chingiz and other figures is not so self-evidently necessary. To argue that the *Secret History* is no more than a panegyric of Chingiz is to encounter difficulties: minor ones – would such a panegyric not have concealed the fact that the young Chingiz was afraid of dogs? – and major ones: as a youth, Chingiz is represented as murdering his half-brother. It is true that this was not wholly without provocation, and that Chingiz's mother is represented as being vexed rather than appalled by the act of fratricide. But there is no pretence that the episode does other than reflect very discreditably on the young Chingiz. This is hardly what one would expect to find in a panegyric, unless perhaps a most strikingly subtle one.[6]

But when we come to Chingiz's rise to power, we find over and over again, according to the *Secret History*, that the other rulers of the steppe double-cross him, and are defeated as the just reward of their perfidy. Chingiz's own political morality is quite irreproachable: he is repeatedly and reluctantly forced to fight, defeat and exterminate the followers of some former ally who has treacherously turned against him. It is hard to take this at face value, and a reading of the events, without the *Secret History's* interpretation, might well suggest that it was in fact Chingiz

---

[6] Para. 66: tr. Cleaves, *The Secret History*, p. 17; paras 76–8, tr. Cleaves, pp. 22–4.

who was the ruthless double-dealer, unwilling to let anyone stand in the way of his absolute supremacy.[7] We shall probably never know with any degree of certainty where the truth lies.

Whatever hesitations historians may have about using the *Secret History* as a record of historical events as such, on one point there can be no doubt: as an insight into the way of life, patterns of thought and beliefs of the thirteenth-century Mongols, the *Secret History* is unique and authoritative. What may be learned on these matters from non-Mongol sources must be regarded as secondary. The *Secret History* is the only major source we have that gives us a realistic appraisal of the Mongol perspective on their conquests. Looking at a map of their empire, we might think that there was some sort of overall plan of world domination in the Mongol mind, and that expansion in all directions was the order of the day. It is true that in the light of their early successes and perhaps under the influence of Turkish or Chinese ideas, the Mongols did come to believe that they had a divine commission to conquer the world,[8] but the world-view revealed by the *Secret History* is rather different. Here it is Mongolia itself, and the internal affairs of the tribes, that really matter most. After that, the important place, far outweighing in interest the whole of the rest of the world, is China. The conquest of China, especially north China, had always been every steppe ruler's dream, and Chingiz was no exception. The account in the *Secret History* of Chingiz's campaigns in the Muslim lands to the west is perfunctory and confused, and the passages on the Mongol invasion of Russia and eastern Europe are still worse. In the eyes of the *Secret History's* author the most interesting feature by far of the campaign in Europe was the feud which developed between some of the Mongol princes who were serving in the invading army. He saw nothing worthy of note in the obscure goings-on of minor potentates like the princes of Russia or the Holy Roman Emperor.

This view of affairs did change in time, especially after the Mongol Empire broke up into a series of, in effect, independent khanates, when the Khāns were anxious for any support they could obtain, even from the once-despised Europeans. But the basic Mongol presupposition, that the really important conquest was China, remained and needs to be borne constantly in mind when Mongol policy is being studied.

---

[7]   See I. de Rachewiltz, *Papal Envoys to the Great Khans* (1971), p. 48.

[8]   I. de Rachewiltz, 'Some remarks on the ideological foundations of Chinggis Khan's empire', *Papers in Far Eastern History*, 7 (1973), pp. 21–36.

Chinese Sources

Invaluable though the *Secret History* is, it stops around 1240: it is severely limited both in the period it covers and in the range of its author's interests. Something similar might be said of the Chinese sources. They are full and essential for the history of Mongol rule in China itself – though the *Yüan-shih* is said to be perhaps the least satisfactory of all the official dynastic histories of China. The *Yüan-shih* conformed to the historiographical pattern that the Chinese had established 1200 years previously. We may note that Chinese civilisation had ample experience in taking barbarian invaders in its stride and taming them. So although China was part of a world empire under Mongol rule, a reader of the *Yüan-shih* would hardly guess it. Like other Chinese sources of the period, it shows almost no interest in any part of the world other than China itself and, as a generous concession, its immediate neighbours. There are no sections on the other Mongol khanates. The affairs of those states appear rarely, and then only in the course of events that are related because they are relevant to China, in the annalistic section of the book. The only foreign countries that rate separate treatment are those that had always received it in the dynastic histories: countries like Japan, Korea or Burma, which had traditional tribute or treaty relations with the Chinese Empire.[9]

Chinese sources, then, though obviously the basis for the study of the most important part of the Mongol Empire, are of limited use for the history of the empire as a whole. It is true, however, that the detailed topical sections of the *Yüan-shih* do have, in at least some instances, a relevance to the study of the Mongol period generally. A number of these chapters have been translated, and those on the economy and on military organisation in particular have wide implications for Mongol policy outside China.[10] It should be said that the introductions and annotations provided by the translators are necessary aids: most chapters of the *Yüan-shih* would be virtually incomprehensible to the non-Sinologist without expert help and interpretation.

The Chinese histories are usefully supplemented by the accounts of several Chinese travellers who visited the Mongols. From among these

[9]   H. Franke, 'Sino-western contacts under the Mongol Empire', *Journal of the Hong Kong Branch of the Royal Asiatic Society*, 6 (1966), pp. 51–2.

[10]   H. F. Schurmann, *Economic Structure of the Yüan Dynasty* (1956); C. Hsiao, *The Military Establishment of the Yuan Dynasty* (1978).

may be singled out the narrative of the journey of the Taoist monk Ch'ang Ch'un, who travelled from China to Afghanistan and back to visit Chingiz Khān in 1221–3; and the reports of two embassies from the Sung government of south China to the Mongols, compiled in 1221 and 1237. These reports are now available in German translation.[11]

Persian Sources

Some sort of history of the Mongol Empire, though a very unsatisfactory one, could perhaps be written without reference to the *Secret History* or to Chinese sources. It is hard to see, however, how anything of worth could be written about the empire as a whole if the Persian chronicles of the period had not survived. To say this does not imply that Persia was of other than secondary importance to the Mongols, when compared with Mongolia itself and China. It is simply a comment on the unparalleled range of some of the Persian chronicles.

Perhaps the character of the Persian histories was partly the result of shock. The Chinese were used to coping with barbarian conquerors who came from outside China and were alien to the Confucian tradition. The Muslims of western Asia, however, had never experienced anything to compare with the Mongol conquests. Those conquests, in a sense, went against the tide of history as the Muslims envisaged it. According to Islamic theory, the world was divided into two parts: the *Dār al-Islām*, the 'Abode of Islam', where the inhabitants would by no means necessarily all be Muslims, but where Islam would rule, where the paramount princes would be Muslims, where all were under the ultimate if somewhat indefinable authority of the Caliph, where Islamic law would prevail; and the *Dār al-ḥarb*, the 'Abode of War', where the infidel reigned supreme, but only for the time being. Muslim expectation was that the Dār al-Islām would gradually expand through the medium of *Jihād*, holy war, until it included the whole world. Any truces made with the infidel could only be of temporary effect. But there was no provision in Islamic theory for the process to go into reverse.

It is true that lands formerly under Muslim rule had previously fallen to the Christian infidel – Sicily, parts of Spain, the Crusader states in Syria – but there had been nothing on the scale of the Mongol onslaught.

---

[11]   A. Waley (tr.), *The Travels of an Alchemist* (1931); P. Olbricht and E. Pinks (trs), *Meng-Ta pei-lu und Hei-Ta shih-lüeh* (1980).

Persia, Iraq and Syria all fell to the Mongol infidel – a type of infidel of whom it could not be said, as it could of the Christians, that they were at least 'People of the Book', guided by genuine if, in Muslim eyes, corrupted sacred scriptures and so with some glimmerings of the truth. At one time, around 1260, there must have seemed little reason to suppose that Egypt and north Africa would not likewise crumble before the Mongol horsemen; could even the holy cities of Mecca and Medina have been regarded as safe? It was, wrote the Arab historian Ibn al-Athīr in the immediate aftermath of Chingiz Khān's first Middle Eastern campaigns, 'a tremendous disaster such as had never happened before. . . . It may well be that the world from now until its end . . . will not experience the like of it again, apart perhaps from Gog and Magog'.[12]

How could a good Muslim make sense of such a catastrophe? Why had God apparently abandoned his people? Muslim historians felt obliged to address themselves to these profoundly disturbing questions. In the process they also found themselves attempting to understand, and therefore to write the history of, the whole Mongol phenomenon.

Jūzjānī, who wrote as an old man in the safe sanctuary of the Delhi sultanate, is of particular importance since he was consequently not obliged to moderate his language so far as the Mongols were concerned. He had himself witnessed the horrors of Chingiz's invasion, 40 years before. He found the explanation in eschatology. Prophecy had indicated clearly that the coming of the Mongols was a sign of the imminent end of the world. Juwaynī, who completed his history in the same year, 1260, as Jūzjānī's *Ṭabaqāt-i Nāṣirī* was finished, considered that the Mongol disaster was God's judgement on the sins of the Muslims. But he was able to discern some silver linings in the Mongol clouds: Islam had spread further than ever before because of the existence of the Mongol Empire, and at least the Mongols had, in 1256, virtually exterminated the hated Muslim sect of the Nizārī Ismāʻīlīs, the sinister Assassins, whom he thought of as being infinitely worse than any outright infidel. But Juwaynī was a much younger man than Jūzjānī. He had not himself experienced the first Mongol invasion. He spent most of his life in the service of the Mongols, the last quarter century of it as Mongol governor of Baghdad and Iraq. It is hardly likely to be chance that, although he was writing in 1260 and in Baghdad, he chose to conclude his book with a great orthodox Muslim triumph, the fall of

---

[12]   C. J. Tornberg (ed.), Ibn al-Athīr, *Al-kāmil fiʼl-taʼrīkh* (1853), vol. 12, p. 234; B. Spuler (tr.), *History of the Mongols* (1972), p. 30.

the Ismā'īlīs. We hear nothing from him of the sack of Baghdad and the murder at Mongol hands of the last 'Abbasid Caliph, two years later in 1258. A degree of tact and caution was doubtless expected of a Mongol government servant.

Juwaynī's book was called 'The History of the World Conqueror', Chingiz Khān, and he tried to make it as comprehensive as he could. He had himself travelled twice to Mongolia, and had gathered large quantities of information. So we learn from him not only about the Mongol invasions of the Islamic lands, but also about the previous dynasties in the territories that formed the Mongol Empire: the Qara-Khitai in Central Asia, the Uighurs further east, the Khwārazm-shāhs in Persia, the Assassins from their first appearance in Persia at the end of the eleventh century. We learn something of the early career of Chingiz Khān, of the Mongols' nomadic way of life, of their methods of warfare, of their laws or customs. His history is an encyclopaedia, if a rather jumbled one, of the early Mongol period, written in a flowery literary Persian which makes one grateful for the existence of a reliable English translation.[13]

But even Juwaynī is eclipsed in importance by Rashīd al-Dīn, perhaps the most remarkable public figure to have been thrown up by the Mongol regime in Persia. A physician by training and a Jew by birth, though converted to Islam, he entered Mongol service at the end of the thirteenth century. This was at the time when the Mongols in Persia had at last accepted the religion of the majority of their subjects. The Īlkhān Ghazan had declared his conversion to Islam after his accession in 1295, and the Mongols under his rule had followed his example with predictable promptitude. Persia and Iraq were once more part of the Dār al-Islām: the intractable problem faced by Jūzjānī and Juwaynī no longer existed. Persia had been conquered by riders from the east before – by the Saljūq Turks in the eleventh century. But by the time the Saljūqs had reached Persia, they were already Muslims. That had made them acceptable, and now the Mongols came into the same category. So Rashīd al-Dīn could regard the Mongol conquest as an accomplished fact, no longer needing justification. Indeed, with the Mongols' conversion to Islam and the gradual growth of identification between them and their subjects, it was now the Mongol rather than the Muslim identity that was in danger. Probably with this in mind, Ghazan asked Rashīd al-Dīn

---

[13] See J. A. Boyle (tr.), 'Aṭā Malik Juvainī, *The History of the World Conqueror* (1958).

to write a history of the Mongols in Persia, possibly as some kind of a permanent *aide-mémoire*.

This he did. He explained in his introduction that the Mongol Empire marked a new era in world history, one that it was necessary to record. Beginning with a history and discussion of the tribes of Mongolia, he proceeded chronologically through the empire's history, using the *Altan Debter* as his source for the earliest period. This was a history of the Mongols themselves, not an Islamic history with Mongol additions. China receives something approaching its due as part of the narrative, and there is much about the great Qubilai, whom the Īlkhāns had been proud to acknowledge as their lord.

But inevitably it is Mongol rule in Persia that receives the most detailed treatment, culminating in Rashīd al-Dīn's immensely complex and problematical account of Ghazan's programme of administrative reforms (see chapter 6). His text preserves Ghazan's reforming edicts in full. If those reforms were as sweeping and successful as Rashīd al-Dīn would have us believe, it is surprising that Mongol rule did not last for a further century. Equally, if Mongol government before Ghazan's accession was quite the shambles that Rashīd al-Dīn's stories suggest, it is remarkable that Mongol power continued to exist at all. We have to remember that Rashīd al-Dīn was Ghazan's chief minister. The true state of affairs is probably indicated, *mutatis mutandis*, by A. H. M. Jones's remarks about the later Roman Empire: 'My own impression is that many, if not most, laws were intermittently and sporadically enforced, and that their chief evidential value is to prove that the abuses which they were intended to remove were known to the central government. The laws, in my view, are clues to the difficulties of the government and not its achievement.'[14]

Ghazan died very young, like most of his line, in 1304. He was succeeded by his brother Öljeitü, who retained Rashīd al-Dīn in office. Seeing that the Mongol history was now complete, and a suitable memorial to his late brother, Öljeitü asked Rashīd al-Dīn to supplement it with an account of all the peoples with whom the Mongols had come into contact. Thus Rashīd al-Dīn's *Jāmiʿ al-tawārīkh*, 'Collection of Histories', came to deserve the title of a world history. It included histories of China, India, the Turks, the Jews, the pre-Islamic Persians, Muḥammad and the Caliphs, even of the Franks, the peoples of western Europe. His method was to use whatever written sources came to hand, and to supplement this information by consulting a learned individual, if possible

---

[14]   A. H. M. Jones, *The Later Roman Empire* (1964), vol. 1, p. viii.

from the people in question. These informants are always named, except in the case of the history of the Franks, a perfunctory work that reflects the characteristic Muslim indifference to the affairs of barbarian Europe (see chapter 7). There was also to have been a geographical appendix, but this, if it was ever written, has yet to come to light.

It is above all because of the existence of the *Jāmiʿ al-tawārīkh* that it is possible to make such large claims for the centrality of the Persian sources for the study of the Mongol Empire's history. No other people produced anything remotely comparable, and indeed there is no other Persian work on the same scale. Rashīd al-Dīn was a many-sided man. As well as his history he wrote voluminously on Islamic theology, works which are orthodox rather than important: their production may have been a necessary precautionary measure for a convert from Judaism. He built lavishly, and the *waqf-nāma*, the deed of religious endowment for the quarter he erected in the Ilkhanid capital of Tabrīz, has been preserved, and is in part written in his own hand. He wrote a long series of letters, mainly of advice, though these present problems of interpretation, and may have been tampered with if they are not actually spurious. He was chief minister of a vast empire.

How did he find time for it all? Another historian of the day, Qāshānī, author of a history of Öljeitü's reign, was in no doubt of part of the answer: he, Qāshānī, was the true author of the *Jāmiʿ al-tawārīkh*, and Rashīd al-Dīn had stolen the credit. Examination of Qāshānī's own work, and comparison with Rashīd al-Dīn's, does little to lend credibility to this claim. Rashīd al-Dīn tells us that he used to write his history between morning prayer and sunrise, not a large proportion of the day. The likelihood is that the great minister had a staff of research assistants, and that like many and eminent historian whose time is taken up mainly with administration, he employed those assistants to do most of the work other than the final writing up. Qāshānī may well have been one of these – a sort of Maurice Ashley to Rashīd al-Dīn's Churchill.[15]

---

[15]   On Rashīd al-Dīn see further J. A. Boyle (tr.), Rashīd al-Dīn, *The Successors of Genghis Khan* (1971), introduction; D. O. Morgan, 'Cassiodorus and Rashīd al-Dīn on barbarian rule in Italy and Persia', *Bulletin of the School of Oriental and African Studies*, 40/2 (1977), pp. 302–20; for a discussion of Jūzjānī, Juwaynī and Rashīd al-Dīn, see D. O. Morgan, 'Persian historians and the Mongols', in D. O. Morgan (ed.), *Medieval Historical Writing in the Christian and Islamic Worlds* (1982), pp. 109–24. On Rashīd al-Dīn's theological writings see J. van Ess, *Der Wesir und seine Gelehrten* (1981).

Rashīd al-Dīn's dominance is so great that it has tended to obscure the major importance of another Persian historian writing at the same time and a little later, Waṣṣāf. Part of the trouble is the almost unbeliev- able complexity of Waṣṣāf's Persian style, compared with the simplicity and clarity of Rashīd al-Dīn's, at least in his narrative sections. It is said that when Waṣṣāf read part of his great work to the Ilkhān Öljeitü, the monarch was unable to make head or tail of it.[16] This is an experience which has been shared, in all probability, by every subsequent would-be reader, Persians not excluded: in 1968 an abridgement of Waṣṣāf, sum- marising the substance of what he actually says, was published in Tehran, in modern Persian and for the convenience of native Persian speakers. It has also proved to be a godsend for foreign historians. Waṣṣāf's incomprehensibility unfortunately did not prevent him from becoming a stylistic model for later Persian historians.

But as the great modern authority on Persian literature, E. G. Browne, remarked in understandable exasperation, 'we could forgive the author more readily if his work were less valuable as an original authority on the period of which it treats, but in fact it is as important as it is unreadable'.[17] Waṣṣāf is worth the effort, and we badly need some self- sacrificing Persian scholar to devote a decade or two of his time to the production of a translation. When his information can be got at, it turns out to be full and reliable, independent of and with a different emphasis from that in Rashīd al-Dīn's work. It is basically a history of Mongol Persia, planned as a sequel to Juwaynī's history; but like Juwaynī it ranges far and wide, including a good deal of material about China as well as much detailed and very instructive information about Fārs, the author's home province where he had served in the financial administra- tion. In 1928 the Russian Orientalist Barthold wrote that 'Juwaynī's work has not as yet been valued at its deserts'.[18] That is no longer true of Juwaynī, but it certainly is of Waṣṣāf, and seems likely to remain so.

The historian who cannot read Persian needs Russian for his Rashīd al-Dīn. Soviet scholars are his best editors, and they have produced translations of much of the *Jāmi' al-tawārīkh*. No more than the section on 'the successors of Genghis Khan' has found its way into English,[19] though other parts are available in French or German. Only Joseph von Hammer-Purgstall has so far tried his hand at Waṣṣāf, putting the first

[16]   E. G. Browne, *A Literary History of Persia* (1928), vol. 3, p. 68.
[17]   Ibid.
[18]   W. Barthold, *Turkestan down to the Mongol Invasion* (1977), p. 40.
[19]   Boyle, *The Successors of Genghis Khan*.

part of the book into German, perhaps the most appropriate language. So the accessibility of these crucially important sources is limited, though the situation is much more satisfactory than that faced by the Mongol historian who cannot read Chinese.

One lesser Persian historian of the period should also be mentioned: Ḥamd Allāh Mustawfī Qazwīnī. Like Qāshānī he was a protégé of Rashīd al-Dīn, who appointed him to high office in the tax administration of the Ilkhanate. He wrote two works of some note: the *Ta'rīkh-i guzīda* and the *Nuzhat al-qulūb*. The first is a general history of the world, the last section of which gives a useful short account of the Mongol period in Persia. The second is a compilation whose geographical section provides us with a mass of material, geographical, historical and financial, about the Ilkhanate, though it also deals, less authoritatively, with other parts of the world. Ḥamd Allāh is important both because he completed his books in 1330 and 1340 respectively, so giving us some insight into conditions during the late Ilkhanid period, for which we have few sources; and because the fiscal information he gives, coming as it does from an official who knew the taxation system from the inside, is likely to be fairly reliable.

European Sources

For European evidence on the Mongols, out most interesting and informative sources are the accounts of travellers in the Mongol Empire. For the most part, European chroniclers took little note of what was happening in remotest Asia except when they were obliged to do so by disasters like the Mongol invasion of Russia and eastern Europe in 1237–42. From such a source as the *Novgorod Chronicle* we can gain a sense of the appalled incomprehension of those who, almost without warning, found themselves bearing the brunt of the Mongol onslaught.[20] By far the fullest chronicler's account is that of Matthew Paris, the St Albans historian. He seems to have had access to some very good information about the Mongols, and his story of how the price of herrings dropped at Yarmouth because the Baltic fleets stayed at home for fear of the Mongols has been famous since Gibbon accorded it a footnote.[21] Mixed in with accurate information is a plentiful supply of legend,

[20]   See R. Michell and N. Forbes (trs), *The Chronicle of Novgorod* (1914).

[21]   E. Gibbon, *The History of the Decline and Fall of the Roman Empire* (1905–6), vol. 7, p. 16, n. 45.

speculation and a fair sprinkling of tall stories. But considered as a whole, Matthew Paris's work gives us a vivid and readable impression of how Europeans reacted to the Mongol threat in the 1240s. He also includes in an appendix an invaluable collection of letters from rulers and others about what should be done to counter the threat, and bewailing the disaster.[22]

In addition to the letters preserved by Matthew Paris, a considerable body of diplomatic correspondence has survived, involving Mongol and European rulers. These letters provide us with precious direct evidence of the changing character of Mongol–European relations. The bulk of the correspondence concerned the Papacy, and most of the letters between the popes and the Mongol rulers have now been conveniently collected together.[23]

Among the travellers, the most acute observers were two Franciscan friars, John of Plano Carpini and William of Rubruck. Carpini was sent to Mongolia in the 1240s, in the aftermath of the invasion of Europe, by Pope Innocent IV. He travelled as papal ambassador through eastern Europe and southern Russia to the camp of the Great Khān, not far from the Mongol capital, Qaraqorum in Mongolia. He received an honourable if slightly frosty welcome; the Mongols made a special point of behaving courteously to ambassadors. In due course he was sent home with a letter from the Great Khān Güyük, demanding the submission of Europe and the attendance of the Pope and other potentates at the Mongol court to pay their homage. This letter – it is written in Persian – still exists in the Vatican archives.

Clearly the main purpose of Carpini's mission was to spy out the land, and the report he compiled, his *Ystoria Mongalorum*, makes no bones about this. He tells us about his journey, and what he was able to discover about Mongol history and customs; he is better on the latter than on the former. But the main concern of his book is its detailed discussion of how the Mongols were organised for war, and how in his

[22]   There is an English translation of Matthew Paris by J. A. Giles: *Matthew Paris's English History* (1852–4). On his Mongol material see J. J. Saunders, 'Matthew Paris and the Mongols', in T. A. Sandquist and M. R. Powicke (eds), *Essays in Medieval History presented to Bertie Wilkinson* (1969), pp. 116–32. The original MS of the *Chronica Majora* in the library of Corpus Christi College, Cambridge, contains some splendid illustrations by Matthew Paris of the Mongols doing disagreeable things to their victims.

[23]   See K. -E. Lupprian (ed.), *Die Beziehungen der Päpste zu islamischen und mongolischen Herrschern im 13. Jahrhundert anhand ihres Briefwechsels* (1981).

opinion the European powers might best prepare to resist them. Two versions of this report are known to exist, Carpini's own and another, with important variants, which is usually called the *Tartar Relation*. It may be based on an account by Carpini's companion Benedict the Pole, who was also responsible for another, very short, account that is extant. The *Tartar Relation* was first discovered, in a unique manuscript, in association with the notorious Vinland Map, now shown to be spurious. But there seems no substantial reason for doubting the authenticity of the *Relation*.

As the first observer to have seen the Mongols not only at first hand but for a lengthy period and in their own homeland, Carpini acquired considerable fame on his return to Europe. We can see from one of the contemporary Franciscan gossip Salimbene's stories that his journeys across Europe took on something of the character of a lecture tour.[24] But he was not the only papal envoy sent to the Mongols at this time. Among the others was Ascelinus, and his journey was recorded by his companion Simon of St Quentin. The journey took them to Mongol territory in the Middle East, but they did not go on to Mongolia. Simon's account has not survived independently, but it was in large part incorporated into a historical encyclopaedia, the *Speculum Historiale* of Vincent of Beauvais. From there it has been painstakingly extracted and published by Professor Jean Richard.[25] It is full of interest, including for example an account of the Great Khān Güyük's enthronement in 1246 that is much more detailed than that of Carpini; though whether that makes it more reliable than Carpini is another matter. Carpini was present at the enthronement and Simon was not.

For some reason that has never been clearly established, the *Itinerarium* of William of Rubruck, later than Carpini's *Ystoria* but longer and much better informed, was destined for obscurity. There are many manuscripts of Carpini's narrative, but only four independent ones of Rubruck's, and they are all in England. This is an oddity that has led to speculation that Roger Bacon, who knew Rubruck and found the Mongols interesting, might have had something to do with their preservation.[26] Rubruck was not, technically, an ambassador. He was sent by Louis IX of France, but Louis, whose previous experience of despatching envoys to the Mongols had not been encouraging, declined to

---

[24] G. G. Coulton, *From St. Francis to Dante* (1972), pp. 135–6.

[25] J. Richard (ed.), Simon de Saint-Quentin, *Histoire des Tartares* (1965).

[26] R. W. Southern, *Western Views of Islam in the Middle Ages* (1962), pp. 51–2.

give him official status. Instead, Rubruck travelled as a missionary, and as such had a less privileged passage through Asia than had been accorded to Carpini. But he reached Qaraqorum, and had meetings with the then Great Khān, Möngke, who had seized the throne in 1251.

Rubruck's book is much more a straightforward travel narrative than Carpini's, and is the work of a far shrewder observer. Overall we have in the *Itinerarium* a much fuller picture of what the Mongol Empire was like. Appropriately for a missionary, he tells us a great deal about the religions he encountered, and is especially interested in Nestorian Christianity, a sect originating in fifth century Antioch which held an unorthodox doctrine of the person of Christ. This church was at the time very widely spread throughout Asia, and was temporarily enjoying a considerable measure of favour at the hands of the Mongols. The great set piece of the book is Rubruck's account of a religious debate held before Möngke, with the local Nestorians, Muslims and Buddhists together with Rubruck himself as protagonists. Rubruck won the argument hands down, according to his own testimony, and there is no doubt that in his opinion it was highly desirable that he and not the Nestorians should represent the Christian cause. Although he never seems to refer to the particular heresy that had originally distinguished Nestorianism from orthodox Christianity, he took a very low view of the character and attainments of the Nestorian priests and monks that he met. Writing of one part of Central Asia, he asserts that 'the Nestorians there know nothing. They say their offices and have their sacred books in Syriac, a language of which they are ignorant ... and this accounts for the fact that they are completely corrupt.'[27] Rubruck returned to Acre in 1255, bringing with him the now customary letter from the Great Khān enjoining prompt submission.[28]

[27]   A. van Den Wyngaert (ed.), *Sinica Franciscana*, vol. 1 (1929), p. 238; tr. C. Dawson (ed.), *The Mongol Mission* (1955), p. 144.

[28]   De Rachewiltz, *Papal Envoys to the Great Khans* is a good account of Carpini, Rubruck and others. The Latin texts of most of their travel narratives are in van Den Wyngaert, *Sinica Franciscana*. Many of them are translated in Dawson, *The Mongol Mission*. A new annotated translation of Rubruck is being prepared for the Hakluyt Society by Dr P. Jackson and myself. See the very interesting discussion, especially of Rubruck, in Southern, *Western Views of Islam in the Middle Ages*, chapter 2, For the *Tartar Relation* see R. A. Skelton, T. E. Marston and G. D. Painter (eds and trs), *The Vinland Map and the Tartar Relation* (1965), which provides a translation as well as a facsimile of the MS and a printed text (usefully making clear what is not found in Carpini). A. Önnerfors (ed.), *Hystoria Tartarorum C. de Bridia Monachi* (1967) is a better edition of the Latin text.

Twenty years later, when Marco Polo travelled to China, the Mongol Empire had to a degree broken up into separate khanates. The Europeans were no longer held in such contempt, and no peremptory summons arrived with him when he returned to Venice from the court of the Great Khān Qubilai in 1295. Marco Polo's book is of course by far the best known ever written about the Mongol Empire, and deservedly so. His merchant's perspective was very different from that of the Franciscan friars. He spent 20 years in Asia, most of it in the service of the Mongols in China. His is a more relaxed account than those of the Franciscans, full of anecdotes and miscellaneous information, often very accurate, though his European contemporaries regarded it as incredible. He saw far more of the empire than his predecessors, none of whom, if they reached China, has left any account of that country; and it is his Chinese information that is the most valuable part of his book. His touch is less sure when he is writing about areas he passed through but did not live in, and when he is repeating what he has heard rather than what he himself saw. Historians of China are impressed with the accuracy of his picture of Chinese society, and he is of particular interest as a representative example of a curious Mongol practice in China: that of using, as far as possible, non-Chinese personnel in high administrative posts. The Mongols, it seems, were anxious to avoid becoming the prisoners of the Chinese bureaucracy, and preferred to employ officials who were entirely dependent on themselves.[29]

Modern Studies

In a sense, the academic study in Europe of the Mongol Empire can be said to have begun with John of Plano Carpini and Matthew Paris. In terms of modern historiography, however, the true beginnings were in the eighteenth century. The first modern study of Chingiz Khān was published in France in 1710: Petis de la Croix's *Historie du Grand Genghizcan*. An English translation followed in 1722, with a dedication

[29]   There are numerous translations of Marco Polo. A. Ricci (tr.), *The Travels of Marco Polo* (1931) has a good index, and is the version I generally use. A. C. Moule and P. Pelliot (trs), *Marco Polo: the Description of the World* (1938) has the highest reputation. The Penguin edition, R. E. Latham (tr.), *The Travels of Marco Polo* (1958), is quite satisfactory. On Polo's Chinese information see e.g. E. Balazs 'Marco Polo in the capital of China', in his *Chinese Civilisation and Bureaucracy* (1964), pp. 79–100.

to the Prince of Wales, the future George II, and a hilarious preface in which the Prince is compared (to his advantage) with Chingiz Khān. This book, even now by no means a contemptible piece of work, was based largely on whatever Persian manuscript sources were available to the author in the library of Louis XIV – such works as those of Rashīd al-Dīn and later histories like the fifteenth-century chronicle of Mīrkhwānd. It is remarkable how influential a basic book like this can be, even after 250 years. The view which it presents of Chingiz Khān's alleged legal code, the *Yāsā* – a largely mistaken one, in my view (see chapter 4) – has in its essentials remained unquestioned ever since. This is despite the fact that it may well be a long time since anyone who has written on the subject actually looked at the *Histoire du Grand Genghizcan*. First in the field, Petis de la Croix's framework passed into the assumptions of all subsequent writers on the history of the Mongol Empire.

The next significant work was also by a Frenchman, Gaubil's *Histoire du Gentchiscan*, published in 1739. Unlike Petis de la Croix's book, this was compiled from Chinese sources, and thus offered a different perspective. There was no full-scale history, however, until in 1824 d'Ohsson published his *Histoire des Mongols* in four volumes, based principally on the Persian sources, but to a greater extent than Petis de la Croix on the earliest and most reliable. To this day it is generally said to be the best full treatment in any European language, though I suspect that it is more often commended than read.

The English contribution to Mongol studies had not so far been substantial, though Gibbon's account (the first part of volume 7 in Bury's edition) is well worth reading. It is characteristically shrewd, even if it does show more than a trace of the eighteenth-century fascination with the supposedly noble savage. The French held the field, and in some ways their most impressive achievement was Quatremère's edition and translation of part of Rashīd al-Dīn's history, published in 1836. Its enormous annotation is still indispensable. The period after d'Ohsson's work was published was one of an increase in the bulk of writing on the Mongols, but perhaps of a decrease in critical acumen. The ubiquitous Joseph von Hammer-Purgstall wrote lengthy works on the Mongols in Russia and in Persia (1840, 1841–3), and the first major English contribution was Howorth's four-volume *History of the Mongols* of 1876–88. This was a compilation that added little if anything to d'Ohsson, and was not based on the primary sources, since Howorth was unable to read any of them except those few that had been translated. Nothing on such a scale has ever again been attempted in English.

Of a very different quality, and one of the great monuments of Victorian scholarship at its impressive best, was Sir Henry Yule's edition of Marco Polo, first published in 1876. The annotation to the 1903 edition ranks with Quatremère's Rashīd al-Dīn in its permanent importance.

The twentieth century has seen the appearance of a number of standard works, securely based on the relevant sources, which have provided a practicable foundation for more detailed studies. Among these, some of the most notable are the great Russian scholar Barthold's *Turkestan down to the Mongol Invasion*, Bertold Spuler's volumes on the Golden Horde and on the Mongols in Persia, and the last two volumes of Otto Franke's *Geschichte des chinesischen Reiches*. A useful summary in English of the current state of studies on Mongol Persia was published in 1968 in the fifth volume of the *Cambridge History of Iran*; and in 1981 there appeared a conspectus of the way in which historians of China are now reassessing earlier views on Mongol rule in China. As the days of the grand-sweep Orientalist are passing, the most useful work is now being done by narrower specialists. But that work still needs its synthesisers. Perhaps the best in recent years has been J. J. Saunders, whose *History of the Mongol Conquests* appeared in 1971. This must now be regarded as the obvious introduction to the history of the Mongol Empire.[30]

Yet there is still a very long way to go. Compared with the study of English or European history, the study of the Mongol Empire is in its infancy. To mention only what was the most glaring lacuna, until 1983 none of the innumerable biographies of Chingiz Khān himself was of any real consequence at all, except for the partial study by H. D. Martin, *The Rise of Chingis Khan and his Conquest of North China*. The writing of a satisfactory new biography needed, ideally, a scholar who was at home equally in Mongolian, Chinese and Persian. An earlier generation possessed such a scholar in Paul Pelliot, a phenomenal figure who wrote innumerable articles and left a vast amount of unpublished work (it is still coming out, though he died in 1945). But he did not

---

[30]   Barthold, *Turkestan down to the Mongol Invasion*; B. Spuler, *Die Goldene Horde: die Mongolen in Russland 1223–1502* (1965); B. Spuler, *Die Mongolen in Iran* (1968: new edition in the press); J. A. Boyle (ed.), *The Cambridge History of Iran*, vol. 5: *The Saljuq and Mongol Periods* (1968); O. Franke, *Geschichte des chinesischen Reiches* (1930–52); J. D. Langlois Jr (ed.), *China under Mongol Rule* (1981); J. J. Saunders, *The History of the Mongol Conquests* (1971).

write books. For all his achievement one cannot avoid the feeling that Pelliot's unparalleled linguistic and critical gifts never quite realised their potential in print.[31] Professor Paul Ratchnevsky, one of Pelliot's pupils, is among the few scholars who do have the necessary skills, though he is obliged to resort to the Russian translations of Rashīd al-Dīn. His recent study of Chingiz Khān has at last filled the gap, and it is much to be hoped that it will receive an English translation.[32]

A word should be said about archaeological evidence. There is not very much of note. The way of life of the Mongols did not lend itself to the laying down of large deposits of material for later generations to dig up: nomadism is no friend to the archaeologist. But after they had conquered most of the known world, the Mongols possessed cities, and some work has indeed been done on what remains. The principal contributors have been Russian archaeologists, who have dug both in Russia itself, notably in the Golden Horde capital of Sarai, and in Mongolia. There they have excavated the site of the imperial capital, Qaraqorum. Their results are available only in Russian, but a useful brief summary may be found in E. D. Phillips's general study.[33]

These excavations apart, there is not a great deal of specifically Mongol relevance that one can point to. As time goes on and medieval archaeology gains ground, especially, one might hope, in Persia and China, there may prove to be more evidence to interest the historian. Who knows, someone might have a stroke of luck: somewhere in the

---

[31]   The same might be said of Professor Joseph Fletcher of Harvard, whose death in 1984 at the age of 49 was in my judgement the greatest loss suffered by the study of Inner Asian history in my lifetime. If pressed he would admit to having learned 15 languages – a process which inevitably took so long that his published historical work, though of remarkable quality, was at the time of his death very small in quantity.

[32]   H. D. Martin, *The Rise of Chingis Khan and his Conquest of North China* (1950); P. Ratchnevsky, *Činggis-Khan sein Leben und Wirken* (1983). Of other biographies in English, the best of an undistinguished lot are B. Y. Vladimirtsov, *The life of Chingis-Khan*, tr. D. S. Mirsky (1930) and R. Grousset, *Conqueror of the World*, tr. D. Sinor and M. Mackellar (1967) (valuable for its annotated bibliography by D. Sinor). Vladimirtsov, a leading Russian Mongolist, is better represented by his important *Le régime social des Mongols*, tr. M. Carsow (1948). R. Fox, *Genghis Khan* (1936) is a lively read, and L. Hambis, *Gengis-Khan* (1973) a useful short account in French (in the 'Que sais-je?' series).

[33]   E. D. Phillips, *The Mongols* (1969).

mountains of north Mongolia is the carefully hidden tomb of Chingiz Khān himself.[34] For the moment, however, it is written evidence that must provide the foundation for the study of this subject, supplemented perhaps by a cautious use of the findings of anthropologists who have studied nomads and nomadism and of the accounts of nineteenth- and twentieth-century travellers in Mongolia. The potentialities of this mass of evidence are not likely to be exhausted for a very long time to come.

[34]   See J. A. Boyle, 'The thirteenth-century Mongols' conception of the after-life: the evidence of their funerary practices', *Mongolian Studies*, 1 (1974), pp. 8–9.

2

Nomads of the Steppe: Asia before Chingiz Khān

Steppe Society

The homeland of the Mongols was in the territory of the modern Mongolian People's Republic, at the eastern end of the vast belt of steppe grassland that stretched as far west as the Hungarian plain. To the north was the impenetrable Siberian forest, the taiga; to the south, desert, and beyond that the lands of settled civilisation – most important, in the nomads' eyes, China. The steppe is treeless pasture, not land that was suitable for agriculture, though there were exceptions, especially the oases along the valley of the river Orkhon in central Mongolia. But it was ideally suited for the pasturing of flocks and herds. The nomads relied above all on sheep and horses. Sheep provided skins for clothing, wool for the manufacture of the characteristic felt tents (*gers*, often called *yurts* in the West) that were the nomads' homes, mutton, milk and cheese for food, and dung for fuel. Horses were the principal means of transport, both of men and goods, and were essential for hunting, which was a major source of food and incidentally a method of military training (see chapter 4); and they were needed for warfare. Their milk, when fermented, provided the staple alcoholic drink, *qumis*, which must have had considerable potency, to judge from the high proportion of Mongol notables who died young from the effects of drink. Less important, but still an integral part of the steppe economy, were camels, and oxen, which were used to pull carts.

As nomads, the Mongols migrated seasonally, typically from summer pastures on the plain to winter pastures in a sheltered valley (for Mongolia itself is a mountainous land, not one of unremitting flatness).

Plate 2.1   An oasis in Mongolia. John Massey Stewart Picture Library

These migrations were not aimless. Every group would, in normal circumstances, move along well-tried routes from one customary pasture to another. Major variations if they occurred, might be the result or the occasion of war. A better pasture was likely to be someone else's pasture. The distances travelled on the seasonal migration would not necessarily be very great: 100 miles or so might not be uncommon.

Man cannot live, or at least does not usually wish to live, on animal products alone. The nomads always had to satisfy some of their needs through trade with the settled societies to the south. Among those needs were grain and a variety of what might be regarded as luxuries, such as tea and textiles. Most important of all, the nomads required metals with which to make their weapons. Reciprocally, settled civilisation could find a use for the nomads' own products: commerce was regarded as mutually beneficial. The relationship between the steppe and the sown should not be envisaged as one of constant hostility, marked by a predatory urge on one side and a fearful defensiveness on the other. In time of peace, however uneasy, it was more a relationship of mutual dependence, though Chinese products were more central to the nomads' needs than anything from the steppes was to the Chinese. This is not to deny that attitudes on both sides were, fundamentally, hostile. In the last analysis the nomads' view of sedentary society was a predatory one, and

Plate 2.2 Chingiz Khān's camp, showing the Mongol felt tents (*gers*). From a Persian miniature. Bibliothèque Nationale de France, Paris, MS. Persian Suppl. 1113, fol. 66v

their predatory instincts were limited only in so far as military circumstances prevented them from indulging them. The nomads had little real understanding of or sympathy with a society based on agriculture and cities, however much they may have valued some of the material products of such societies.[1]

This general statement should, however, be qualified by considering the extent to which any particular group of nomads had first-hand experience of what settled society was like. The Chinese, always very aware of the threat from the north, categorised the nomads into 'cooked' and 'uncooked' barbarians: the cooked ones were those who lived nearer to China and were more influenced by Chinese civilisation. These tended to be the tribes that lived on the southern side of the Gobi desert, in the vicinity of the frontier that was later demarcated by the Great Wall of China. In the twelfth century the government of north China maintained fairly close control of the frontier zone,[2] but much attention was also paid to the more remote barbarians, since they were likely to prove the most dangerous. There was a standard imperial Chinese policy for dealing with them. They would be carefully watched, and if one nomadic chief seemed to be gaining power and influence at the expense of others, Chinese subsidies, recognition and titles would be offered to one of his rivals, who would be encouraged to cut the upstart down to size. Should the new protégé in his turn seem to be becoming dangerously powerful, the process would be repeated. The Chinese had a good record of success in such enterprises; but when they did not work, as in the case of Chingiz Khān's Mongols, the consequences might be fateful or indeed fatal.

The nature of the nomadic clan and tribe is still a topic of lively debate among anthropologists. It is at least clear, however, that we shall misunderstand nomadic society if we think of it as composed of tribes whose membership is determined exclusively by blood relationship. Theoretically they were so determined, and this is no doubt the

---

[1]   All general accounts of the Mongols contain some discussion of their physical habitat and of steppe nomadism. Particularly helpful are J. J. Saunders, *The History of the Mongol Conquests* (1971), chapter 1, and E. O. Reischauer and J. K. Fairbank, *East Asia: the Great Tradition* (1958), chapter 7. As a general study of Mongol society over the centuries, S. Jagchid and P. Hyer, *Mongolia's Culture and Society* (1979) is in something of a class of its own.

[2]   P. D. Buell, 'The role of the Sino-Mongolian frontier zone in the rise of Cinggis-Qan', in H. G. Schwarz (ed.), *Studies on Mongolia: Proceedings of the First North American Conference on Mongolian Studies* (1979), pp. 63–4.

explanation of plethora of patently spurious genealogies that litter the contemporary and later literature. In reality, however, the tribe was a rather 'open' institution, its membership created more by shared political interests than by descent from a common ancestor. It is only in this way that it is possible to explain the fact that Chingiz Khān was able to organise the nomads of Central Asia, an extraordinarily disparate collection of groupings whether considered 'racially' or linguistically, into a unified and effective war machine. Chingiz Khān may have manipulated the nomadic tribal structure on a larger scale than any of his predecessors, but in essence he merely followed accepted precedent.[3]

In his analysis of Mongol society in the twelfth century, Owen Lattimore divides the clans (*oboq*) that constituted the larger groupings, the tribes, into subordinate – their subordination resulting from military defeat or from the need for protection – and ruling clans.[4] Within the ruling clan, kinship was certainly on principle of organisation; but even that included provision for a 'free choice' of kinship, the institution of *anda*, or sworn brotherhood. In the *Secret History of the Mongols* Chingiz Khān is represented as enjoying an especially close relationship with his *anda*, and later principal rival, Jamuqa. He is also able to profit politically, when his fortunes are at a low ebb, from the fact that his father had been *anda* to Toghril of the Keraits, one of the most powerful of the steppe rulers. *Anda*-ship, then, was the voluntary equivalent of blood relationship between equals.

More overtly voluntary was attachment by an individual to a leader of his own choice. In order to do this, he would have to forswear his blood loyalty to his own clan. He would become his new leader's *nöker*. This is a difficult term to translate; perhaps 'associate' or 'comrade' is better than 'follower', though as time went on the latter connotation became more prominent. The word entered the Persian language during the Mongol period, and now, by a not uncommon process of descent down the terminological social scale, means 'servant'. It was certainly not that in twelfth-century Mongolia. The *nöker* system became one means whereby a gifted but politically insignificant warrior could build up a following, if he had the qualities of leadership and personal mag-

---

[3] I have been greatly influenced here by R. P. Lindner, *Nomads and Ottomans in Medieval Anatolia* (1983), chapter 1, and 'What was a nomadic tribe?', *Comparative Studies in Society and History*, 24/4 (1982), pp. 689–711.

[4] O. Lattimore, 'Inner Asian frontiers – defensive empires and conquest empires', in his *Studies in Frontier History* (1962), pp. 506ff.

netism that would attract other warriors to his banner. Again the *Secret History* illustrates vividly how in just this way the young Chingiz Khān acquired many of his early adherents, some of whom would later become his greatest generals. Lattimore contends that the increasing prevalence of individuals to abandon their own clan so as to become *nöker* to some chosen leader has significance in what he regards as the transition, then in progress, from tribal to 'feudal' organisation among the steppe peoples. We may perhaps doubt whether the concept of feudalism as an explanatory device for understanding nomadic society is likely to prove helpful: no doubt much depends on what is meant by 'feudalism'.[5] But to introduce it does at least emphasise that we are not dealing with a society whose structure is determined wholly by descent. It should be added that the openness of the clan structure was further aided by the universal practice of exogamy (marriage outside the clan).

It has already been implied that the position of a chief was very much dependent on his own individual merit, as that was perceived by his actual or potential followers. This did not quite mean that anyone could become a chief if he could attract enough support. The tribes had their noble families. Chingiz Khān himself was a member of such a family, some of whom had been powerful khāns in earlier years. This was enough to make him a possible candidate for chieftainship, but not by any means enough to guarantee success. Among the nomads, chieftainship was an *ad hoc* institution, existing for the convenience, very largely, of those 'ruled'. There had to be an accepted arbitrator for the resolution of disputes; there was need of a war leader in whom the warriors had confidence. So chiefs were made, not simply born. Incompetence meant instant *de facto* disqualification. When a chief died, his effective successor might well be that one of his family who had succeeded in wiping out the other contenders, and who had thus demonstrated his efficiency: a process to which Professor Fletcher has applied the term 'tanistry'.[6] Even then, in normal circumstances, a chief's power was closely circumscribed. He could expect to be obeyed without question in time of war, but his interference in peoples' lives during peacetime would not be welcomed.

In the *Secret History's* account of Chingiz Khān's election as khān of the Mongols, his new and voluntary subordinates are represented as

[5]   Cf. P. Anderson, *Passages from Antiquity to Feudalism* (1974), pp. 219–20.

[6]   J. F. Fletcher, 'Turco-Mongolian monarchic tradition in the Ottoman Empire', *Harvard Ukrainian Studies*, 3–4 (1979–80), pp. 236–51.

promising him the pick of captured women and horses, as well as of animals killed in the hunt. But the only obedience they commit themselves to – and that is absolute obedience – is in time of war. So far as peacetime is concerned, they undertake only to refrain from acting in any way that is contrary to the khān's interests. The promise of obedience in battle was taken seriously: three of the subordinate chiefs subsequently disobeyed an order not to delay in battle for the purpose of looting. Their plunder was confiscated.[7]

Such was the foundation of Chingiz Khān's rule; which is not to say that his power, or that of his family, was so circumscribed once they had become would conquerors. Yet even then the Mongol Empire was not an autocracy, with rule determined by primogeniture or any other blood principle. Chingiz Khān's nomination of his third son, Ögedei, as his successor was indeed in due course accepted after the founding father's death, such was Chingiz's prestige; but the family seems to have run the empire on something of a consultative basis.

This is in fact what one would have been led to expect by a study of earlier Central Asian (whether Mongolian or Turkish) conceptions of the nature of political rule. Not only was the extent of a khān's power limited, but that power was seen rather as a family than as a personal possession. The choice of a successor was in theory decided by a *quriltai*, an assembly of Mongol notables; and these were indeed convened. But after Ögedei died in 1241, his own nomination of a grandson as successor was ignored, and much disputation ensured. Not until 1246 was Ögedei's son Güyük able to secure his own elevation; and only his early death in 1248 averted the outbreak of open conflict within the Chingizid family. After that, the throne was seized by another branch of the family in a *coup d'état* that was a perfect demonstration of 'tanistry', though it was legitimised by a *quriltai*; and the next vacancy was similarly settled, in this case by a civil war, at the outset of which both candidates were duly elected by *quriltais* of their supporters (see chapter 5).

It is interesting to note that during both interregnums, 1241–6 and 1248–51, the empire was headed by the late Great Khān's widow as regent. This did not prevent Güyük's widow from being executed when her branch of the family was ultimately the loser in the succession struggle, but it is a significant indication of the relatively high position held by women in Mongol society. This is illustrated too in the *Secret*

[7]   Paras 123 and 153: F. W. Cleaves (tr.), *The Secret History of the Mongols* (1982), pp. 54–5 and 81–2.

History's stories of the respect shown by Chingiz Khān to the opinions of his mother and chief wife – neither of whom, of course, came from Chingiz's own tribe. Indeed, his mother had been acquired by his father by force, which was one way of observing the custom of exogamy. Women played an important role, not only at times in political affairs, but also on occasion in warfare, and always in the management of the family's flocks and herds.[8] Polygamy flourished among those able to afford it, but the chief wife of a ruler had a special status: only Chingiz Khān's sons by that wife were regarded as eligible for the succession.

Mongol Religious Beliefs

The Mongols' religious beliefs and practices come into the category that is usually called Shamanism. Quite what this amounted to in the twelfth and thirteenth centuries is not, in detail, always easy to determine, for we possess no systematic contemporary exposition of it. A good deal, however, may be deduced from such sources as the *Secret History*; and otherwise our best body of information is probably the often acute observations of the early European travellers, especially Carpini and Rubruck. Some elements, only half understood, are to be found in the Islamic sources. The difficulty is that religious belief as such seems to have sat rather lightly on the Mongols: it was not long before they took the line of least resistance and adopted, in the various parts of their empire, a more developed religion learned from their conquered subjects. Hence they embraced Islam in Persia and in the lands of the Golden Horde, and a Tibetan variety of Buddhism in China. Buddhism was influential, too, among the Mongols of Persia before their conversion to Islam.

The Mongols' lack of religious fervour is well demonstrated in one of their most lauded characteristics, their firm policy of religious tolerance, which so appealed to writers of the eighteenth century. 'The Catholic inquisitors of Europe', wrote Gibbon in a celebrated passage, 'who defended nonsense by cruelty, might have been confounded by the example of a barbarian, who anticipated the lessons of philosophy and established by his laws a system of pure theism and perfect toleration.' He goes on to add, in a footnote, 'a singular conformity may be found

[8]   See M. Rossabi, 'Khubilai Khan and the women in his family', in W. Bauer (ed.), *Sino-Mongolica: Festschrift für Herbert Franke* (1979), pp. 153–8.

between the religious laws of Zingis Khan and of Mr Locke.'[9] This is rather to overstate the case. Toleration there certainly was, but it was determined not so much by high-mindedness as by indifference, by a feeling that any religion might be right and that therefore it would be sensible to have every subject praying for the khān; and also by the fact that nomadic society in the steppes was accustomed to the practice of many religions. Buddhism was well known; Muslim merchants passed to and fro; many of the Uighur Turks, those influential intermediaries between sedentary civilisation and the steppes, were Manichaeans; and several of the tribes of Mongolia professed Nestorian Christianity.

There is an essential supplement to the contemporary sources for the understanding of Mongol Shamanism. This is the large number of orally transmitted hymns and prayers, dating from later periods and pain-stakingly collected in this century by such scholars as Professor Walther Heissig, whose book on *The Religions of Mongolia* is the best introduction to the subject.[10] The problem with this body of evidence is that in the sixteenth century the Mongols were converted to the Lamaistic Buddhism of Tibet. This did not mean that Shamanism withered away, but it did result in the thorough penetration of Shamanism by Lamaistic elements. Scholars have therefore to filter these out if they are to be able to see clearly what was there before the advent of Buddhism. This is obviously a potentially hazardous process, but the results that Heissig and his colleagues have produced do seem convincing.

Shamanism appears to have originated from ancestor worship. Images of the ancestors called *ongghot* (singular *ongghon*), were kept in the family's tents, and were thought to provide protection if propitiated. Further elaboration followed. At the head of the supernatural hierarchy was the Blue (*Köke*) or Eternal (*Möngke*) Heaven (*Tengri*). The earth and fertility deity was as usual a goddess, Itügen. Below Heaven, and of more immediate importance in daily life, was the world of spirits. The shaman acted as a mediator between man and this mysterious realm. He was a seer who communicated with the spirits while in trance. He had an elevated position in society, dressed in white and rode a white

---

[9]   E. Gibbon, *The History of the Decline and Fall of the Roman Empire* (1905–6), vol. 7, p. 4 and n. 8.

[10]   W. Heissig, *The Reigions of Mongolia* (1980), chapter 2. See also, more generally, M. Eliade, *Shamanism* (1964). J. A. Boyle, 'Turkish and Mongol Shamanism in the Middle Ages', *Folklore*, 83 (1972), pp. 177–93 and other articles gathered in J. A. Boyle, *The Mongol World Empire 1206–1370* (1977) are useful on matters of detail.

horse, and carried as insignia a staff and a drum. His functions were intercession with the spirits, various kinds of exorcism, the recital of blessings over herds, hunters, children and so forth, and prophecy. The last was carried out by burning the shoulder-blades of sheep and examining the cracks the resulted (the procedures have been tested extensively by Professor Charles Bawden).[11]

The shaman was sometimes a powerful figure. There is a fascinating story in the *Secret History* of a conflict between Chingiz Khān and the leading shaman Kököchü in the period just after Chingiz had, partly through the instrumentality of Kököchü, attained acknowledgement of his supreme power at the *quriltai* of 1206.[12] The impression given is that Chingiz may have been faced at this juncture with a priestly challenge to his authority, and that the shaman was aiming at establishing himself at the very least as the effective power behind the throne. At any rate we are presented with the picture of a very nervous Chingiz who did not feel secure until the shaman had been safely done away with; and even then a supernatural story was concocted to explain the disappearance of his body as divine judgement on him.

Notable among the shamanist devotee's rituals was the worship of high places, since from such there was uninterrupted access to Tengri. The devotee would kneel nine times on top of the chosen hill, with his head uncovered and his belt around his neck. Chingiz Khān himself is represented in the *Secret History* as performing this ritual at a crucial stage during his early career.[13] Indeed, the Persian historian Waṣṣāf has an account of an exactly similar occurrence, the significance of which evidently escaped him, many years later on the shores of the Persian Gulf. Other rituals of importance were the sacrifice of meat or of whole horses suspended on poles,[14] and the practice of purification by fire: John of Plano Carpini was disconcerted when required to pass between two fires before being allowed inside Batu Khān's tent.[15]

---

[11]   See W. Heissig, *A Lost Civilisation: the Mongols Rediscovered* (1966), p. 24.

[12]   Paras 245–6: tr. Cleaves, *The Secret History*, pp. 178–82; see Hülegü's later confirmation of Kököchü's role at the *quriltai* in his letter to St Louis: P. Meyvaert, 'An unknown letter of Hulagu, Il-Khan of Persia, to King Louis IX of France', *Viator*, 11 (1980), pp. 245–59, esp. p. 252–3 and n. 36.

[13]   Para. 103: tr. Cleaves, *The Secret History*, p. 37.

[14]   J. A. Boyle, 'A form of horse sacrifice amongst the 13th- and 14th-century Mongols', *Central Asiatic Journal*, 10 (1965), pp. 145–50.

[15]   A. van Den Wyngaert, *Sinica Franciscana*, vol. 1 (1929), p. 109; tr. C. Dawson (ed.), *The Mongol Mission* (1955), p. 56.

Shamanism was, it would seem, exclusively concerned with the material needs of the present life. It may be this that in part at least explains the willingness of the Mongols to entertain the possibility of other religions being true. Heissig writes of Shamanism that it is 'a religion bound to specific goals, directed only to the past and the present. Ideas concerning the future' – in the sense of a future life – 'are foreign to it'.[16] So Buddhism, Christianity or Islam were not necessarily seen by the Mongols, even if they had accepted one of them, as excluding some sort of shadowy belief in and practice of Shamanism. Elements of it therefore continued to exist long after the Mongols had, at least in theory, defected to some other religion. The Mongols believed in taking out as much celestial insurance as possible.

The Mongols' Steppe Predecessors

We have seen in chapter 1 that the Mongol Empire needs to be viewed in the context of previous steppe confederations. The longest lasting of these earlier empires was that of the Hsiung-nu, which reached its apogee in the third and second centuries BC, but survived to trouble the Chinese until the fourth century AD. By this time a section of the Hsiung-nu may possibly have put in an appearance at the other end of the Eurasian steppe, if the identification Hsiung-nu = Huns is accepted. The break-up of east Asian steppe empires was not infrequently followed by the departure of fragments of the defeated confederation westwards: the short-lived Juan-juan empire of the sixth century had its last lease of life in the shape of the Avars of Hungary.

The most formidable of the pre-Mongol empires was probably that of the Turks in the sixth and seventh centuries AD. It was exclusively a steppe empire, but was of such dimensions that it is possible to study its history from both Chinese and Byzantine sources. None of these empires, however, can be said to have exercised any direct influence on the rise of the Mongol Empire, unless we wish to posit, as is plausible enough, some kind of intangible 'steppe political tradition'.[17] The empires of two other peoples are another matter entirely.

[16]   Heissig, *The Religions of Mongolia*, p. 11.
[17]   On these early empires see G. Hambly (ed.), *Central Asia* (1969); R. Grousset, *The Empire of the Steppes*, tr. N. Walford (1970) and W. M. McGovern, *The Early Empires of Central Asia* (1939).

In the aftermath of the dissolution of the Turkish Empire, Mongolia and the eastern steppes came in the mid eighth century under the control of the Uighur Turks, who had their capital in the valley of the Orkhon, near the site of the later Mongol capital, Qaraqorum. It was this kingdom that in 762 adopted the Manichaean faith as its official religion, as a contemporary inscription records. After the fall of their empire in 840, some of the Uighurs migrated south-westwards to the oases of the Tarim basin, in present-day Sinkiang, where they established several minor kingdoms. These, by paying tribute when necessary to more powerful neighbours and generally minding their own business, contrived to survive until they were peacefully incorporated into the Mongol Empire, nearly four centuries later. They developed in the Tarim basin a culture of considerable sophistication, and finally came into their own when their skills, especially the administrative skills of a people who had a respectable steppe pedigree but knew how to organise a sedentary state, came to the notice of Chingiz Khān. We have seen how Chingiz took over the Uighur script for the writing of Mongolian, previously an unwritten language. The Uighurs' chancery practice and scribal tradition, too, had their part to play in the organisation of the Mongol Empire in its formative period (see chapter 4).

At the beginning to the tenth century Mongolia and north China were conquered by a semi-nomadic people from north of the 'Great Wall' frontier, the Khitans, who subsequently as a Chinese dynasty took the name of Liao.[18] This was by no means an unusual development in Chinese history; it was the fulfilment of every Turko-Mongolian nomad chief's fondest dream, the conquest rather than merely the temporary plunder of the rich lands of north China. The Chinese had proved themselves amply capable of taming such conquerors through the complexity and resilience of their civilisation. The Khitan language, in so far as it is understood, seems to be a form of what would later be called Mongolian; and this points to the Khitan people's affinity to the later and greater conquerors. Under the Khitan regime, 'Chinese' direct rule extended further into Mongolia than had been customary, even when the Chinese dynasty was of barbarian origin. The Khitans garrisoned the oases of the Orkhon valley, and the independent-minded Turkish tribes of those parts, if they would not submit, were driven to the west.

[18]   See K. A. Wittfogel and C. Fêng, *History of Chinese Society: Liao 907–1125* (1949).

In eastern Mongolia, behind the Khitan defensive screen, there were now significant developments. It is in this period that for the first time it is possible to detect the emergence of a specifically 'Mongol' people that had direct continuity with the Mongols of Chingiz Khān.

In the 1120s the Khitans were displaced in their turn by a new wave of invaders from the north, the Jürchen of Manchuria (ethnically related to the Manchus who in the seventeenth century provided China with its last imperial dynasty to date, the Ch'ing). The Jürchen ruling family took the dynastic name of Chin, 'golden'. Many Khitans were driven out of China, though others stayed and took service under the Chin. For Mongolia the most important consequence of the Chin conquest of north China was that direct Chinese rule in Mongolia disappeared. The Chin withdrew the Orkhon garrisons: they were more interested in China itself, and indeed they succeeded in conquering and holding far more of China than had ever been under Khitan rule. The Chin became something like an authentic Chinese dynasty, whereas the Khitans had always kept one foot in the steppe. The 'Great Wall' frontier once again became a real one. Meanwhile, in Mongolia, a power vacuum had been created by the end of Khitan rule. Power therefore fell to those on the spot who were in a position to seize it – the mobile mounted nomads, among them the ancestors of Chingiz Khān. For their control of the steppe and its dangerous inhabitants the Chin reverted to the traditional Chinese policy of divide and (indirect) rule.[19]

But the last had not been heard of the Khitans. At the time of the Chin conquest one of the princes of the Khitan royal house had managed to gather together a large group of followers who were unwilling to submit to the new rulers. They had headed westwards into Central Asia, where they succeeded in setting up a new empire in the vast tract of territory that now forms the Soviet and Chinese Central Asian republics and autonomous regions. This empire is known as Qara-Khitai, which might be translated 'Black Cathay' – for it was the Khitans who gave the word 'Cathay' to European languages. Here, in 1141, the new Khitan emperor met in battle the last Great Saljūq sultan of Persia, Sanjar. The Saljūq forces were heavily defeated, and the battle of the Qatwān steppe, near Samarqand, momentous enough in history, entered legend. Distorted accounts of the conflict are thought to have given rise

---

[19]   See O. Lattimore, 'The geography of Chingis Khan', *Geographical Journal*, 129/1 (1963), pp. 1–7, for the emergence of the Mongols.

to the legend of Prester John, or at least to have been 'the peg on which it has been hung'.[20] Prester John, it was believed, had been hastening to the aid of the hard-pressed Christians in the Holy Land; for he was himself the greatest of Christian kings of the Orient. It is not hard to see how optimistic Christians might have assumed that any king who was at war with the Muslims, as the Qara-Khitai ruler indeed was, must himself be a Christian and thus a potential ally.[21]

The Qara-Khitai empire was a curious body politic, still very little known and understood: the study of its history requires a knowledge of Arabic, Persian and Chinese. Administratively it seems to have been a blend of Khitan (steppe 'Mongol'), Central Asian (Turkish) and Chinese elements. The Chinese element was perhaps dominant, and in Chinese historiography the Qara-Khitai have a respectable place in the imperial scheme of things: the dynasty is known as Hsi Liao, western Liao. Chinese, in which all coins were inscribed, was an official language of administration, but Persian and Uighur Turkish were also used. The Qara-Khitai army, on the other hand, gradually lost most of its Chinese characteristics and became more and more a cavalry force of the traditional steppe type, organised decimally as the Liao army and indeed most steppe armies had been. The Qara-Khitai empire was not a rigorously centralised state. Large areas were left to enjoy a considerable measure of autonomy under their local dynasties, especially at the western end of the empire, in Transoxania. Furthermore, as befitted a state with large communities of Buddhists, Manichaeans, Christians and Muslims among its subjects, the Qara-Khitai rulers adhered to a policy of religious toleration.[22]

The Qara-Khitai endured until the Mongol conquest. Like the Uighur lands that formed a part of its dependent territories, their empire fell into Mongol hands without a serious struggle (see chapter 3); and its people can even be said to have welcomed the Mongols, a distinction that gives them some claim to uniqueness. This occurred in 1218, and

[20]   C. F. Beckingham, *The Achievements of Prester John* (1966), p. 5.
[21]   On Prester John see Beckingham, *The Achievements of Prester John* and 'The quest for Prester John', *Bulletin of the John Rylands University Library of Manchester*, 62/2 (1980), pp. 291–310; I. de Rachewiltz, *Papal Envoys to the Great Khans* (1971), pp. 30–40.
[22]   The best information of Qara-Khitai is in W. Barthold, *Turkestan down to the Mongol Invasion* (1977), chapter 3, and Wittfogel and Fêng, *History of Chinese Society*, appendix 5, pp. 619–74.

it can plausibly be argued that the acquistion of the Qara-Khitai territory was one of the most significant steps in the establishment of the
Mongol Empire. For if there is one group of people whose influence on
the organisation and administration of the early Mongol Empire was
even more pervasive than that of the Uighurs, it is the Khitans. Much
of the Khitan influence may well have come from China, where many
Khitans still in Chin service defected to the Mongols, or from the old
Khitan homeland north of the 'Great Wall' frontier. But in the Qara-
Khitai empire the Mongols had taken over, virtually intact, a major state
that had been ruled by a people with strong affinities to the Mongols
and with an illustrious imperial tradition. It would hardly be surprising
if evidence were found of the continuance of Qara-Khitai institutions
in a Mongol guise; and such institutional borrowing is indeed readily
apparent (see chapter 4). With the conquest of the Qara-Khitai following
the employment of numbers of gifted and experienced Khitan officials
from China, the Mongols had an institutional framework available on
which they could and did draw. There is a sense in which the Mongol
Empire was a successor state, on a much grander scale, to the Qara-
Khitai empire.

Asia at the Beginning of the Thirteenth Century

We have seen that Chingiz Khān, after he had succeeded by 1206 in
unifying the tribes of Mongolia under his rule, had to deal with the
Chin dynasty in north China, with the Qara-Khitai, and with the
Uighurs. A more general look at the political map of Asia around
the year 1200 will serve to identify the other major states with which
the new Mongol confederation had to contend.

In accordance with Mongol priorities, China must be considered first.
By the thirteenth century China proper had not constituted a unified
state for a very long time. It is perhaps the Mongols' most enduring
positive legacy to China that they brought the country back under the
rule of one government, as it has remained ever since, except during
periods of civil war. In 1200 'China' comprised three states: the Chin
Empire, already referred to, in the north, Hsi-Hsia in the north-west,
and the Sung Empire in the south. The rulers of Hsi-Hsia were the
Tanguts, a people of Tibetan origin according to the Chinese sources
that form the principal body of information about them. The population, however, included also Chinese, Uighurs and others. It was a partly
sedentary, partly nomadic land, organised largely on Chinese lines, and

deriving most of its governmental revenue from trade, for it was strategically situated across the main east–west trade routes of Asia.[23]

The Sung Empire was in a certain sense the real China, even though the great Chinese dynasties of the past had all had their capitals in the north, whereas the Sung had been driven south. But its dynasty was a native Chinese one, long established, and possessing cultural and administrative continuity with its mighty predecessors, the Han and the T'ang. It occupied the bulk of Chinese territory, and contained the greater part of the Chinese population. It was an agricultural land; there was no nomadism at all. Essentially Sung China was a traditional Chinese empire, run on age-old Confucian principles – a state of great cities and major rivers that provided the necessary irrigation for rice cultivation.

The Sung had never reconciled themselves to the loss of the north, and their metropolis, Hang-chou, was officially known as the temporary capital. 'Temporary' it may have been, but it was still without much doubt the greatest city in the world at that time, with a population of around one million. There happen to be very full Chinese accounts of life in Hang-chou in the period before the Mongol conquest. These, supplemented by the well-informed discussion in Marco Polo's *Travels*, from rather later, have made it possible to reconstruct in some detail the patterns of life in a city whose size, complexity and level of culture were beyond the wildest dreams of anyone in the Christian or Islamic worlds of the day.[24] Unfortunately for the Sung, their empire was not as formidable militarily as it was culturally or administratively. Nevertheless it proved to have considerable staying power, and the Mongols were still fighting in south China in the 1270s, well after their empire had ceased to expand in any other direction.

Westwards, beyond the sub-Chinese empire of the Qara-Khitai lay the Dār al-Islām. The empire of the Saljūq Turks had not, as a whole, long survived the death of Sanjar in 1157. In Persia the principal

---

[23]   For the Tanguts the most up-to-date and accessible information is probably that in L. Kwanten, *Imperial Nomads: a History of Central Asia, 500–1500* (1979); but the reader should be warned that this book, generally considered, is a minefield of conceptual oddities and factual inaccuracies: see, *inter alia*, C. Hung, 'China and the nomads: misconceptions in western historiography on Inner Asia', *Harvard Journal of Asiatic Studies*, 41/2 (1981), pp. 597–628 and D. O. Morgan, 'The Mongol Empire: a review article', *Bulletin of the School of Oriental and African Studies*, 44/1 (1981), pp. 120–5.

[24]   A. C. Moule, *Quinsai, with other notes on Marco Polo* (1957); J. Gernet, *Daily Life in China on the Eve of the Mongol Invasion* (1962).

successors to the Saljūqs were another Turkish family, the Khwārazm-shāhs. Khwārazm is the very fertile province in the area where the river Oxus flows into the Aral Sea, and its ruling dynasty was descended from the provincial governor appointed to that province by the Saljūq sultan in the eleventh century. In 1200 the Khwārazm-shāh, the ruler who had in due course have to face, or rather to flee from, the Mongol onslaught, was 'Alā' al-Dīn Muḥammad II. The Khwārazm-shāhs had originally been obliged to accept a position of subordination to the rulers of the Qara-Khitai, but Muḥammad embarked on an expansionist policy that allowed no place for subjection to any other ruler. Within 15 years he had seized control of most of Persia, and in 1210 he had taken Transoxania from the Qara-Khitai, who as we shall see were much weakened in their last years by internal troubles. He then transferred his capital to Samarqand, the greatest city of his new province.

In 1215 Muḥammad conquered much of what is now Afghanistan from the Ghurid sultans. The Ghurids are perhaps the least well known of all the significant Islamic dynasties. The capital of their empire was at Fīrūzkūh, in the almost inaccessible centre of Afghanistan (its site was identified with reasonable probability only in the 1950s). They also possessed territories in northern India, however, and although the Ghurid dynasty itself did not long survive its defeat at the hands of the Khwārazm-shāh, Ghurid generals did succeed in holding the Indian lands. These formed the nucleus of what was to become a powerful state, the Delhi sultanate.

Around the year 1215, then, the empire of the Khwārazm-shāh must at first sight have seemed very formidable. Indeed, had it not had the evil fortune, almost immediately, to have to confront the Mongols, it might conceivably have proved as enduring and successful as its Saljūq predecessor. But the empire had no chance to coalesce, to recover from its very pronounced growing pains. The state's weaknesses were speedily revealed under such a strain. Part of Muḥammad's problem was his mother, a princess of the Qipchaq or Qangli Turks, originating from the lands to the north of Khwārazm. She exercised more effective power in Khwārazm itself than her son, and the loyalty of the bulk of the Khwārazm-shāh's army, which was made up of Qipchaq and Qangli mercenaries, was primarily to her. This, taken together with the acute tensions that existed between the Turkish and the Persian elements in the army, seems to have made Muḥammad reluctant to concentrate his forces against the Mongols, lest his army's first act should be his own deposition. He therefore distributed his troops around the empire as garrisons – a decision that may have been unavoidable, but was certainly to prove disastrous. Not for the last time in Persian history, a large and well-equipped army showed itself to be an inadequate basis of support for an unpopular shāh.

The Khwārazm-shāh had other troubles. If he could not rely on the loyalty of his army, he could look nowhere else for help. The mass of the people were likely to regard his government at best with indifference, at worst with outright hostility. Its predatory nature is likely to have been seen as its most conspicuous characteristic, though it probably differed in this respect more in degree than in kind from most Persian governments down the ages. Nor could he rely on the religious classes, whose approval was important to a regime that sought legitimacy. He was in open conflict with the 'Abbasid Caliph al-Nāṣir in Baghdad, and by way of reprisal was drifting towards heterodox Shī'ī Islam. He had provoked further opposition by having a noted holy man murdered. One way and another, Muḥammad needed a long breathing space if his regime was to achieve stability. He was not to be granted anything of the sort.[25]

To the west of the Khwārazm-shāh's shaky empire the Caliph al-Nāṣir had, in the vacuum that followed the collapse of Saljūq rule, established the Caliphate as a real political power in Iraq for the first time for centuries. It had generally been treated, as an essential institution, with respect by those who held the reins of power, but territorial rule had eluded it. This was to be a final flowering of power and influence before the last 'Abbasid was put to death by the Mongols in 1258. There is a story that al-Nāṣir, in pursuance of his feud with the Khwārazm-shāh, wrote to incite the Mongols to attack the lands of Islam. It would have been a grim irony, but in fact there seems to be no real basis for the accusation.

Further west again, the successors of Saladin ruled in Syria and Egypt, and fought among themselves and against the remnants of the Crusading states that maintained a precarious foothold on the Syrian coast. In Anatolia the Saljūq (Seljük) sultanate of Rūm, last representative of a once great and far-flung dynasty, disputed territory with a Byzantine Empire that was shortly to fall victim to its friends from the Christian west in the Fourth Crusade.[26] Apart from those few who took

---

[25]   On the empire of the Khwārazm-shāhs see Barthold, *Turkestan down to the Mongol Invasion*, chapter 3; J. A. Boyle (ed.), *The Cambridge History of Iran*, vol. 5, chapter 1 (C. E. Bosworth).

[26]   See R. S. Humphreys, *From Saladin to the Mongols* (1977); C. Cahen, *Pre-Ottoman Turkey* (1968).

Prester John seriously, none of the contenders in the political maelstrom of western Asia gave a thought to events in the Far East whose consequences were soon to engulf most of them: just as, when an earlier disaster befell that same part of the world, 'in the days that were before the flood they were eating and drinking, marrying and giving in marriage . . . and knew not until the flood came, and took them all away'.[27]

---

[27]   Matthew xxiv, 38–9.

3

Chingiz Khān and the Founding of the Mongol Empire

Chingiz Khān's Rise to Power

We do not know with any certainty exactly when the future Chingiz Khān was born. According to some traditions it was in a Pig year of the animal cycle, which would mean 1155 or 1167. Another version is 1162, and this was the date celebrated in the Mongolian People's Republic, in 1962, as the 800th anniversary. It happened to fall during a brief period in which Chingiz was enjoying Marxist respectability.[1] The usual scholarly preference, which has the advantage of not making him improbably old at the end of his career, is for 1167.[2] This lack of certainty usefully serves to point to the considerable degree of imprecision that afflicts our knowledge of the details of Chingiz's career before he commenced his attack on the great sedentary states of Asia. The broad lines and the general character of Chingiz's early life are clear enough. But any attempt to provide a detailed chronological narrative is in my view a hazardous project, unless the historian is prepared simply to offer a paraphrase of the *Secret History of the Mongols*, and to call that history.

But we do admittedly have the earlier sections of the chronicle of Rashīd al-Dīn, which draws on the other, lost, Mongolian source, the *Altan Debter* – as, in a more abbreviated form, do the Chinese *Sheng-wu ch'in-cheng lu* and parts of the *Yüan-shih*. So there is a sufficient check on the *Secret History* for us at least to be sure that we are unlikely to be dealing with mere fiction when we read its account of Chingiz

---

[1] C. R. Bawden, *The Modern History of Mongolia* (1968), pp. 417–19.
[2] P. Pelliot, *Notes on Marco Polo* (1959–73), vol. 1, pp. 284ff.

Khān's rise to power. Paul Ratchnevsky, in his magisterial study of Chingiz, has provided an account of this phase of the hero's life that takes all these sources into account.[3] Nevertheless I remain a little sceptical, and I shall here offer no more than what seems to me a reasonably secure general conspectus of the conqueror's formative years.

Of the Mongols themselves, called by that name, we know very little prior to the twelfth century, though the name under the form Mong-wu is perhaps to be recognised in Chinese sources of the T'ang dynasty (618–907). The Mongols of Chingiz Khān's period are in all probability, as was suggested earlier, a people whose definitive formation should be ascribed to the time of the Khitan domination of Mongolia. During the twelfth century, according to the *Secret History*, they did have powerful khāns, notably Qabul Khān, who fought the Chin of north China in mid century and who was among Chingiz Khān's immediate ancestors. But Chingiz's family, thought of high rank, does not seem to have exercised power of a very far-flung kind. The Mongols were one among many peoples of the steppe, and not by any means the most important.

The tribes of Mongolia in the twelfth century have to be described as 'Turko-Mongol', since it is by no means clear in all cases which were Turkish and which Mongol. Even this would mean no more than that they spoke Turkish or Mongolian respectively. In any case, the tribes intermarried freely, in accordance with exogamous custom. The most important of the tribes were perhaps the Tatars, living like the Mongols in eastern Mongolia; the Keraits in the centre; the Merkits to the north of them; and the Naimans to the west. A tribal map of Mongolia would also have to fit in the Qonggirats, the Önggüts, the Kirghiz, and others.

At the time of Chingiz Khān's birth the Tatars were probably the most influential of the tribes: they were the people who had Chin support. Unfortunately they were also something of a hereditary enemy of the Mongols. In due course, we are told, Chingiz Khān in the days of his power virtually exterminated the Tatars, who ceased to exist as an identifiable tribe, though individuals can be traced. Of these the most notable was Shigi-Qutuqu, whom Chingiz's mother adopted as her son when the tribe was destroyed.[4] In these circumstances it is odd that

[3]   P. Ratchnevsky, *Činggis-Khan sein Leben und Wirken* (1983), chapters 1 and 2.

[4]   See P. Ratchnevsky, 'Šigi-qutuqu, ein mongolischer Gefolgsmann im. 12–13. Jahrhundert', *Central Asiatic Journal*, 10 (1965), pp. 88–120.

'Tatar' should have become so widely the name by which the conquerors as a whole were known. This has never been satisfactorily explained, though in Europe Tatar, if spelt Tartar, had the convenient advantage of suggesting that the Mongols emanated from Hell, Tartarus. Matthew Paris ascribes the pun to Louis IX of France.[5] It has been suggested on philological grounds that in the context of the Mongol Empire, 'Tatar' carried the implication of 'people who have become (politically) Mongol'.[6] This might solve the puzzle if the point is valid historically as well as philologically. It seems just as likely, however, that perhaps because of the former prominence of the Tatars, the name had become for outsiders a conventional general label for the peoples of Mongolia, and that the label stuck. It is worth noting that the Sung envoy Chao Hung in 1221 described all the 'Mongols' as Tatars, dividing them into Black, White and Wild.[7]

Chingiz Khān's father, Yesügei, was a minor chieftain of noble descent, not of sufficient status to rate the title of Khān, though Chingiz is shown referring to him posthumously as Yesügei Qan. He named his son, the future Chingiz Khān, Temüchin, after a Tatar he had defeated shortly before his son's birth.[8] In due course, however, he was himself murdered by the Tatars, and this while Temüchin, his eldest son, was still a small boy. The feud with the Tatars had to be left till later: mere survival was the immediate problem, for Yesügei's followers promptly and unsurprisingly took themselves off. No one wanted a nine-year-old chieftain. Years of struggle, we are told, then ensued for Temüchin, his mother and his siblings. They were at times reduced to living on berries and on what they could grub up from the earth. In addition to all this they are said to have had a good deal of trouble with another Mongol clan, the Tayichi'uts, who feared that if Temüchin was left to grow up in peace, he might some day make a nuisance of himself. However, failing to have the courage of their convictions, they neglected to kill

---

[5]   J. J. Saunders, 'Matthew Paris and the Mongols', in T. A. Sandquist and M. R. Powicke (eds), *Essays in Medieval History presented to Bertie Wilkinson* (1969), p. 124.

[6]   O. Pritsak, 'Two migratory movements in the Eurasian steppe in the 9th–11th centuries', in *Proceedings of the 26th International Congress of Orientalists, New Delhi 1964*, vol. 2 (1968), p. 159.

[7]   P. Olbricht and E. Pinks (trs), *Meng-Ta pei-lu und Hei-Ta shih-lüeh* (1980), p. 3.

[8]   *Secret History*, paras 177 and 59: tr. F. W. Cleaves, *The Secret History of the Mongols* (1982), pp. 104 and 14.

Plate 3.1   Chingiz Khān. A portrait in the Chinese Imperial Portrait Gallery. National Palace Museum, Taipei, Taiwan, Republic of China

Temüchin when they had captured him, and in due course, with characteristic resource, he was able to make his escape.

What we are to make of these Mongolian tales of the hero's childhood is extremely hard to say. Taken as a whole they present a picture of a child who triumphs over all adversity to fulfil his destiny and to reclaim his birthright and more; who enjoys the favour, if somewhat erratically vouchsafed, of Heaven; and who shows immense ingenuity as well as nascent powers of leadership in overcoming all the disadvantages resulting from his father's sudden death and his followers' faithlessness. Perhaps it is rather too good to be true. But on the other hand the boy who later became Chingiz Khān is no doubt likely, in reality, to have been remarkable enough; and we have seen before that the *Secret History* does not shrink from relating such tales, discreditably though they may be to the young hero, as that of his murder of his half-brother Bekter. So again I would propose reserving judgement on some of the details while accepting the probable general truth of the picture presented.

The Tatars may, during Temüchin's youth, have been temporarily the most powerful tribe, but they did not dominate, still less rule, Mongolia. Both the Keraits and the Naimans were serious rivals for primacy. Since there was nothing that even approximated to a 'central government', and because the tribal structure was apparently in something of a fluid state, circumstances were propitious for a successful young nomad warrior to build up a following of his own, if he could once make a start. This is what Temüchin appears to have done. By his audacity, his success in raiding those more powerful than himself, his personal magnetism – whatever it may have been – he began to attract like-minded young warriors to his standard. He acquired as *anda* another Mongol of noble blood, Jamuqa, and an increasing number of less well-born individuals renounced their own tribal allegiance in order to become Temüchin's *nökers*. This group ultimately became the nucleus of his imperial guard, and supplied many of the generals who carried the Mongol name across Asia and Europe.

Eventually Temüchin had established his position sufficiently for it to be possible for him to take two important steps: to marry his long-betrothed wife, Bortei of the Qonggirat tribe, and to make an alliance with the greatest of the anti-Tatar rulers of the steppe, Toghril, Khān of the Keraits. The pretext for this alliance is supposed to have been that Toghril had been *anda* to Temüchin's father, Yesügei. When reminded of this fact and given a suitable present, Toghril showed himself favourably disposed towards his old comrade's son. Be that as it may, Temüchin's following was evidently by now considerable enough for him to be worth taking on by the Kerait khān as a junior partner. Later, the Chin government came to feel that their protégés, the Tatars, were becoming over-mighty. So, following customary Chinese practice, they looked around for a counterweight, and found one in Toghril. Aided by Temüchin, he inflicted a defeat on the Tatars, and as a reward received from the Chin emperor the title of Wang, king. Hence he is usually known in the sources as the Wang-Khān or (Mongolised) the Ong-Khān. Temüchin received a lesser title for his lesser services.[9]

[9] *Secret History*, paras 94, 96 and 134: tr. Cleaves, pp. 32–3 and 63.

Temüchin's rise to power still had its marked ups and downs, but he was eventually recognised as khān of Mongols, and it may have been at this time rather than later that he assumed the title of Chingiz ('Oceanic' = universal?) Khān. The Tatars were finally subjugated. Jamuqa turned against his *anda* (or vice versa, or both) and at a later date was executed – at his own request, according to the *Secret History*; possibly this is evidence that its author had a sense of humour.[10] The parting of the ways with Toghril also came, and he too met his end, allegedly at the unwitting hands of a Naiman scout. The Naimans were next to be dealt with, but more was to be heard of them: Küchlüg, son of the Naiman khān, escaped and fled to the Qara-Khitai court. Well treated and given sanctuary, he reciprocated by overthrowing his bene-factor and setting himself up as ruler. He was to be the last. He had apparently been brought up as a Nestorian Christian, but in the Qara-Khitai empire he was converted to Buddhism, and he became a militant, persecuting Buddhist. This may suggest that his Buddhist education had been deficient in some respects. The majority of the Qara-Khitai subject population was Muslim, and these Küchlüg alienated by his vigorous persecution. The foolishness of this policy was noted with interest by the Mongols.

In the years before 1206, then, the tribes of Mongolia were one by one brought under Mongol rule, though the process was not one of unbroken Mongol success. In some cases large numbers of the defeated tribesmen were massacred. The Tatars could expect no mercy, and Temüchin had a score to settle with the Merkits. They had kidnapped his chief wife Bortei just nine months before the birth of Jochi, his eldest son, and the uncertainty over Jochi's true parentage remained to trouble the Mongol royal house. But for the most part the tribes, once defeated, were neither killed nor driven out: their manpower was potentially far too useful for that. They were incorporated into the new Mongol mili-tary machine. As the author of the *Tartar Relation* wrote in the 1240s, 'he had acquired the invariable habit of conscripting the soldiers of a conquered army into his own, with the object of subduing other coun-tries by virtue of his increasing strength, as is clearly evident in his successors, who imitate his wicked cunning'.[11]

---

[10]   *Secret History*, para. 201: tr. Cleaves, pp. 138–41.
[11]   R. A. Skelton, T. E. Marston and G. D. Painter (eds and trs), *The Vinland Map and the Tartar Relation* (1965), p. 56.

Chingiz Khān's Campaigns of Conquest

By 1206 Temüchin had largely completed the task of conquering, or of unifying by force, the tribes of Mongolia. A great *qūrīltāi* was held, at which Temüchin was acclaimed as supreme khān of all the Turko-Mongol tribes of the area. Some have seen the *qūrīltāi* as an elective assembly, and it may on occasion have been that. But such elections rarely had more than one candidate before them, and acclamation is probably a more accurate characterisation of the proceedings. The *Secret History* has a long account of what went on at the *qūrīltāi* of 1206.[12] Essentially it seems to have been concerned with laying the organisational foundations of the new regime, and with the granting by Chingiz Khān (who now received that title if he had not had it before) of rewards to his most faithful and long-standing followers. Those most favoured were the few who had remained true to Chingiz when his fortunes had been at their lowest ebb, three years previously; they had withdrawn with him to the lake or river of Baljuna, reaffirming their allegiance in the 'Baljuna covenant'.[13]

The question that had to be faced was: what now? The tribes of the Mongolian steppelands, not for the first time, had a supreme ruler. Chinese policy had been circumvented: they had failed to keep the tribes at each others' throats. But unless something decisive was done with the newly formed military machine, it would soon dissolve into quarrelling factions again, and Mongolia would revert to its earlier state. This, to my mind, is at least one explanation for the beginnings of the Mongols' astonishing career of conquest. A superb army, potentially invincible in the field in thirteenth-century conditions, had been successfully created. But if it was not used against external enemies, it would not remain in being for long. The only matter that required a decision was in which direction the armies were to advance.

There can have been little doubt about the answer. A children's strip cartoon version of the life of Chingiz Khān depicts the following scene: 'Men, after some thought, I have decided to conquer Cathay. Are you with me?' 'Yes, sir, a good scheme.' Indeed, the decision was inevitable, since China was always the target of any successful ruler in Mongolia,

---

[12]   Paras 202–34: tr. Cleaves, *The Secret History*, pp. 141–71.
[13]   F. W. Cleaves, 'The historicity of the Baljuna covenant', *Harvard Journal of Asiatic Studies*, 18 (1955), pp. 357–421.

Plate 3.2 The enthronement of Chingiz Khān at the *quriltai* of 1206. From a manuscript of Rashīd al-Dīn's *Jāmiʿ al-tawārīkh*. Bibliothèque Nationale de France, Paris, MS. Persian Suppl. 1113, fol. 44v

and since the Chin government of north China was the new Mongol state's principal antagonist. It would do whatever it could to destroy Chingiz Khān's power, if he did not strike first.

The years immediately after 1206 were spent in tying up loose ends. The remnants of tribes still in 'revolt', such as the residue of the Naimans and the Merkits, were dealt with. In the meantime preparations were made for the great expedition south. The Chin allegiance of the peoples of the Sino-Mongolian borderlands was already weakening, and those territories would provide a springboard for the Mongol assault on China.[14] Two small-scale attacks had already been made on the Tanguts of Hsi-Hsia, and it was decided to mount a major campaign against them before attempting to tackle the more formidable enemy, the Chin. This would serve two purposes. It would be something of a practice run against a state which was organised largely on Chinese lines, and if successful it would open a western route into China to add to the more direct northern path of invasion. No doubt the Mongols, always alive to the importance of commerce, were also interested in the control of the major trade routes that passed through Hsi-Hsia.

Hsi-Hsia was attacked in 1209, and speedily brought to submission. But it was not at this stage conquered. Its native rulers remained in power, now subject to Chingiz Khān and no longer a danger on the flank of the projected assault on the Chin. The great invasion of Chin began in 1211, and campaigns in the north Chinese empire continued until in 1234, some years after Chingiz Khān's death, it was finally subjugated. According to one story, the invasion of China quickly revealed a serious weakness in Mongol military effectiveness: a cavalry force such as the Mongol army could be supreme in the field, but it was not an adequate instrument for the taking of the walled cities of China. We are told that, faced with a formidable city for the first time, Chingiz Khān offered to raise the siege if he were given 1000 cats and 10,000 swallows. These were duly handed over. Material was tied to their tails, and this was set on fire. The animals were released and fled home, setting the city ablaze, and in the ensuing confusion the city was stormed. This was an excellent stratagem, but not one that Chingiz could expect to succeed very often. The story comes from the seventeenth-century Mongol chronicle of Sagang Sechen, hardly a contemporary source.

[14]   P. D. Buell, 'The role of the Sino-Mongolian frontier zone in the rise of Cinggis-Qan', in H. G. Schwarz (ed.), *Studies on Mongolia: Proceedings of the First North American Conference on Mongolian Studies* (1979), pp. 66–8.

Indeed, the tale is, in slightly variant forms, a frequently recurring motif in medieval sources, being attached to Princess Olga of Kiev, Harald Hardrada of Norway, Guthrum the Dane and Robert Guiscard the Norman among others.[15] But whatever the truth of the story, the Mongols certainly soon found it necessary to add a train of Chinese siege engineers to their forces.

The detailed marching and counter-marching of the north Chinese campaigns, the successive invasions and withdrawals, the sackings and lootings, are perhaps not of great interest except to the military historian. They are ably recounted in H. D. Martin's distinguished study.[16] At first the Mongols do not seem to have been aiming at conquest and permanent occupation of the Chin Empire. Loot appears to have been their object, and a great deal of it was indeed secured. Treaties were made, and the Mongols were offered and accepted bribes to induce them to return to Mongolia; then back they came with the new campaigning season. That they seem to have experienced little difficulty in breaking through the Great Wall of China, which has sometimes puzzled historians, is less of a problem now that we know that although the Chin had indeed erected walls, well to the north of the present line, the Great Wall as such was not there at the time.[17]

Despite the Mongols' run of victories, the Chin Empire proved a hard nut to crack. The emperors were not inclined to surrender without a prolonged struggle, and their resources and manpower appeared to be virtually limitless. The Mongol raids gradually turned into conquest, however. Peking, or rather the city on a site near modern Peking which was the Chin northern capital, fell to the Mongols in 1215. But this city was in an exposed position, too near to Mongolia, and the Chin emperor had already moved to K'ai-feng, in the south on the Yellow River, where the capital remained until the dynasty fell. The later stages of the war were conducted by Chingiz Khān's general Muqali, for the Great Khān's own attention had been drawn away by events further west.

By this time the conquest of China was already ceasing to be an operation that could be manned solely by Mongol forces. Large armies

[15]   J. R. Krueger (tr.), Sagang Sechen, *A History of the Eastern Mongols to 1662* (1964), part 1, p. 50; H. R. Ellis Davidson, *The Viking Road to Byzantium* (1976), pp. 215–16.

[16]   H. D. Martin, *The Rise of Chingis Khan and his Conquest of North China* (1950), chapters 5–10.

[17]   A. N. Waldron, 'The problem of the Great Wall of China', *Harvard Journal of Asiatic Studies*, 43/2 (1983), pp. 654, 656.

were constantly needed, and there were calls elsewhere on the available Mongol troops. There were not enough Mongols to go round. Nor was China ideally suited to the Mongol style of warfare. The problem of the conduct of sieges had to be dealt with; and although the north China plain lent itself more readily to cavalry warfare than, later, did the lands of the Sung Empire with their numerous waterways, it was still not comparable with campaigning on the steppe. Hence native Chinese troops were welcomed if they chose, as many did, to defect to what was evidently proving the winning side. It has to be remembered that not every subject of the Chin emperor had very good reasons for remaining loyal to the dynasty. The Khitans, who had been ousted from power by the Chin, were open to offers; and the Chinese had not forgotten that the Chin themselves were alien, barbarian conquerors from Manchuria who had ruled in China for only a century. Nor were some Chin officials unwilling to abandon what increasingly seemed a lost cause. As we shall see, such officials, whether of Chinese or Khitan origin, had a part to play in the setting up of the new empire's organisational framework (see chapter 4).[18]

Küchlüg the Naiman, last survivor of Chingiz Khān's old enemies, was now at least nominally ruling the Qara-Khitai territory, and remained to be dealt with. But quite apart from the internal troubles provoked by Küchlüg's seizure of power and subsequent short-sighted policies, the Qara-Khitai empire was no longer what it once had been. A substantial part of its lands, Transoxania with its great cities of Samarqand and Bukhārā, had already been occupied by the Khwārazm-shāh in 1210. In fact the Qara-Khitai empire did not prove to be a serious problem for the Mongols. They were well informed about local conditions, and had had for some years a foothold inside Qara-Khitai borders: the Uighurs of Turfan had made their submission to Chingiz Khān in 1209, after which date a Mongol garrison was stationed in their territory.[19] In 1218 Chingiz's general Jebei Noyon was sent to dispose of Küchlüg once and for all. Jebei promptly ended Küchlüg's religious persecution and restored freedom of worship to the Muslims. The people

---

[18]   See I. de Rachewiltz, 'Personnel and personalities in north China in the early Mongol period', *Journal of the Economic and Social History of the Orient*, 9 (1966), pp. 88–144; P. D. Buell, 'Sino-Khitan administration in Mongol Bukhara', *Journal of Asian History*, 13/2 (1979), pp. 121–51.

[19]   T. T. Allsen, 'The Yüan Dynasty and the Uighurs of Turfan in the 13th century', in M. Rossabi (ed.), *China among Equals: the Middle Kingdom and its Neighbors, 10th–14th Centuries* (1983), pp. 246–7.

turned against Küchlüg's troops. He fled, later to be hunted down and killed, and the Qara-Khitai lands were added to the Mongol Empire almost without opposition.[20]

Chingiz Khān's frontiers now marched with those of the Khwāraam-shāh 'Alā' al-Dīn Muḥammad. It is difficult to be certain what Chingiz's intentions towards this apparently powerful neighbour were. He is said to have informed the Khwārazm-shāh that he recognised him as the ruler of the west, as he was himself the ruler of the east, and to have expressed the hope that peace would be maintained and trade promoted between the two empires. But Chingiz pointedly referred to the Khwārazm-shāh as his 'son' – hardly a declaration that he accepted their equality as monarchs. There had been a small military clash between the two powers, when a Khwarazmian army attacked a Mongol force which had been pursuing a group of fugitive Merkits. But this could have been written off as an accident, and did not need to be the occasion of war. It may indeed be that Chingiz had no wish to involve himself militarily with the Khwārazm-shāh, at least at this stage. He had his hands full in China, and had already acquired a considerable empire which he had yet fully to absorb and organise. No doubt, to judge from later Mongol history and the ultimate extent of their conquests, Khwārazm would ultimately have been attacked in any case. But as things were, the Khwārazm-shāh took the matter out of Chingiz Khān's hands, and by his own actions made war inevitable.

In 1218 a caravan of 450 Muslim merchants from Mongol territory arrived at the Khwārazm-shāh's frontier city of Utrār. The governor of the city, asserting, no doubt correctly, that these so-called merchants were in fact spies, had them all killed and their property confiscated. One man is said to have escaped the massacre and to have returned to Chingiz with the tale. Three ambassadors were sent to the Khwārazm-shāh to demand reparation and the punishment of the governor of Utrār. The Khwārazm-shāh's response was to kill one envoy and – almost as serious an insult – to shave off the beards of the other two. In Mongol eyes the person of an ambassador, especially one of their own, was sacrosanct. No reply was possible but war. The Khwārazm-shāh's act was either the occasion or the perfect excuse for the perpetration of what was probably the greatest calamity ever to befall the people of the eastern Islamic world.[21]

---

[20] W. Barthold, *Turkestan down to the Mongol Invasion* (1977), pp. 402–3.

[21] Ibid., pp. 393–400.

The Khwārazm-shāh had established his capital at Samarqand, in the territory he had so recently seized from the Qara-Khitai. It was this land, Transoxania – broadly the modern Soviet republic of Uzbekistan – that was to be the first to feel the effects of Chingiz Khān's self-righteous anger. In 1219 he launched a three-pronged attack. This baffled the Khwārazm-shāh who, both for that reason and because he could not trust his troops, failed to meet the Mongols in the field, although his army is reputed to have been colossal. Leaving his forces split up in garrisons where they could be mopped up piecemeal, he fled. A Mongol detachment followed at his heels; he eluded his pursuers, taking refuge on an island in the Caspian Sea, where he died. It was not a distinguished performance, and it is far from clear why he did not even attempt effective resistance to the Mongols. The fact that so large a part of his territories had been acquired only very recently may have been a factor in reducing effectiveness. But the Khwārazm-shāh's military record up to this time had not been wholly unimpressive; and after all, if what the sources tell us is true, he had himself quite unnecessarily provoked the war which he now failed to fight. To understand the Khwārazm-shāh we need some insight into his state of mind at the time; but he is not available for psychiatric analysis.[22]

The killing and destruction that was visited on Transoxania at Chingiz Khān's hands was evidently appalling. A worse fate still was in store for the Khwārazm-shāh's eastern Persian province of Khurāsān, which was comprehensively wrecked over the next few years by Chingiz's youngest son, Tolui. It seems that Chingiz did not at this juncture envisage fully incorporating the Khwārazm-shāh's empire into his own, though Mongol viceroys were appointed and exercised some sort of rule over parts of the area for the next three decades. He was concerned to inflict punishment on the Khwārazm-shāh and his people, and perhaps to remove permanently any danger there might have been of the Khwārazm-shāh's empire becoming a centre of power in Asia able to rival his own. Resistance was maintained for some years in the Khwārazm-shāh's former dominions by his son, Jalāl al-Dīn, who became and has remained something of an epic figure. Jalāl al-Dīn was a gifted field commander who might indeed, in the absence of the main Mongol army, have achieved much had he been prepared to concentrate

[22]   See ibid., pp. 403ff., and J. A. Boyle in J. A. Boyle (ed.), *The Cambridge History of Iran*, vol. 5: *The Saljuq and Mongol Periods* (1968), pp. 360ff., on these events.

on the Mongols instead of dissipating his energies in attacks on a variety of other powers of the region. As it was, he was ultimately killed, having made no permanent mark on Mongol dominance. Groups of Khwaraz-mian soldiers continued to rampage about the Middle East for some years; one of these possesses a small niche in history as the Muslim force that (more or less incidentally) finally evicted the Crusaders from Jerusalem in 1244.

Chingiz Khān's stay in the Islamic world has left one curious literary memorial, mentioned in chapter 1. Feeling his age, and realising that there were lands still to conquer and people yet left unmassacred, he enquired whether there was available any medicine of immortality. With this aim in view he summoned from China to the Hindu Kush a famous Taoist sage, Ch'ang Ch'un. The sage admitted that he knew of no such medicine, though he suggested that Chingiz's life might be to some extent prolonged if he gave up hunting and slept alone from time to time. Whether because of or in spite of this advice, Chingiz was impressed with the old man, had long talks with him, and granted valuable privileges to the Taoist sect he headed. One of Ch'ang Ch'un's disciples and companions on the journey wrote an account of it, which has survived and which gives a vivid picture of the condition of Asia in the immediate aftermath of Chingiz's campaigns.[23]

The Mongol force which had pursued the Khwārazm-shāh went home the long way round, heading through the Caucasus and returning to Mongolia by a route north of the Caspian Sea. It had defeated all comers and had acquired valuable intelligence for use when, in the late 1230s, the great Mongol expedition against Russia and eastern Europe was mounted (see chapter 6). Chingiz himself departed for Mongolia in 1223. He had set himself one final task: the complete subjection of Hsi-Hsia, whose ruler had failed to contribute troops for the campaign in the west, as he was under an obligation to do. This time the Tanguts were thoroughly subjugated, though their destruction and the execution of their ruler did not take place until just after Chingiz's own death, which occurred in 1227. His body was taken back to be buried, so Rashīd al-Dīn says, in a secret spot on a Mongolian mountain which he had himself chosen many years before.[24]

---

[23]   See A. Waley (tr.), *The Travels of an Alchemist* (1931).
[24]   J. A. Boyle, 'The burial place of the Great Khan Ögedei', *Acta Orientalia* 22 (1970), pp. 45–7.

Plate 3.3 Lamentation at the bier of Chingiz Khān. From a manuscript of Rashīd al-Dīn's *Jāmiʿ al-tawārīkh*. Photo: Khalili collection, Warburg Institute, MS. D. 31 fol. 90v

So ended one of the most remarkable careers of military conquest known to history. How Chingiz should be rated when compared with Alexander the Great, Caesar, Napoleon or other generals I am not competent to judge. That able commentator Sir Basil Liddell Hart rated him very highly indeed, and included a chapter on him, together with his greatest general Sübodei, in his *Great Captains Unveiled*.[25] Nor is it an easy matter to discern whether or not there was some overall strategy behind Chingiz's campaigns, as Owen Lattimore maintains in a wide-ranging and provocative short article that has already been referred to. According to Lattimore, Chingiz was anxious to avoid the classic mistake of previous barbarian rulers of the steppe who, as soon

[25] B. H. Liddell Hart, *Great Captains Unveiled* (1927), chapter 1.

as they had formed an effective nomadic confederation, succumbed to the temptation to invade north China and to establish themselves there. This sequence of events generally created, he suggests, a power vacuum on the steppe. This was duly filled by the next nomadic general to form a confederation, and he in his turn would then invade China and expel his predecessor. By contrast Chingiz's strategy, in Lattimore's opinion, was first to form his confederation, secondly to neutralise temporarily the danger from China (the campaigns against Hsi-Hsia and the Chin), and then to return to the steppe to mop up and incorporate all the remaining Turko-Mongol peoples, thus ensuring that no power vacuum would be created and that, when China was conquered, the steppe would be retained as well. This achieved, it would now be safe to proceed to the permanent conquest and occupation of China – though this part of the alleged grand design had to be left for Chingiz's successors to implement since, having failed to become immortal, he ran out of time.[26]

This is certainly a fair description of what in fact happened, and Lattimore may be right. The difficulty lies in the absence of any evidence whatsoever for the grand strategic plan except for the events themselves. Lattimore's theory is very attractive, but inevitably it remains no more than a theory.

The Effects of the Mongol Conquests

The immediate effects of Chingiz Khān's conquests, seen from the point of view of those who bore the brunt of them, were undeniably catastrophic, though this has not prevented some modern historians from arguing that the destruction and loss of life have been greatly exaggerated. But one should not be distracted by admiration for the later achievements of Qubilai in China, or by respect for the attempts of Ghazan to put matters right in Persia, from recognising that the Mongol conquests were a disaster on a grand and unparalleled scale. North China was subjected to a series of destructive campaigns over a period of 25 years. According to one oft-repeated if possibly apocryphal story, the Mongols seriously considered wiping out the whole population of the former Chin Empire so as to turn the land over to pasture: they were

---

[26]   O. Lattimore, 'The geography of Chingis Khan', *Geographical Journal*, 129/1 (1963), pp. 6–7.

only dissuaded when their Khitan adviser Yeh-lü Ch'u-ts'ai pointed out
to them how much income in taxation they could expect to extract from
an unmassacred Chinese people.[27] To the west, Transoxania and more
particularly eastern Persia had to endure something that must have
seemed to approximate very nearly to attempted genocide.

Contemporary historians were unanimous when they wrote about the
horrors that accompanied the Mongol invasion of the Khwārazm-shāh's
empire. Ibn al-Athīr, quoted earlier, is perhaps the best known and the
most vivid of them.[28] Jūzjānī wrote a similar account in his Delhi sanctuary. Jalāl al-Dīn's secretary, Nasawī, who accompanied that last of the
Khwārazm-shāhs in his campaigns and wanderings, conveys much the
same impression, as do such sources as the local history of Harāt, Sayfī's
Ta'rīkh-nāma-i Harāt. The figures that these writers quote for the
numbers of people massacred are beyond belief. Sayfī tells us that
1,600,000 were killed at the sack of Harāt, and 1,747,000 at Nīshāpūr.
Jūzjānī puts the Harāt death toll even higher, at 2,400,000.[29]

What are we to make of such figures? One difficulty is that no one
has a clear idea of what size the population of a great Islamic city may
have been in the early thirteenth century. It does not seem likely, however,
that Khurāsān possessed so many cities with more inhabitants than the
Sung Chinese capital, Hang-chou, which as we saw is estimated at about
one million people. Moreover, not enough Islamic archaeology has been
comprehensively undertaken to enable us to estimate population from
the remains now on or under the ground. Nīshāpūr, frequently afflicted
as it was by earthquakes, had an inconvenient habit of moving around
the plain where it is situated, which in itself points to an architectural
peculiarity of that part of the world. Mud-brick buildings, which would
form the majority of the houses in any such city, do not respond well
to repair. If they are badly damaged it can be easier to start again somewhere else than to try to rebuild on the spot.[30]

---

[27]   See e.g. D. O. Morgan, 'Who ran the Mongol Empire?', *Journal of the
Royal Asiatic Society*, 1982/2, p. 126 and n. 7.

[28]   On Ibn al-Athīr see D. S. Richards, 'Ibn al-Athīr and the later parts of
the *Kāmil*: a study of aims and methods', in D. O. Morgan (ed.), *Medieval
Historical Writing in the Christian and Islamic Worlds* (1982), pp. 76–108.

[29]   M. Z. al-Ṣiddīqī (ed.), Sayfī Harawī, *Ta'rīkh-nāma-i Harāt* (1944), pp.
60 and 63; 'A. Ḥabībī (ed.), Minhāj al-Dīn Jūzjānī, *Ṭabaqāt-i Nāsirī* (1964–5),
vol. 2, p. 121; tr. H. G. Raverty, *Ṭabakāt-i-Nāṣirī* (1881), vol. 2, p. 1038.

[30]   On Persian vernacular building see E. Beazley and M. Harverson, *Living
with the Desert* (1982).

Plate 3.4   The Timurid tomb-complex of Shāh-i zinda, at the edge of the site
of pre-Mongol Samarqand. Photo by the author

In Harāt, however, the city walls do still exist in part. They are the
post-Mongol walls, but it seems reasonable to assume that they follow
the line of their predecessors.[31] No one who has visited Harāt will
believe that the area enclosed could have contained two million people,

[31]   K. Fischer, 'From the Mongols to the Mughals', in F. R. Allchin and N.
Hammond (eds), *The Archaeology of Afghanistan from the Earliest Times to
the Timurid Period* (1978), p. 379.

Plate 3.5   The fifteenth-century shrine of Abū Naṣr Parsā, Balkh. Photo ©
Edgar Knobloch

even temporarily, during a siege. Perhaps the most eloquent site is
Samarqand. When the city was rebuilt, it ultimately became the great
metropolis of the empire of Tīmūr, Tamerlane. But Timurid Samarqand
is some distance from the old site, which was never fully restored. What
now exists on the old site is what appears to be a plateau. On closer
inspection, the sides of the plateau are seen to be the pre-Mongol mud-
brick walls, still rising to a considerable height and enclosing nothing
but the *Shāh-i zinda*, a beautiful series of Timurid religious structures
leading up the wall to a Muslim shrine just inside. Apart from that,
there is a vast panorama of emptiness, with only house foundations to
be seen. Balkh is hardly less evocative: a mere village squats amid
massive ruined medieval ramparts. These are all imposing sites, but they

are hardly big enough to have accommodated the populations of which our sources speak.[32]

It is possible, indeed likely, that the great walled cities of Khurāsān had to find room at the last minute for large numbers of refugees from the countryside. This may be part of the explanation for the chroniclers' huge numbers. But it is no more a total solution than the glib assertion that 'chroniclers always exaggerate'. Very similar chroniclers reported the Saljūq invasions of the eleventh century, and if they indulged in exaggeration of its (admittedly much lesser) horrors, that exaggeration was kept within strict limits. On the other hand, the sorts of figures just quoted cannot be reproduced as though they were reliable statistics. Even if our chroniclers had been present at the massacres, how would they have been in a position to calculate the numbers involved? It seems more reasonable to regard these figures not as statistical information but as evidence of the state of mind created by the character of the Mongol invasion. The shock induced by the scale of the catastrophe had no precedent: hence these enormous figures. This must imply that the death and destruction which produced that shock had no precedent either.

But not everything can be explained in such terms. The next generation of Persian historians, whose principal representative is Juwaynī, tell a similar tale when relating events of which they were not themselves contemporaries. So do even later writers such as Rashīd al-Dīn and Ḥamd Allāh Mustawfī, who lived under a Mongol regime that had long been an established fact: indeed, in Ḥamd Allāh's day Mongol rule was beginning to fade away. Nor is the general tenor of these sources something peculiar to Muslim writers. Travellers like the Franciscan emissaries Carpini and Rubruck, Marco Polo, and Ch'ang Ch'un's disciple seem to have formed much the same view of what the first Mongol invasion of western Asia had been like.

The impression that the available sources give us is, then, virtually as unanimous as it could easily be. This should not lightly be set aside: but is there anything to be said in mitigation? One objection to belief in our sources may speedily be dealt with: the well-known argument that history does not repeat itself, it is simply that historians repeat each other. This is always possible, and indeed in the Islamic historical tradition it was standard practice to copy out one's distinguished predeces-

---

[32]   My impressions of Harāt, Balkh and Samarqand derive from visits to Afghanistan and Uzbekistan in 1974 and 1978, respectively.

sors' material as far as was feasible. But in the case of the Mongol invasions, such an explanation fails when we look at two of the most important sources: Jūzjānī and Juwaynī. Their story, though they differ from one another in detail, is in its account of the horrors inflicted by the Mongols much the same in tone. Juwaynī was the younger man, not a witness of the invasion as Jūzjānī had been. Can he then have copied Jūzjānī's material? It would appear not. For they finished their histories at about the same time, in the year 1260, and as far from each other as Delhi and Baghdad. Jūzjānī, a contemporary of the events, writing outside Mongol-held territory and from an extremely hostile standpoint, and Juwaynī, recording what had occurred before he was born and writing as a Mongol employee within their empire, tell essentially the same tale. It does not seem unduly credulous to suppose that this is because that tale is, in fact, largely true.

Professor Bernard Lewis, something of a revisionist on this matter of the Mongol horrors, has suggested that in the twentieth century we are better able to judge man's destructive capacity than were our Victorian forebears, to whom the Mongol conquests seemed terrible beyond normal human experience. For, Lewis points out, we have seen the havoc wreaked in Europe between 1939 and 1945; and we have also seen the speed of Europe's recovery. Hence, he feels, we should resist the temptation to believe that the Mongols, whose apparatus of destruction was so primitive compared with what was available to Hitler, could have devastated the Islamic world so totally as the historians of the time would lead us to suppose.[33]

On the face of it this seems persuasive. But we should ask ourselves what it was that was destroyed in Europe during the Second World War. Europe's was an urban, industrial civilisation, and it was this that was rebuilt after 1945. The agricultural, food-producing capacity was not so seriously affected – nor, in European conditions, could it be. No amount of bombing of European cities will make it impossible to grow corn on a European field. In Persia the situation was very different. It is true that what we hear most about is the slaughter and demolition in the great cities of Khurāsān. But more serious, in the long run, was the effect of the Mongol invasions on agriculture.

The Persian plateau is largely lacking in great rivers. Consequently agriculture is, or was until very recently, dependent on a locally devised

[33] B. Lewis, 'The Mongols, the Turks and the Muslim polity', in his *Islam in History* (1973), pp. 179–98 and 324–5.

Plate 3.6   An aerial view of the line of a *qanāt*, a Persian underground irrigation channel Photo © Roger Wood/Beltmann Corbis

form of artificial irrigation, the *qanāt* – an underground water channel that brings the water, often many miles, to where it is needed. Some of these were destroyed during the invasions, and without effective irrigation much of the land would soon revert to desert. But a more long-term consideration is that *qanāts*, even if not actually destroyed, quickly cease to operate if they are not constantly maintained. Hence if peasants were killed in large numbers, or fled from their land and stayed away, land would suffer irreparable damage simply through neglect of the *qanāts*. With their pasture-oriented minds, the Mongols were not the people to do anything to remedy this in time. Without the agricultural hinterland, the cities could not adequately be supported and would therefore not be rebuilt to anything approaching their previous size. So a brief invasion, if sufficiently destructive, could in fact have permanent consequences on a scale to which twentieth-century Europe offers no parallel.

The later invasion of Iraq by Hülegü in the 1250s (see chapter 6) is often credited with the destruction of the ancient irrigation system of Mesopotamia and with causing the end of the fertility that had made the land between the Tigris and the Euphrates the cradle of civilisation. It is true that the work of R. M. Adams on the Diyāla plain, the 'land behind Baghdad', suggests that decline had been going on since the Arab conquest in the seventh century, and that the Mongols were among many contributors. Adams's findings have recently been disputed, partly on methodological grounds: they were based both on written sources and on archaeological evidence, but the latter consisted of what could be learned from surface surveys rather than actual excavation.[34] In any case, although Iraqi irrigation was river rather than *qanāt* based, again the Mongols could have contributed much to decay, whatever should be laid at the door of their predecessors, simply by allowing the irrigation canals to be neglected.

I believe, therefore, that the testimony of contemporaries should be accepted so far as it concerns Transoxania and Khurāsān. We have a description of Khurāsān from the pen of the geographer Yāqūt, written a few years before Chingiz Khān's invasion.[35] Yāqūt's Khurāsān is a fertile, rich and phenomenally flourishing province, quite unlike Khurāsān in later centuries or today. It is certainly possible that some of the decline should be ascribed to the effects of later warfare between the different Mongol khanates (for Khurāsān became a disputed frontier zone), to the campaigns of Tamerlane, the Ṣafawid-Özbeg wars of the

---

[34] R. M. Adams, *Land behind Baghdad* (1965). See A. M. Watson, 'A medieval green revolution: new crops and farming techniques in the early Islamic world', in A. L. Udovitch (ed.), *The Islamic Middle East, 700–1900: Studies in Economic and Social History* (1981), p. 53, n. 29.

[35] C. Barbier de Meynard (tr.), *Dictionnaire géographique, historique et littéraire de la Perse* (1861).

sixteenth century or the political chaos of the mid eighteenth. But the consequences of the Mongol invasion and of their subsequent unenlightened occupation must surely have been decisive.

Another of Lewis's points, however, may be readily conceded: that even if the devastation was great in the Islamic world, it was not universal. Only Transoxania and Khurāsān had to suffer Mongol wrath at its worst. Other parts of Persia were less affected at the time, and in the case of south Persia were never subjected to a full-scale assault. This may have been either as a result of timely submission on the part of the local rulers or because the terrain was too hot, and had insufficient grassland, to tempt the Mongols into regarding it as suitable for settlement rather than the extraction of tribute. Our sources tend to bear out this impression of patchiness. Ch'ang Ch'un's disciple, while showing very clearly how Transoxania had been damaged, makes it no less evident that other parts of Central Asia were prospering under Mongol rule. Towards the end of the thirteenth century, Marco Polo, and rather later Ibn Baṭṭūṭa, noticed on their travels that although some cities had not yet recovered from the Mongol assault, others were flourishing. However, recovery by these dates, no doubt following the line of the Mongol Empire's trade routes, need hardly influence a verdict on the initial effect of the invasions.

We shall see in chapter 6 that recent work on the history of Russia in the thirteenth century has confirmed the same general impression: that the Mongol invasions were a truly awful, frequently a final, experience for those who had the misfortune to be in the way of the armies' advance; but that the impact was patchy, with some areas escaping fairly lightly or even completely. Similarly the destructiveness of the Mongol campaigns in the Chin Empire was not matched when the time came to undertake the conquest of the Sung. In south China the aim of the Mongols, and of Qubilai in particular, was to take over as intact a country as possible (see chapter 5). Yet even in China we have to explain a drop in population, if the figures are right, from over 100 million in Sung and Chin times to 70 million in the 1290s and 60 million in 1393, after the Mongols had been expelled.[36] The word 'disease' is much bandied about nowadays, and no doubt justifiably (see chapter 5); but the suspicion must remain that Mongol policies and actions may have something to answer for.

[36]   J. D. Langlois Jr (ed.), *China under Mongol Rule* (1981), introduction, p. 20.

The Mongol invasions and conquests continued for many years after the death of Chingiz Khān in 1227. The final limits of the empire were not fixed until around 1260 in western Asia and 1279 in the Far East. Nor did the Mongols at those dates concede that expansion had permanently halted. Modern historians, looking perhaps at the *Travels of Marco Polo* or the fourteenth-century merchants' handbook by Pegolotti, and reflecting on the proportion of the earth's surface that had come under the control of one family, have been fond of talking about the *Pax Mongolica*. But as Professor Franke deflatingly if accurately remarks, 'the Pax Mongolica is no more than one of those brilliant simplifications that can serve as chapter titles for world history books'.[37] If the concept is derived from the *Pax Romana*, the most appropriate comment belongs rightly to a Roman historian, Tacitus, speaking through the mouth of a British chieftain: 'Solitudinem faciunt, et pacem appellant' – 'they make a desolation, and call it peace'.[38]

[37] H. Franke, 'Sino-western contacts under the Mongol Empire', *Journal of the Hong Kong Branch of the Royal Asiatic Society*, 6 (1996), p. 50.
[38] *Agricola*, 30.

4

Nature and Institutions
of the Mongol Empire

The Mongol Army

The Mongol Empire was the creation of military conquest, and it was military supremacy that sustained it. There may have been truth in the old Chinese saw that Yeh-lü Ch'u-ts'ai is said to have repeated to the Great Khān Ögedei: that although the empire had been conquered on horseback, it could not be ruled from horseback. But without the Mongol army, no amount of efficient administration would have kept the Mongol Empire in being. The army must therefore be regarded as the basic and most essential of imperial institutions.[1]

The nature of nomadic society on the steppe was such that to speak of the Mongol army is really no more than to speak of the Mongol people in one of its natural aspects. For the whole of life was a process of military training. The same techniques that were necessary for survival in a herding and hunting environment were, with very little adaptation, those used in warfare.

This was particularly true of hunting. The Mongols mounted an annual expedition for the acquisition of meat to tide them through the hard Mongolian winter. This took the form of a *nerge*, a vast ring of hunters, which gradually contracted, driving the game before it. Any hunter who allowed an animal to escape from the ring, or who killed

---

[1] The best accounts of the Mongol army in English are H. D. Martin, 'The Mongol army', *Journal of the Royal Asiatic Society*, 1943/1–2, pp. 46–85, and *The Rise of Chingis Khan and his Conquest of North China* (1950), chapter 2; C. Hsiao, *The Military Establishment of the Yuan Dynasty* (1978), part 1; and P. D. Buell, 'Kalmyk Tanggaci people: thoughts on the mechanics and impact of Mongol expansion', *Mongolian Studies*, 6 (1980), pp. 41–59. See also, more generally, D. Sinor, 'The Inner Asian warriors', *Journal of the American Oriental Society*, 101/2 (1981), pp. 133–44.

one before the appointed time, was punished. At the end the khān would loose the first arrow, and the slaughter would commence. A few 'emaciated stragglers' would ultimately be spared. Juwaynī remarks that 'war – with its killing, counting of the slain and sparing of the survivors – is after the same fashion, and indeed analogous in every detail'.[2] Or as Gibbon, in his extraordinarily vivid account of the hunt, sums up: 'The leaders study, in this practical school, the most important lesson of the military art: the prompt and accurate judgment of ground, of distance, and of time. To employ against a human enemy the same patience and valour, the same skill and discipline, is the only alteration which is required in real war; and the amusements of the chase serve as a prelude to the conquest of an empire.'[3]

Mongols learned to ride very young indeed; and a Mongol who could ride was a potential soldier. All male Mongol adults below the age of 60 were liable for military service. There was no such thing as a civilian. Juwaynī says that the Mongol army 'is a peasantry in the dress of an army, of which, in time of need, all, from small to great, from those of high rank to those of low estate, are swordsmen, archers or spearmen'.[4] The Mongol rulers therefore had available to them a cavalry force which could be speedily mobilised, was highly trained, and consisted in theory – and even to some extent in practice – of the entire adult male population.

Can this be part of the explanation of the enormous size – if we are to believe our sources – of the Mongol armies? It must certainly have been of great significance that the Mongols could mobilise so much greater a proportion of their manpower than was possible in the sedentary states that they invaded. Other explanations have been offered. Marco Polo took the view that more men were to hand because of the Asiatic custom of polygamy. According to him the result of this was that more children would be born than under a monogamous system[5] – a somewhat dubious proposition if the ratio between the sexes was more or less equal. More plausibly it might be pointed out that the very

[2]   M. M. Qazwīnī (ed.), 'Aṭā Malik Juwaynī, Ta'rīkh-i Jahān Gushā (1912, 1916, 1937), vol. 1, p. 21; tr. J. A. Boyle, The History of the World Conqueror (1958), vol. 1, p. 29.
[3]   E. Gibbon, The History of the Decline and Fall of the Roman Empire (1905–6), vol. 3, p. 77.
[4]   Qazwīnī (ed.), Ta'rīkh-i Jahān Gushā, vol. 1, p. 22; Boyle, The History of the World Conqueror, vol. 1, p. 30.
[5]   A. Ricci (tr.), The Travels of Marco Polo (1931), p. 154.

Plate 4.1   Chingiz Khān in pursuit of his enemies. From a Persian miniature. Bibliothèque Nationale de France, Paris, MS. Persian Suppl. 1113, fol. 49

manoeuvrability of the Mongol forces would incline their enemies to overestimate the numbers involved. The Mongols themselves were not above employing tricks to suggest that they were present in overwhelming strength. Each Mongol went on campaign with a string of several horses. The number quoted varies, but something of the order of five horses per man would seem not to have been unusual. The mounting of dummies on spare horses, a device sometimes used, could have the effect, on the battlefield, of multiplying the apparent size of the army and increasing the terror in the hearts of the enemy soldiers.

It is probably impossible to arrive at a really accurate estimate of the size of the Mongol army. The two most valuable figures in the sources are those that can be extracted from the *Secret History* and from the *Altan Debter*, via Rashīd al-Dīn. Both sources offer a detailed breakdown of the Mongol military formations at their respective dates, and it is possible that the totals may have some relation to reality. The *Secret History*'s figures refer to the army at the time of the *quriltai* of 1206, and seem to suggest an army of around 105,000 men. Rashīd al-Dīn is concerned with the forces inherited by Chingiz Khān's sons at his death in 1227. According to him the size of the army in Mongolia proper was 129,000 men.

"Aw c'mon, Genghis – we need one more to make up a horde!"

Plate 4.2 Historians' difficulties in estimating the size of the Mongol army vividly illustrated. Reproduced by permission of Punch, Ltd. www.punch. co.uk

Chroniclers writing from outside the Mongol Empire tend to quote much higher figures. Jūzjānī variously reports Chingiz Khān's army that attacked the Khwārazm-shāh as being 700,000 or 800,000 strong. The Mamlūk fourteenth-century writer al-'Umarī estimated the number of soldiers on the registers of the Ilkhanate in his day at 200,000 to 300,000. He says that an army from the Golden Horde that invaded Transoxania around the end of the thirteenth century consisted of 250,000 men, each having not only five horses but also two slaves, a weapon waggon, and 30 head of sheep and goats.[6]

It does not seem likely that such figures should be treated literally, though it is only fair to point out that some scholars think that they

[6]   D. O. Morgan, 'The Mongol armies in Persia', *Der Islam*, 56/1 (1979), pp. 83–4, 85–6 and n. 35.

should.[7] If Chingiz Khān's army in around 1220 was indeed 800,000 strong, and if for the sake of argument al-'Umarī's remarks are taken as representing some kind of norm, then theoretically some four million horses, to say nothing of 24 million sheep and goats, may have been on the move through Transoxania and Khurāsān. The Mongols certainly developed considerable expertise in solving logistical problems, as Juwaynī's account of the elaborate arrangements made by Hülegü for the supply of his army shows.[8] But however efficient the sturdy Mongol horse may have been at feeding itself in the most unpromising circumstances, it is hard to believe that eastern Persia could have sustained an influx of animals on anything remotely approaching this scale. I have tried elsewhere to show that one of the reasons for the repeated Mongol failure to conquer Syria was the inadequacy of the pasture there.[9] Khurāsān would have been a great deal better than Syria in this respect, but scarcely sufficiently so.

No one can doubt, however, that at least by the standards of European armies of the period, the Mongol forces were very large indeed, though in fact they were probably smaller than those at the disposal either of the Khwārazm-shāh or the Chin and Sung emperors. The Mongols had large armies, certainly; but the Mongol conquests were not, essentially, won by the sheer weight of numbers. It is the character rather than the size of the Mongol army that is crucial.

The best-known fact about the Mongols' military administration is that they organised their forces according to a decimal system, with units of 10, 100, 1000 and 10,000. Of these the *tümen* of 10,000 was the major fighting unit, but the individual Mongol trooper would probably identify most readily with his thousand. This may be illustrated in the name 'Hazāra', that of a people of central Afghanistan, Persian-speaking but with a very Mongolian look about it, and which is thought to descend from Mongol military settlers. *Hazāra* is Persian for one thousand.

---

[7]   See J. M. Smith Jr, 'Mongol manpower and Persian population', *Journal of the Economic and Social History of the Orient*, 18/3 (1975), pp. 271–99, and his reply to Morgan, 'The Mongol armies in Persia', in J. M. Smith, 'Ayn Jālūt: Mamlūk success or Mongol failure?' *Harvard Journal of Asiatic Studies*, 44/2 (1984), pp. 308–9.

[8]   Qazwīnī (ed.), *Ta'rīkh-i Jahān Gushā*, vol. 3, pp. 91–4; Boyle, *The History of the World Conqueror*, vol. 2, pp. 608–10.

[9]   D. O. Morgan, 'The Mongols in Syria, 1260–1300', in P. W. Edbury (ed.), *Crusade and Settlement* (1985); and see chapter 6 in this book.

So straightforward and uniform a system was no doubt convenient, though one may wonder how many units actually had the precise round number of men that they were supposed to have, or anything like it. In Yüan China *tümens* were classified into those with 7000, 5000 and 3000 men.[10] The decimal system of army organisation was very far from being an innovation on Chingiz Khān's part: it had for many centuries been standard practice in steppe armies. What may have been more significant is what Chingiz Khān did with it.

Although the succession to the Mongol Great Khanate and to the various successor khanates was contested frequently and more often than not bloodily, there is one very striking fact about such contests: no candidates appear to have been considered except for properly authenticated descendants of Chingiz Khān. There was no attempt to set up an alternative ruling house of, say, Kerait or Tatar origin. This is presumably to be explained partly in terms of the almost sacred prestige that accrued to the house of the founder the empire. But it may be suspected that there was more to it than this, and that Chingiz Khān's radical reconstruction of the old tribal pattern in Mongolia provides the main explanation.

Chingiz Khān reorganised the whole Turko-Mongolian man-power of Mongolia into his new decimal military structure. Old tribal identities were not wholly ignored, and tribes which had been allies of the rising Chingiz retained at least some of their integrity as groupings: hence there were Önggüt and Qonggirat thousand formations. But the 'enemy' tribes – Tatars, Merkits, Keraits, Naimans and so forth – were broken up, and such of their men as had not been killed during the process of tribal unification were distributed among other units. So there were no Kerait *tümens* in existence that might have posed a threat to Mongol and Chingizid supremacy. Instead, Chingiz seems to have created what might be described as an artificial tribal system, in which old tribal loyalties were superseded by loyalty to the individual soldier's new military unit. Beyond that the Mongol royal house became the ultimate focus of obedience and allegiance.

Over and above the ordinary fighting formations, Chingiz Khān created an imperial guard (*keshig*). Its nucleus was his original and most faithful followers, the *nökers* of his early days of struggle. As time passed its functions multiplied, as did its numbers. By 1206 it was 10,000 strong. It was recruited across tribal boundaries, and

---

[10] Hsiao, *The Military Establishment*, pp. 170–1, n. 27.

membership was regarded as a supreme honour. The enlistment of high-born guards from all the tribes of Mongolia enabled Chingiz to treat his imperial guard corps as a useful form of honourable hostage taking.[11] The guard in effect constituted Chingiz's household too, and as such provided the machinery and personnel through which the empire was administered in its early stages. Any trooper in the imperial guard took precedence, if necessary, even over a commander of a thousand in the army proper. The imperial guard formed the nursery of the new empire's ruling class.

Originally the Mongol soldier received no pay other than booty, which was divided up according to fixed principles. Military service was not regarded as a job. Indeed, the Mongol soldiers themselves paid contributions in kind, called *qūbchūr*, to their commanders for such purposes as the maintenance of poor or disabled troopers. However, this did not prove to be a workable system once the empire had ceased its rapid expansion and when plunder was no longer so readily available. Ultimately the Mongol troops in China were salaried, at least so far as the officers were concerned; and they were able to pass on their military offices to their heirs. In Persia the reforming Īlkhān Ghazan, after trying out various methods of providing for the Mongols' needs, attempted to meet the problem by utilizing a traditional Persian device, the *iqtā'*, whereby the soldiers were allotted assignments of agricultural land, receiving the produce in lieu of salary.[12]

In the first instance a cavalry force, the army consisted essentially of light cavalry archers, using the standard compound bow of the steppes, which was made of layers of horn and sinew on a wooden frame. This bow required a pull much stiffer than the English longbow, even though it was fired from horseback. It had impressive range and power of penetration.[13] It was a very long time indeed before the hand gun could match the compound bow in range, penetration or rate of fire; we should be wary of assuming that the invention of gunpowder immediately made the steppe archer obsolete. The Tatar archers of the Crimea were still campaigning successfully in eastern Europe in the seventeenth century.[14]

---

[11]   Ibid., pp. 36–7.

[12]   Ibid., pp. 25–7; Morgan, 'The Mongol armies in Persia', pp. 91–6.

[13]   See J. Chambers, *The Devil's Horsemen: the Mongol Invasion of Europe* (1979), p. 57.

[14]   L. J. D. Collins, 'The military organisation and tactics of the Crimean Tatars during the sixteenth and seventeenth centuries', in V. J. Parry and M. E. Yapp (eds), *War, Technology and Society in the Middle East* (1975), pp. 257–76.

In addition to their light cavalry the Mongols also used some armoured heavy cavalry, equipped with lances. Both the Chinese and Middle Easterners provided units of siege engineers.

It would not have been possible to conquer such enormous areas if the Mongol army proper had alone been available. From very early days, Chinese troops were used in large numbers, and the Sung Empire, with its vast walled cities, its numerous waterways and its rice paddy fields, could hardly have been taken by any number of cavalry manoeuvres. Chinese forces were used mainly as infantry and as garrison troops once the conquest was completed. In Persia, similarly, native Persian troops were utilised for garrison duty and to guard passes. Ghazan is said to have organised them decimally.[15]

A further use of non-Mongols was as a rather disagreeable tactical device. When prisoners were taken at the fall of a city they were compelled to undertake dangerous siege works, or were driven in front of the Mongol assault troops at the storming of the next city. The expectation was that the defenders would be reluctant to slaughter their own compatriots, or at least that casualties among the Mongols themselves would be minimised. Other tactics included encirclement (after the pattern of the hunt); the use of surprise, especially through appearing by an unexpected (sometimes a supposedly impossible) route; the efficient synchronisation of forces that were far apart; the ancient steppe device of the feigned flight, which could usually be counted on to work; and terror. Unlike many other Asiatic conquerors the Mongols did not generally indulge in wanton cruelty as such. Countless thousands of innocent people were killed, but normally this was done as quickly and efficiently as possible, without the use of torture. Specific cases might require a different approach: the Khwārazm-shāh's governor of Utrār, against whom the Mongols had a particular grievance, was put to death with uncharacteristic refinements. But normally Chingiz Khān had neither the time nor the inclination for such expedients as cementing people alive into towers, which Tamerlane is said to have enjoyed.

Chingiz's principle seems to have been much the same as President Truman's over Hiroshima and Nagasaki. The apparent rationale was that if the population of one city was subjected to a frightful massacre, the next city would be more likely to surrender without resistance, thus avoiding unnecessary Mongol casualties. The morality of this approach to warfare is no doubt open to discussion, but there can be no disputing that it worked. The Mongols' policy was that any city which surrendered

---

[15]   Morgan, 'The Mongol armies in Persia', p. 89.

without fighting would be spared, but that those who caused the Mongol army to suffer casualties could expect no mercy. The Mongols usually kept their word, and the message, to judge from the number of cities that did surrender on demand, seems speedily to have spread.

An important organisational feature of army's structure was what was known as the *tamma* or *tanma* system. A *tamma* force was an army of contingents allotted from the total available Mongol manpower. Its purpose was to maintain and if possible to extend Mongol rule in conquered territory, and it was usually stationed, at least initially, on the steppe–sedentary borderlands. *Tamma* forces were originally established by order of the central imperial government. Hence when Hülegü invaded Persia and Iraq in the 1250s, his brother the Great Khān Möngke granted him a *tamma* army supposedly consisting, according to Juwaynī, of two out of every ten available Mongol soldiers.[16] A similar allocation was made for the armies which were simultaneously to invade and conquer the Sung Empire.

Some *tamma* armies ultimately became the nuclei of the permanent military forces of the empire's subsidiary khanates, such as Hülegü's Ilkhanate in Persia. The Great Khanate itself had had, within the army, a central 'core' army (*qol*), of which the imperial guard was the inner elite. From the outer armies were found the forces necessary to provide the armies of the patrimonies (*ulus*) which were granted to the sons of Chingiz Khān and their descendants and were the basis of the subsidiary khanates. These armies were recruited on the *tamma* principle.

We happen to be able to see in some detail how the *tamma* system worked in one instance as a result of some remarkable research by Professor Jean Aubin.[17] He set himself to try to solve the long-standing problem of a group known as the Qaraunas, whose origin and identity had puzzled historians; even the awesome Pelliot failed to clarify it satisfactorily. The Qaraunas were a group or groups of marauding Mongols who operated in the area between eastern Persia and the borderlands of India – in effect, modern Afghanistan – and who in their bandit capacity were encountered by Marco Polo when he was passing that way in 1272.[18] Aubin's examination of the sources showed that they were in

---

[16] Qazwīnī (ed.), *Ta'rīkh-i Jahān Gushā*, vol. 3, p. 90; Boyle, *The History of the World Conqueror*, vol. 2, p. 607. See Buell, 'Kalmyk Tanggaci people', on the *tamma* system.

[17] J. Aubin, 'L'ethnogénèse des Qaraunas', *Turcica*, 1 (1969), pp. 65–94.

[18] Ricci, *The Travels of Marco Polo*, pp. 42–3.

origin a *tamma* formation, sent first of all in the reign of Ögedei, and stationed on the Indian borders. The names of some of their commanders can be identified. They prove to have come from a very wide diversity of tribes – an interesting illustration of the reconstruction by Chingiz Khān of tribal allegiances into military formations which was discussed earlier. The Qaraunas became, in fact, one of the newly minted synthetic tribes.

Their appearances in the sources for the history of Persia in the thirteenth century usually show them as enemies of the Ilkhanate. This appears to be so because they contained a section, commanded by a Golden Horde general called Negüder (Nīkūdar in Persian), which had been joined by the survivors of the Golden Horde's contingent in the Mongol army allotted to Hülegü's expedition. When in 1261 or 1262 warfare broke out between Hülegü and Berke of the Golden Horde, the Qaraunas (or Nīkūdarīs, as the Persian historians often call them) formed as it were an independent section of the Golden Horde's army in the enemy's rear. In due course some Qaraunas became loyal to the Ilkhanate, and others to the Chaghatai khanate of Central Asia; but the details of the story are too complex to pursue here.[19]

Law

It has been asserted that when a new steppe empire is inaugurated, the conqueror will usually 'mark the foundation of his polity by the promulgation of laws'.[20] The ascription of such a legal code to Chingiz Khān is common form, and indeed his 'Great *Yāsā*' has long been seen as one of the essential institutional foundations of the Mongol Empire. Never-

[19]   It is intriguing to note that in parts of Afghanistan today, especially in villages near the city of Harāt in the west of the country, there still exist groups of Mongolian speakers. They do not look in the least Mongoloid, having (unlike the Hazāras) intermarried with the local indigenous population. But they have retained the Mongolian language in an archaic form that has been lost in Mongolia itself. The odd feature is that they apparently call themselves Nīkūdarīs – to say the least a very curious coincidence.

[20]   P. Crone, *Slaves on Horses: the Evolution of the Islamic Polity* (1980), p. 20.

theless there seems to me to be little evidence for the conventional view, and I shall present here a rather different interpretation.[21]

To summarise what is usually said: Chingiz Khān laid down a code of laws, probably at the *quriltai* of 1206, though perhaps supplemented later. This, the Great *Yāsā*, was written down, copies were kept for consultation in the treasuries of the Mongol princes, and it was regarded as permanently binding. No complete copy now survives, but it may to a considerable extent be reconstructed by assembling and classifying such fragments as are quoted in a variety of sources. The crucial figure in all this is Chingiz Khān's adopted brother (or, according to Rashīd al-Dīn,[22] adopted son), the ex-Tatar Shigi-Qutuqu. He was made chief judge (*yarghuchi*) at the 1206 *quriltai*, and according to the received doctrine the *Yāsā* was entrusted to him. As I suggested in chapter 1, this formulation of the supposed sequence of events appears to date from the publication of Petis de la Croix's biography of Chingiz Khān in 1710.

The matter can best be approached under two heads: the origins of the *Yāsā*, and its contents. There are two prime sources for the original institution: the account of the *quriltai* of 1206 in the *Secret History*, and the *Altan Debter* material used by Rashīd al-Dīn. The first thing to notice is that in the *Secret History* section the word *Yāsā* is not used, though it does appear elsewhere in the book in the sense of 'order' or 'decree'. In fact a closer look at what was said to Shigi-Qutuqu reveals that he was indeed granted the right to exercise judicial functions, with reference to cases of robbery or fraud and to the distribution of subject peoples among the Mongol royal family. He was to write his decisions in a blue book (*kökö debter*), and such decisions were to be regarded as binding. He was to keep, then, a record of *ad hoc* decisions and perhaps to begin the evolution of a kind of case law. None of this has anything

---

[21]   The following section summarises the argument of D. O. Morgan, 'The "Great *Yāsā* of Chingiz Khān" and Mongol law in the Īlkhānate', *Bulletin of the School of Oriental and African Studies*, 49/1 (1986), pp. 163–76, where a more detailed discussion may be found and where full references are given. The most learned recent presentation of a more 'positive' view of the *Yāsā* than the one I give here is in P. Ratchnevsky, *Činggis-Khan Sein Leben und Wirken* (1983), pp. 164–72. See also P. Ratchnevsky, 'Die Yasa (Jasaq) Činggis-khans und ihre Problematik', *Schriften zur Geschichte und Kultur des alten Orients 5: Sprache, Geschichte und Kultur der altaischen Völker* (1974), pp. 471–87.

[22]   B. Karīmī (ed.), Rashīd al-Dīn, *Jāmiʿ al-tawārīkh* (1970), vol. 1, p. 414.

to do with a general legal code, or much connection with the known 'fragments' of the *Yāsā*.[23]

In the case of Rashīd al-Dīn we find that the standard account of his material in Riasanovsky's *Fundamental Principles of Mongol Law*,[24] which as used by Riasanovsky largely confirms the supposed *Secret History* evidence, both misdates and mistranslates it. Rashīd al-Dīn's discussion of the 1206 *quriltai* contains no reference to the *Yāsā*; the account of an earlier *quriltai* (which Riasanovsky thinks refers to 1206) is speaking of individual decrees, not a legal code; and the only reference which is at all germane is a very brief remark which might possibly presuppose some kind of legal code in Rashīd al-Dīn's account of a *quriltai* in the 1218.[25] Since these are the two sources on which the argument has always been founded, I conclude that we have insufficient evidence, unless something new can be produced, for believing that Chingiz Khān instituted the Great *Yāsā* in 1206.

The death-blow to the process of fragment classifying, of which again Riasanovsky was the leading exponent, was inflicted by Professor David Ayalon, who showed that all the significant fragments derived, with or without acknowledgement, from one source, Juwaynī.[26] But in fact when Juwaynī is examined, we find that he is not discussing the Great *Yāsā* either. His chapter is an account of Mongol military training, communications, taxation of conquered territories and such matters. Chingiz Khān's decrees on this kind of affair were, according to Juwaynī, written down and preserved for consultation. This is very likely, but again has nothing to do with a general legal code.[27]

There seems really to be very little convincing evidence that a written legal code ever did exist. But there was certainly something, and that something was later believed to have been the Great *Yāsā*. There are many references which seem to indicate the prevalence of a belief in such

---

[23]   Para. 203: F. W. Cleaves (tr.), *The Secret History of the Mongols* (1982), pp. 143–4.

[24]   V. A. Riasanovsky, *Fundamental Principles of Mongol Law* (1965), p. 27.

[25]   I. N. Berezin (ed. and tr.), Rashīd al-Dīn, *Sbornik Letopisei, Trudy vostočnago otdêlenija Imperatorskago Russkago Arkheologičeskago Obščestva* 13 (1868), pp. 238–9; 15 (1888), p. 65.

[26]   D. Ayalon, 'The Great *Yāsā* of Chingiz Khān: a re-examination', A, *Studia Islamica*, 33 (1971), pp. 97–140.

[27]   Qazwīnī (ed.), *Ta'rīkh-i Jahān Gushā*, vol. 1, pp. 17–18; Boyle, *The History of the World Conqueror*, vol. 1, p. 25.

a thing, but a fog of vagueness and uncertainty appears to engulf the contemporary historians when it comes to explaining exactly what it amounted to. Ayalon explains this by suggesting that the text of the *Yāsā*, like the *Altan Debter*, was regarded as taboo. But such a theory involves us in believing that the Mongols imposed and enforced a legal code, the contents of which were unknown and unknowable to many of those who were expected to obey it. This does not seem very plausible.

I would suggest that there may have been several possible bases for the later belief that Chingiz Khān had laid down a Great *Yāsā*. One is that there undoubtedly was a body of unwritten Mongol customary law. In our sources, Chingiz Khān's second son Chaghatai is represented as its stern upholder. This would have been an evolving body of custom, beginning long before Chingiz's time and being added to long after. In this context it is interesting to note that some Chinese sources ascribe the institution of a *Yāsā* to Ögedei rather than to Chingiz; and a number of Persian sources contain references which appear to equate in authority *yāsās* promulgated by later Great Khāns with those of Chingiz himself.

A second element is the recollection of Chingiz Khān's utterances – his maxims, or *biligs*. These were certainly remembered and recorded, and Rashīd al-Dīn has a long chapter detailing them, though he has nothing whatever on the contents of the Great *Yāsā*. A third possibility relates again to Shigi-Qutuqu's activities. From the *Dastūr al-kātib*, a source of the late Ilkhanid period in Persia, we learn that in certain cases involving disputes between Mongols a written record of the case, a *yarghū-nāma*, was kept.[28] Now according to Rashīd al-Dīn, Shigi-Qutuqu's practice as *yarghuchi* set the pattern that was always to be followed in Mongol legal proceedings.[29] It is not impossible, then, that for a period of a century or more after Shigi-Qutuqu's time written records were kept of the decisions taken in certain kinds of dispute. This may have helped give rise to the otherwise dubious notion that there existed a written Great *Yāsā*.

It is not feasible at this stage to state with certainty that the Great *Yāsā* did not exist: only that the sources which have so far been used

[28]   A. A. Alizade (ed.), Muḥammad ibn Hindūshāh Nakhjawānī, *Dastūr al-kātib fī taʿyīn al-marātib*, vol. 2 (1976), pp. 29–35.
[29]   A. A. Romaskevich, L. A. Khetagurov and A. A. Alizade (eds), Rashīd al-Dīn, *Jāmiʿ al-tawārīkh*, vol. 1, part 1 (1965), p.180.

to demonstrate the proposition that it did do not show anything of the sort. But if my argument is right, at least one institutional foundation of the Mongol Empire will be left looking a little shaky. This is perhaps salutary: historians have tended overmuch to discern system in the Mongol approach to empire. Often this can only be achieved by bending some parts of the evidence and ignoring others.

Taxation

In nothing has this over-schematisation been more evident than in discussions of Mongol taxation.[30] Can what the Mongols did in this sphere be dignified with the name of 'system'? I am inclined to doubt it. From his examination of the Persian sources of the Mongol period Petrushevsky concluded that around 45 different terms for taxation were used, though this does not imply that there were 45 distinct taxes, since terminology varied at different times and places.[31] Traditional nomadic taxation was divided into tribute (*alba*) and levy (*qūbchūr*). Such taxes were paid in kind, as we have seen in the case of the payments of *qūbchūr* made by the individual Mongol soldier. *Qūbchūr* may be taken as the most characteristic Mongol tax. It was a 1 per cent levy on flocks and herds, paid by the nomads to the ruler. It could be an *ad hoc* levy. For example, according to the *Secret History* Chingiz Khān on one occasion levied a *qūbchūr* from his followers for the support of the Ong Khān of the Keraits, who had arrived at Chingiz's camp in a state of some distress.[32]

---

[30]   The standard discussion of Mongol taxation is H. F. Schurmann, 'Mongolian tributary practices of the thirteenth century', *Harvard Journal of Asiatic Studies*, 14 (1956), pp. 304–89, supplemented and revised by J. M. Smith Jr, 'Mongol and nomadic taxation', *Harvard Journal of Asiatic Studies*, 30 (1970), pp. 46–85, though as I indicate in the text I am not convinced of the existence of the system which he discerns. The best discussion as far as the Islamic world is concerned is A. K. S. Lambton, 'Mongol fiscal administration in Persia' (forthcoming in *Studia Islamica*), the conclusions of which are to some extent foreshadowed in her *EI²* article 'Kharādj II – in Persia'. See also my 'Ḳūbčūr', in *EI²*.

[31]   I. P. Petrushevsky, 'The socio-economic condition of Iran under the Īl-Khāns', in J. A. Boyle (ed.), *The Cambridge History of Iran* (1968), vol. 5, p. 529.

[32]   Para. 152: tr. Cleaves, *The Secret History of the Mongols*, pp. 80–1.

Qūbchūr appears again in a rather different context. From around the year 1252 it was the term used for a poll-tax, flat rate or graduated, imposed on the conquered sedentary population of Persia and Central Asia. Its incidence was determined on the basis of a census. This is as different from the original variety of *qūbchūr* as it would be possible to be; and it is far from clear why the Mongols should have elected to cause endless confusion among historians by using the same term for the two taxes. I once suggested that it might be 'an indication of conservative Mongol thinking',[33] but since I wrote those words a more interesting possibility has been put forward. In an article on the Uighurs, Professor Thomas Allsen has pointed out that Uighur documents of (if the dating is right) before the Mongol period contain references to the two most typical 'Mongol' taxes, *qalān* (of which more shortly) and *qūbchūr*. The population of the Uighur lands, though ultimately of nomadic origin, was settled; and this pre-Mongol *qūbchūr* appears to be the sedentary, poll-tax variety.[34] If this is correct, we may now know from where the Mongols derived the idea of such a tax; and of how the ambiguous usage of the word *qūbchūr* may have arisen. Indeed it would be no great surprise in the light of their conspicuous institutional and cultural indebtedness to the Uighurs.

There can be no doubt that of all the Mongol exactions, *qūbchūr* and *qalān* were the most resented in the conquered lands of the Islamic world. This comes through strongly even in poetry of the period.[35] Yet it is some indication of the obscurity of the subject that it is still not certain precisely what *qalān* was. Professor John Masson Smith believes that it was a catch-all term for pre-Mongol, Islamic taxation,[36] which would be tidy and convenient if true. But unfortunately too much of the evidence will not fit into this particular system. The most likely explanation at present would seem to be that it was a general term for occasional exactions of a specifically Mongol character, imposed on the sedentary population and including some kind of corvée. Such exactions would

---

[33]   D. O. Morgan, 'Who ran the Mongol Empire?', *Journal of the Royal Asiatic Society*, 1982/2, p. 127.

[34]   T. T. Allsen, 'The Yüan Dynasty and the Uighurs of Turfan in the 13th century', in M. Rossabi (ed.), *China among Equals: the Middle Kingdom and its Neighbors, 10th–14th Centuries* (1983), pp. 263 and 278, n. 141.

[35]   V. Minorsky, 'Pūr-i Bahā and his poems', in his *Iranica* (1964), pp. 292–305.

[36]   Smith, 'Mongol and nomadic taxation'.

tend to fall unpredictably and at random, and this would go far to explain *qalān's* peculiar unpopularity.

The third most frequently mentioned of the characteristic Mongol taxes presents fewer problems. This was *tamghā*, a tax apparently levied usually at a rate of 5 per cent on all commercial transactions. It included some kinds of services as well as sales – prostitution, for example – and had something of the nature of VAT. Its existence testifies to the importance attached by the Mongols to trade and its profits. They may have had difficulty in adjusting to the idea that there was some point to agriculture and city life, but they needed no persuasion that it was in their interests to encourage the greatest possible amount of trading activity in their dominions and with the lands beyond.

The purpose of the taxes imposed on the conquered populations was quite simply the maximum conceivable degree of exploitation. There was little pretence that in Mongol eyes their subjects had any justification for their existence except as producers of revenue. As a rule exploitation was limited only by the consideration that it was sensible to leave the peasants sufficient to permit their survival till the next year, so that a further year's taxes could be levied. In the early days of excessive zeal the Mongols did not in fact always stop even at that point. Mongol taxation was more a pragmatic series of exactions as seemed appropriate and profitable than any kind of fixed system. To judge from the experience of the Islamic lands that fell under Mongol rule, the burden of taxation on the peasants was probably appreciably heavier than it had been even under such unenlightened rulers as the Khwārazm-shāhs. But as the Mongols increasingly entrusted the day-to-day administration of government to Persian bureaucrats, many of whom had at least a realistic appreciation of practical possibilities, there may have been some mitigation. This is likely to have been especially true for a time after the reforms of Ghazan Khān in Persia (see chapter 6). Throughout, the burden was increased in that all these 'Mongol' taxes were additional. The peasants were still required to continue paying the Islamic taxes that had been extracted from them by the pre-Mongol regimes.

In China too, exploitation to the limit and beyond was the norm, particularly in the early years of Mongol rule. The Sinicised Khitan Yeh-lü Ch'u-ts'ai was able to use his influence over both Chingiz Khān and his successor Ögedei to moderate the worst effects of Mongol oppression. But considerations of income would always take precedence over any question of humanitarian treatment. In 1239 a Central Asian Muslim merchant, 'Abd al-Raḥmān, came to Ögedei with the proposal that if he were given the right to farm the taxes of north China, he would be able to double the government's income from them. The temptation was too much even for Ögedei, though he had the reputation of being an unusually benevolent ruler of his conquered subjects by the not very exacting Mongol standards of benevolence. The protests of Yeh-lü Ch'u-ts'ai were ignored, and 'Abd al-Raḥmān was left to extract taxation at the new levels as he thought appropriate.[37] No doubt the rule of Qubilai was less burdensome, but as Professor Langlois remarks, 'Mongol rule in China, like Mongol rule elsewhere, was the rule of conquerors. The Mongols' aim was to enrich themselves. Their perception of how best to accomplish that aim changed over time, but Mongol superiority and enrichment remained their chief concerns in China.'[38]

Communications

It would hardly have been possible to rule an empire the size of the Mongols' effectively without an adequate system of communications. Such a system, called the Yām,[39] was therefore created by the Mongols, and its organisation and efficiency were among the features of Mongol government that most impressed European observers. Marco Polo was particularly taken with it, and his account of how it worked is one of our most valuable sources of information.[40] The purposes served by the Yām network were various. It was designed to facilitate the travels of envoys going to and from the Mongol courts; it was used (especially on the route between north China and Mongolia) for the transportation of goods; it ensured the speedy transmission of royal orders from one part of the empire to another; and it provided a framework whereby the Mongols could receive intelligence as quickly as possible. By abuse it

[37]   I. de Rachewiltz. 'Yeh-lü Ch'u-ts'ai (1189–1243): Buddhist idealist and Confucian statesman', in A. F. Wright and D. Twitchett (eds), *Confucian Personalities* (1962), p. 207; M. Rossabi, 'The Muslims in the early Yüan Dynasy', in J. D. Langlois Jr (ed.), *China under Mongol Rule* (1981), pp. 265–6.
[38]   Langlois, *China under Mongol Rule*, introduction, p. 9.
[39]   P. Olbricht, *Das Postwesen in China unter der Mongolenberrschaft im 13 und 14 Jahrhundert* (1954) is a useful monograph in German on the Yām system in China, but there is very little in English except the somewhat tertiary account in F. Dvornik, *Origins of Intelligence Services* (1974), chapter 5, and short sections in general histories of the Mongols.
[40]   Ricci, *The Travels of Marco Polo*, pp. 152–7.

was also used by merchants and by travelling Mongol notables who had with them a sufficient following to enable them to enforce the compliance of the *Yām* officials. The frequency of edicts forbidding such practices is an index of how prevalent they were.

We are told nothing about Chingiz Khān's own arrangements for communications. It may be that in a career of perpetual motion he was able to deal with the matter only on an *ad hoc* basis. Our sources for the beginnings of the *Yām* system are as usual the *Secret History of the Mongols* and Rashīd al-Dīn.[41] According to both of these the system was instituted by Chingiz's successor, the Great Khān Ögedei, in 1234. The *Secret History* tells us that the passage of couriers before 1234 had imposed an unacceptable burden on the areas through which they travelled because of their commandeering of horses and provisions. A properly organised network was supposed to deal with this. Ögedei seems initially to have set up the new machinery in the territories subject to his own direct rule. It was them extended to include the lands of his brothers Chaghatai and Tolui and his nephew Batu. This is in itself interesting in that it shows the old steppe notion of family sovereignty at work: Ögedei may have been Great Khān, but he was not a dictator. If a new institution were to be set up throughout the empire, this would be done after consultation between the different branches of the Chingizid family.

The responsibility for maintenance of the *Yām* system fell to the army units in the various parts of the empire. The necessary horses and supplies were contributed by the local population. However, at least in theory this was done on a regular rather than an arbitrary basis, the incidence of exaction being determined by reference to the census returns.

The structure of the system was based on the erection of post stations at stages equivalent to a day's journey. According to Marco Polo this meant about every 25 or 30 miles (more in desolate areas). Other sources quote similar figures. The stations held stocks of horses and fodder for the use of authorised travellers. Proper authorisation would be a tablet of authority, a *paiza* (Chinese *p'ai-tse*, Mongolian *gerege*). This might be of wood, silver or gold, and in some cases have a tiger or a gerfalcon

---

[41]   *Secret History*, para. 279: tr. Cleaves, *The Secret History of the Mongols*, p. 225; A. A. Alizade (ed.), Rashīd al-Dīn, *Jāmi' al-tawārīkh*, vol. 2, part 1 (1980), pp. 121–2, 143–4; tr. J. A. Boyle, Rashīd al-Dīn, *The Successors of Genghis Khan* (1971), pp. 55–6 and 62–3; note that the translation has gone astray on p. 62, line 18.

Plate 4.3   A Mongol *paiza* (tablet of authority) in the Uighur script. Discovered in the former lands of the Golden Horde. From E. D. Phillips, *The Mongols*, London: Thames & Hudson, 1969

at its head, depending on the rank and importance of the holder. Normally, then, traffic might move at about 25 miles a day; but urgent messages could go very much faster. Marco Polo speaks of 200–300 miles per day, and Rashīd al-Dīn mentions 60 *farsakhs*, probably about 200 miles.[42] Such express couriers travelled swathed around the middle and the head, and either wore a belt of bells or carried a horn which they would sound as they approached a *Yām* station. Thus a horse would be made ready for them in advance, and they could change horses and go straight on without stopping. A further refinement was that in

[42]   Ricci, *The Travels of Marco Polo*, p. 157; A. A. Alizade (ed.), Rashīd al-Dīn, *Jāmiʿ al-tawārīkh*, vol. 3 (1957), p. 484.

some areas the horse post was supplemented by runners. Marco Polo says that in China these were placed at intervals of three miles between post stations, and Rashīd al-Dīn says that in Persia each *Yām* station was supposed to possess two resident runners.[43]

The impression we receive from our sources is that on the whole the *Yām* system worked very well in China.[44] In Persia, on the other hand, what we hear most about is the appalling abuse to which it was subject. But this may well represent the preoccupations of some of the writers rather than a real contrast that was quite so stark. For example, Marco Polo was concerned to relate the marvels of the east, Rashīd al-Dīn the need for reform. Considered as a whole, the *Yām* system was probably the most effective of Mongol imperial institutions after the army. By and large it seems to have worked, though with interruptions caused by warfare among the Mongol khanates, and its influence was widespread. The *barīd*, the horse post system of Mamlūk Egypt, is usually said to have been modelled on it; and to judge from the Arab traveller Ibn Baṭṭūṭa's account, a similar claim could be made in respect of the courier system in the Delhi Sultanate.[45] The long-lived *ulak* system of the Ottoman Empire may well have been a direct descendant of the *Yām* as it functioned in Ilkhanid Persia.

The question must arise: did the Mongols devise this remarkable institution themselves, or did they derive the idea from someone else? It may perhaps first be worth saying that the search for 'influences' can sometimes get out of hand, and that anyone who is faced with the running of a large empire is likely to think, without being prompted, that a system of efficient couriers might be an idea worth considering. But in this case, as it happens, the evidence for direct influence on the Mongols by others is very strong.

The possibility of Middle Eastern influence on the Mongols may be discounted: the celebrated *barīd* of the 'Abbasid Caliphs had disappeared long before the thirteenth century. The source is further to the east. According to Clauson's dictionary of early Turkish, the word *yām*

---

[43]   Ricci, *The Travels of Marco Polo*, p. 154; Alizade (ed.) *Jāmi' al-tawārīkh*, vol. 3, p. 484.

[44]   See Olbricht, *Das Postwesen in China*, p. 39.

[45]   J. Sauvaget, *La poste aux chevaux dans l'empire des Mamelouks* (1941), p. 13; and see D. Ayalon, 'On one of the works of Jean Sauvaget', *Israel Oriental Studies*, 1 (1971), pp. 298–302; H. A. R. Gibb (tr.), *The Travels of Ibn Baṭṭūṭa*, vol. 3 (1971), p. 594.

itself derives from the Chinese *chan*, 'to stop; a stage on a journey'.[46] In China the mounted postal courier network had a history stretching back many centuries before the arrival of the Mongols. More directly to the point, the system operated in north China by the Khitan Liao dynasty had similarities to the *Yām* which are too striking to be coincidental. The Khitan dynastic history has descriptions of courier stations, their use for the reception of foreign envoys, and the issue of silver tablets of authority to the couriers: these tablets are clearly the immediate ancestors of the Mongol *paiza*.[47]

Not for the first time, then, we encounter the marked influence of Khitan institutions on the administration of the Mongol Empire. The Mongols must be given the credit for extending the *Yām* concept to cover the whole of their empire; but it is in this, the adoption and enlargement of an already existing idea, rather than in institutional innovation, that the Mongol genius must be said to lie.

The Mongol Approach to Government

The Mongols were undoubtedly pragmatists.[48] They were not too proud to learn from other peoples, especially from peoples who had both a

[46]   G. Clauson, *An Etymological Dictionary of pre-Thirteenth Century Turkish* (1972), p. 933.

[47]   See I. de Rachewiltz, 'Personnel and personalities in north China in the early Mongol period', *Journal of the Economic and Social History of the Orient*, 9 (1966), pp. 111–12; Morgan, 'Who ran the Mongol Empire?', p. 130.

[48]   There is an extensive literature on the Mongol approach to administration, of which P. D. Buell, 'Sino-Khitan administration in Mongol Bukhara', *Journal of Asian History*, 13/2 (1979), pp. 121–51, I. de Rachewiltz, 'Yeh-lü Ch'u-ts'ai (1189–1243): Buddhist idealist and Confucian statesman' and 'Personnel and personalities in north China', J. W. Dardess, 'From Mongol Empire to Yüan Dynasty: changing forms of imperial rule in Mongolia and Central Asia', *Monumenta Serica*, 30 (1972–3), pp. 117–65, D. M. Farquhar, 'Structure and function in the Yüan imperial government', in Langlois, *China under Mongol Rule*, pp. 25–55, and I. P. Petrushevsky, 'Rashīd al-Dīn's conception of the state', *Central Asiatic Journal*, 14 (1970), pp. 148–62, are among the most important items. My own views are given in more detail in D. O. Morgan, 'Cassiodorus and Rashīd al-Dīn on barbarian rule in Italy and Persia', *Bulletin of the School of Oriental and African Studies*, 40/2 (1977), pp. 302–20 and 'Who ran the Mongol Empire?'

respectable steppe pedigree and experience in the techniques necessary for administering a great empire. This was the more true once the empire had come to include a sedentary sector. It is clear enough (see chapter 2) how pervasive was the influence, above all, of the Uighurs and the Khitans. It has rightly been said that 'because the Uighurs were the first of the advanced sedentary societies to come under Mongol control, they exercised a profound influence on the institutional and cultural life of the empire in its formative stages'.[49] But although the Uighurs will be especially remembered because of the Mongols' use of their alphabet and of their chancery practice, Khitan influence, as was suggested earlier, was probably of even greater importance though it is more difficult to trace in detail.

The careers of a number of Khitan defectors to the Mongols have been perceptively traced,[50] and two of them have been tracked as far west as Bukhārā. These were mentioned by the Persian historian Juwaynī, who conflated them into one individual whom he called 'Tūshā the *bāsqāq*'. This, it transpires, is not as was previously assumed a personal name, but a garbled Persianisation of the two Khitans' Chinese official title, *t'ai-shih*, 'grand preceptor'.[51] *Bāsqāq* is a Turkish term, the Mongolian equivalent of which is *darugha* or *darughachi*. This is a term that is not easy to define: it might (especially a little later in the Mongol period) mean a provincial governor or a Mongol resident in partly autonomous territory, whose murder would customarily mark the inauguration of a local revolt. But in the empire's early stages the *darughachi* was the most important all-purpose Mongol official in conquered territory; the office appears as an offshoot of the imperial guard and household discussed earlier. The *darughachi's* role has been interestingly studied by Professor Buell and others, and there can be little doubt about its Khitan origins. The subdivisions of the Qara-Khitai empire had been under the supervision of officials who seem very similar to the later *darughachi*, and they are called, in Persian sources, *shahna*, which is an Arabic term used as an equivalent for *bāsqāq* and *darugha*. As additional confirmation they are called, in Chinese sources, *pa-ssŭ-ha* among other things. *Pa-ssŭ-ha* is derived, it appears, from *bāsqāq*.[52] Buell's legitimate general conclusion is that 'it was the Khitan, more than any

---

[49]   Allsen, 'The Yüan Dynasty', p. 266.
[50]   De Rachewiltz, 'Personnel and personalities in north China'.
[51]   Buell, 'Sino-Khitan administration', pp. 122–4.
[52]   Morgan, 'Who ran the Mongol Empire?', p. 129.

other group, who provided the needed expertise and guidance in the rise of the Mongols, and it was from the Khitan, above all, that the Mongols borrowed conceptions, vocabulary and institutions'.[53]

Although this is of immense importance if we are to understand how the Mongols, having acquired an empire, were able to make it work, it refers essentially to the government of the early empire. When Persia and China had been conquered, the Mongols became the masters of great sedentary societies that had complex administrative traditions of long standing. Were the Mongols to make a clean sweep, introducing *darughachis* and the like wholesale and disregarding the machinery already in existence, or were they to permit at least some degree of administrative continuity to be maintained?

The Mongols do not seem to have considered a uniform approach to Persia and China appropriate to their requirements. Initially in Persia, Non-Persians did often hold the highest offices, especially during the period between Chingiz Khān's invasion and the setting up of the Ilkhanate in the 1250s. Mongols like the Oirat Arghun Aqa and Uighurs like Körgüz exercised great power. Even after Hülegü's day, members of minority groups such as the Jew Sa'd al-Dawla were influential at times. But throughout the period of the Ilkhanate the administration seems to have rested largely in the hands of members of the old Persian bureaucracy. The historian Juwaynī was governor in Mongol-ruled Baghdad for many years, and his brother was the chief minister of successive Īlkhāns. When the latter ultimately fell from power, the Juwaynī family had been in high office virtually continuously for 80 years, serving Khwārazm-shāhs and Mongols in turn.

The most notable of all Ilkhanid government servants, Rashīd al-Dīn, did not come from an old bureaucratic family like the Juwaynīs, but he can certainly be regarded as a representative of the Persian governmental tradition, and he did his best to found a bureaucratic dynasty. Several of his sons were made provincial governors, and one of them himself became chief minister a few years after his father's death. All in all, the machinery seems to have continued working much in the traditional fashion, though perhaps with less efficiency than before, and subject to more interference. Indeed, we are given the distinct impression that the Mongols in Persia were reasonably content to leave the job of administration to their Persian officials, so long as the revenue from taxation continued to roll in. We should however remember that our chief sources

---

[53] Buell, 'Sino-Khitan administration', p. 124, n. 15.

for that impression are such historians as Juwaynī, Waṣṣāf, Rashīd al-Dīn and Ḥamd Allāh Mustawfī, all of whom were not only Persians but also members of the bureaucracy.

[But in China the Chinese were very pointedly not left to run affairs to anything approaching the same extent.] China was so large and complex a society that the lower-ranking civil servants had to be allowed to continue with their job if government was to function at all. In fact the Mongols do not appear to have set up a rigidly centralized government in China, as was once thought (see chapter 5).[54] They were, however, very disinclined to appoint Chinese to the highest offices: there was no Chinese equivalent to Rashīd al-Dīn. Instead, foreigners – Middle Eastern and Central Asian Muslims, Khitans, Uighurs, Europeans like Marco Polo and so forth – were preferred. This may have been because, as Marco Polo shrewdly suggested, they were regarded by the Great Khan as more trustworthy since they had no local loyalties: they 'belonged to his train, and were faithful to him'.[55] Professor Rossabi thinks that part of the reason for the extensive use of foreign Muslims in the business of tax collection may have been the wish for a scapegoat, an identifiable non-Mongol group on which Chinese resentment might be focused.[56]

Although Qubilai, that (by and large) enlightened ruler, restored much of the traditional administrative framework after his accession in 1260, he did not appoint Chinese to the great offices of state, and the old examination system for entry into the civil service, which tested the candidates' knowledge of the Chinese classics, was not revived. Yeh-lü Ch'u-ts'ai had failed in an attempt to restore it in 1238, and no more examinations were held until 1315. Even then they did not regain the importance that had been theirs before the Mongol conquest.

The Mongols, then, would adopt any institution and employ and potential servant that seemed likely to facilitate effective government; the effectiveness would be measured chiefly by the revenue receipts. There is little that can be regarded as identifiably 'Mongol' in the governmental institutions of the Mongols' empire, except for the way in which they put it all together and made such an extraordinarily disparate assemblage actually work. The principal constraint on this free and easy approach was the consideration that nothing should be allowed to

[54]   Farquhar, 'Structure and function in the Yüan imperial government'.
[55]   Ricci, The Travels of Marco Polo, p. 127.
[56]   Rossabi, 'The Muslims in the early Yüan Dynasty', p. 277.

endanger Mongol military supremacy. Yüan emperors may have made appropriate noises about the Mandate of Heaven, and Rashīd al-Dīn may have liked to call Ghazan the *Pādishāh-i Islām*, 'the king of Islam'. But few if any Mongol rulers can have supposed themselves to be ruling with the consent of their non-Mongol subjects. It was above all essential that the man on horseback should succeed in staying there.

5

The Mongols in China

Chingiz Khān's Successors

The death of Chingiz Khān in 1227, uncharacteristically, as later events were to show, was not followed by a major succession crisis.[1] Chingiz had in his lifetime indicated that his third son Ögedei should succeed him as Great Khān, and the *quriltai* that was duly held in 1229 confirmed this apparently without much argument. It has however been suggested that Ögedei's younger brother Tolui was not entirely happy about the outcome, and that this explains the two-year delay in electing Ögedei.[2] The three other potential candidates already had *uluses* of their own to rule under the Great Khān's suzerainty. Chingiz's eldest son, Jochi, had died just before his father, but Jochi's son Batu inherited his allotment of territory, which was the land to the west as far as the hoof of Mongol horse had trodden. The traditional steppe nomad practice of granting the grazing lands furthest away from the home camp to the eldest son was thus upheld, though in this instance the pastures available would prove to be unusually extensive. Batu was not in fact Jochi's eldest son. This was Orda, the founder of a Mongol khanate to the east of Batu's future Golden Horde and known as the White Horde. Very little indeed is known about its history. Chingiz's second son Chaghatai received territory in Central Asia, roughly the former lands of the

---

[1]   The best account of the political evolution of the Mongol Empire in the decades after Chingiz Khān's death is to be found in W. Barthold, *Turkestan down to the Mongol Invasion* (1977), chapter 5 (not included in editions of the book published before 1968).

[2]   Barthold, *Turkestan*, p. 463; I. de Rachewiltz, 'Turks in China under the Mongols: a preliminary investigation of Turco-Mongol relations in the 13th and 14th centuries', in M. Rossabi (ed.), *China among Equals: the Middle Kingdom and its Neighbors, 10th–14th Centuries* (1983), p. 293.

Plate 5.1   Ögedei, son and successor of Chingiz Khān (reigned 1229–41). From the Chinese Imperial Portrait Gallery. National Palace Museum, Taipei, Taiwan, Republic of China

Qara-Khitai, to which Transoxania was added during Ögedei's reign. The youngest son, Tolui, received the original Mongol home in Mongolia, the 'hearthlands', birthright of a nomad chief's youngest son.

Ögedei was on the whole a more generous and tolerant man than his brothers. If the numerous anecdotes about him in the Persian sources are to be believed he spent a good deal of his time in inventing expedients whereby individuals who had fallen foul of Chaghatai's stern enforcement of Mongol ancestral custom might evade the death penalty. Indeed, he is represented as being somewhat in awe of Chaghatai, as in the endearing story which tells how, when Chaghatai taxed him with drinking to excess, he submissively agreed to limit the number of cups of wine he drank daily, and to accept the presence of a supervisor (*shahna*) who would ensure that he kept his word. He evaded the spirit of his terrifying brother's injunction by drinking out of an unusually large cup.[3]

Under Ögedei's leadership the Mongol Empire continued to expand. Some fighting occurred in northern Persia, where armies under the generals Chormaghun and Baiju campaigned from 1229. But the main achievements of the reign were the invasion of Russia and eastern Europe and the establishment of the Golden Horde (see chapter 6), and the completion in 1234 of the conquest of the Chin Empire in north China and modern Manchuria. It was in Ögedei's reign, too, that the Mongol Empire acquired a capital – Qaraqorum, in the Orkhon valley of central Mongolia, the area formerly dominated by the Naimans. The city was first walled by Ögedei in 1235, though Chingiz Khān seems previously to have used the site as a base camp.[4] It was not much of a place by the standards of imperial capitals. William of Rubruck, who visited it in the 1250s, contrasted it unfavourably with the village of St Denis outside Paris which, he said, was bigger if the area of the Khān's palace was not taken into account.[5] The ruins were extensively pillaged in the sixteenth century to provide building materials for the erection of a Buddhist monastery nearby, but the site was excavated in 1948–9 by Russian archaeologists.[6] If Qaraqorum was not an especially impressive city, this is no doubt because the Mongols at that time were very far from being natural city dwellers. Now that they had acquired an empire, however, it was useful for them to possess a centre for commerce, the receipt of tribute and for imperial administration.

The death of Ögedei in 1241 led to a long interregnum. He had himself hoped to be succeeded by his grandson Shiremün, but because of Shiremün's youth this proposal attracted little support. In any case Ögedei's prestige was not sufficient to give his nomination great weight.

[3]   A. A. Alizade (ed.), Rashīd al-Dīn, *Jāmiʿ al-tawārīkh*, vol. 2, part 1 (1980), pp. 150–1; tr. J. A. Boyle, Rashīd al-Dīn, *The Successors of Genghis Khan* (1971), p. 65.

[4]   P. Pelliot, *Notes on Marco Polo* (1959–73), vol. 1. pp. 165–9.

[5]   A. van Den Wyngaert (ed.), *Sinica Franciscana* (1929), vol. 1, pp. 285–6; tr. C. Dawson (ed.), *The Mongol Mission* (1955), pp. 183–4.

[6]   See E. D. Phillips, *The Mongols* (1969), pp. 94–103.

Plate 5.2   A pavilion in Qaraqorum, the Mongol imperial capital. From a manuscript of Rashīd al-Dīn's *Jāmi' al-tawārīkh*. Photo: Warburg Institute, MS. D. 31 fol. 21v

In the end Ögedei's son Güyük managed to secure election as Great Khān, but this did not occur until 1246. The election was strongly disapproved of by Batu, who had clashed bitterly with Güyük during the Russian campaign. Güyük's enthronement, at his camp near Qaraqorum, was attended by John of Plano Carpini and we have

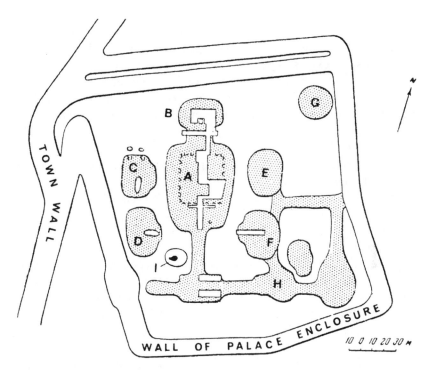

Plate 5.3   Plan of the palace at Qaraqorum as revealed by excavation. From E. D. Phillips, *The Mongols*, London: Thames & Hudson, 1969. Shaded areas represent raised ground. *Key: A*, site of main palace; *B*, site of private apartments; *C–F*, storehouses or treasuries; *G*, possible site of the Khān's Great Ger; *H*, gate guardhouse and other buildings; *I*, stone tortoise (after Kiselev)

already referred to the more detailed account by Simon of St Quentin.[7] Only Güyük's early death in 1248 prevented the outbreak of hostilities between him and Batu.

Güyük's widow undertook the regency, as had Ögedei's before 1246. But this was not enough to ensure the retention of the throne by the house of Ögedei. There was no new Great Khān until 1251, when the throne was seized by the junior branch of the Chingizid family, the descendants of Tolui. Our sources for this struggle, notably Juwaynī's

[7]   Van Den Wyngaert, *Sinica Franciscana*, p. 119; C. Dawson, *The Mongol Mission*, p. 63. Simon: J. Richard (ed.), Simon de Saint-Quentin, *Histoire des Tartares* (1965), pp. 90–2; B. Spuler (tr.), *History of the Mongols* (1972), pp. 87–8, ascribing the account to Carpini.

history, are for the most part written by employees of the victors, but even so we are left in no doubt that this was a bloody *coup d'état*, organised by Batu (who himself declined election) in collaboration with the Toluids. An extensive purge of the families of Ögedei and Chaghatai ensued, and the Great Khanate remained from that date a perquisite of the house of Tolui. In return for his support of Möngke, the successful candidate, Batu was conceded virtual autonomy in his own *ulus* of the Golden Horde.

Once settled on the throne, Möngke at a *quriltai* considered the further territorial expansion of the empire. His brother Hülegü was sent to the Middle East (see chapter 6), while he himself with another brother, Qubilai, undertook the conquest of Sung China. The Sung proved a hard nut to crack, and there was still a long way to go when Möngke died on campaign in 1259. His death precipitated the inevitable succession crisis.

There were now three surviving Toluid brothers: Hülegü, away fighting in Syria; Qubilai, in command of the Mongol forces in northern and western China; and Ariq-böke, in Mongolia. Hülegü did not propose himself as a candidate, and it is not at all clear which of his brothers he was at first inclined to back. Both Qubilai and Ariq-böke held *quriltais* of their supporters, and were duly elected. A four-year civil war followed, in which Qubilai was victorious, largely because Ariq-böke lacked the necessary resources for continuing the struggle successfully.[8] By 1264 it was all over, and Qubilai had commenced the glorious reign that was to last until 1294.[9]

The Reign of Qubilai

But even after defeating Ariq-böke, Qubilai was not to have things all his own way. At least when viewed in retrospect, Ariq-böke can be seen as representing an influential school of thought among the Mongols, which Qubilai through his actions and attitudes after 1260 opposed.

[8]   P. Jackson, 'The accession of Qubilai Qa'an: a re-examination', *Journal of the Anglo-Mongolian Society* 2/1 (1975), pp. 1–10.

[9]   No adequate study of the career of Qubilai is yet available, though one by Professor M. Rossabi is in preparation. In the meantime see M. Rossabi, 'Khubilai Khan and the women in his family', in W. Bauer (ed.), *Sino-Mongolica: Festschrift für Herbert Franke* (1979), pp. 153–80. For the history of Yüan China I have depended heavily on the articles in J. D. Langlois Jr (ed.), *China under Mongol Rule* (1981), especially the editor's introduction (pp. 3–21).

Plate 5.4 Qubilai, fifth Great Khān, grandson of Chingiz Khān and founder of the Yüan Dynasty in China (reigned 1260–94). From the Chinese Imperial Portrait Gallery. National Palace Museum, Taipei, Taiwan, Republic of China

Some Mongols felt that there was a dangerous drift towards softness, typified in those like Qubilai who thought that there was something to be said for settled civilisation and for the Chinese way of life. In the traditionalist view the Mongol centre ought to remain in Mongolia, and the Mongols' nomadic life be preserved uncontaminated. China ought merely to be exploited. Ariq-böke came to be regarded as this faction's figurehead. After his defeat, leadership of the old guard fell to a member of the house of Ögedei, Qaidu, who succeeded in establishing himself in Central Asia, and in inducing the Chaghataids to recognise his supremacy. Apart from a feeling for the old way of doing things, Qaidu and the house of Chaghatai also had their common hostility to the Toluids to bind them together.

Qaidu remained a serious menace until his death in 1303;[10] and, as affairs worked out, Qubilai was not able to secure for his dynasty any lasting control of Central Asia, despite constant effort. Even the Uighur lands were abandoned by Qubilai's successors, to fall into the Chaghataid sphere of influence. Part of the difficulty was caused by Qubilai's transference of the capital of the Great Khanate to Peking. It has been persuasively argued that in the circumstances of the time, the various parts of the empire could only be controlled effectively if they were within a certain radius of the capital. The Uighur lands, and north China, were near enough to Qaraqorum to be held from there. Likewise, Mongolia could be controlled from Peking: but the Uighur lands were too far away.[11] So in the end Central Asia had to be abandoned, and what resources were available were concentrated on reinforcing the link between Mongol China and Mongolia itself, which in the course of time became a rather privileged and special province of the Chinese Empire.

Despite troubles to the north and west, Qubilai was not to be deflected from his conquest of the Sung. But it occupied him for many years: Hang-chou, the capital, fell in 1276, and not until 1279 was resistance at an end. The Mongols had taken almost 70 years to complete their occupation of China, which was by far the most formidable enemy they ever had to face. The final conquest could hardly have been accomplished without massive defections from the Chinese side, including the commanders of the Sung fleets; for control of the seaboard and the internal waterways was essential.

Qubilai's treatment of south China bore little resemblance to the way in which his predecessors had dealt with the north. Qubilai understood very well – too well, some Mongols thought – the virtues of agriculture and city life. These was a minimum of destruction. The southern Chinese landowners' loyalty to the new regime was assured by their being left in undisturbed possession of their estates. As for the peasants, the enormous majority of the population, they were no more consulted than they had ever been. Only 90 further years were to pass before Mongol rule had come to an end; and the Mongols' eviction took their Ming successors a very much shorter time than it had taken the invincible Mongols to wipe out the Chin or the Sung.

[10]   M. Hambly (ed.), Qāshānī, Ta'rīkh-i Ūljāytū (1969), p. 32, for the date.
[11]   J. W. Dardess, 'From Mongol Empire to Yüan Dynasty: changing forms of imperial rule in Mongolia and Central Asia', Monumenta Serica, 30 (1972–3), pp. 117–65.

Despite his domestication in China, Qubilai did not forget that he was a Mongol. He is said to have had a patch of steppe grass planted in the garden of his palace in Peking, as a reminder of his origins. Nor, even after the fall of the Sung, was he by any means exclusively a peaceful ruler. The military traditions of his ancestors were still very much alive in Qubilai. He did not, however, have very great success in the field, except in fending off challenges from other Mongols to the north and west. Expeditions were mounted into mainland south-east Asia, and even to Java, but the damp jungles of those lands were the last parts of the world to be appropriate to the Mongol style of warfare, even as modified for the conditions of south China. Qubilai did, however, succeed in conquering the non-Chinese kingdom of Nan-chao, the modern south-western Chinese province of Yunnan; and the incorporation of Yunnan into China, which was permanent, is one of the Mongols' enduring legacies.

The really tempting target, once the Sung were clearly heading towards defeat, was Japan. The difficulty was that Japan could not be reached by a cavalry charge, even though the Mongols' control of Korea put them within a fairly short distance of the islands. The Mongols had managed with a surprising degree of success to a accustom themselves to fighting in ships during the south China campaigns, however, so Qubilai determined that Japan too should succumb to the Mongol yoke. Two amphibious expeditions, in 1274 and 1281, were mounted; and both were disasters, very largely because the weather appeared to be on the side of the Japanese. The expedition of 1281 was much the larger of the two. It fell victim to a typhoon, the 'divine wind' or 'kamikaze', a victory the Japanese were not to forget. Such Mongol troops as contrived to struggle ashore were easily mopped up by the Japanese forces, and no further attempts were made to add Japan to the Mongol Empire.

The two acts which marked most clearly the comparative transformation of Mongol rule over China under Qubilai's aegis were his adoption of a Chinese dynastic title and his foundation of the new imperial capital at Peking. In 1272 Qubilai issued an edict[12] which declared that the Mongol dynasty would henceforth take the title of Yüan, 'the origin'. The title is said to have been suggested to Qubilai by his Chinese adviser

---

[12] Translated by Langlois, *China under Mongol Rule*, introduction, pp. 3–4.

Liu Ping-chung,[13] and marked a departure from Chinese precedent in that previous dynastic titles had tended to have a geographical derivation, referring to the dynasty's own place of origin. Possibly it was felt that in the case of the Mongols such a title would be lacking in tact, if it was hoped that they would come to be accepted by their subjects as legitimate rulers. In practice, although some Sung loyalists withdrew into affronted retirement after 1279 and declined to serve China's new masters, there was no essential difficulty about accepting Mongol rule once it had become an established fact. The Chinese doctrine of the Mandate of Heaven allowed, other things being equal, for the presumption that the fall of one dynasty and the accession of another was in itself evidence that the Mandate had passed from the one to the other. But although the form of the Mongol dynastic title was innovative, in another way it cleverly reflected Chinese tradition. What Qubilai had done through his choice of the name Yüan was to seize 'an ideologically sound and prestigious symbol' from the Chinese classics. This is made quite explicit in the text of the edict. Professor Langlois would go further: 'Identifying the dynasty with the generating principle of the cosmos enabled Khubilai to extend the universal pretensions of the traditional Chinese monarchy to their natural limits.'[14] The edict is a very Chinese document, which no doubt helped the people who mattered – the Chinese literati – to accept that China now had a new but legitimate dynasty. Indeed, that legitimacy was not to be seriously challenged even by the Yüan's Ming supplanters, who would interpret their own success as meaning that the Mandate of Heaven had passed to them, not that the Yüan had never truly possessed it.

The same year, 1272, saw an edict of Qubilai's which renamed the imperial capital (on the site of Peking) Ta-tu, the 'great capital', though whether the Mongols themselves normally called it that is open to doubt: Marco Polo refers to the city as Cambaluc, that is, Khan-baliq, Turkish for 'city of the Khān'. Further north, in inner Mongolia, was the summer capital of Shang-tu, Coleridge's Xanadu, where the *quriltai* that acclaimed Qubilai as Great Khān in 1260 had been held. Building work at Peking had begun in 1266, and the plan that was followed in laying out the city was, once again significantly, 'drawn up on the basis of the capital city outlined in the ancient Chinese classic of government, the

---

[13]   See H. Chan, 'Liu Ping-chung: a Buddhist-Taoist statesman at the court of Khubilai Khan', *T'oung-pao*, 53 (1967), pp. 98–146.

[14]   Langlois, *China under Mongol Rule*, introduction, pp. 4 and 5.

Chou li.[15] The Mongol Empire now had a capital that was a fixed city, built to a Chinese plan, and situated on Chinese soil. No step could have been more momentous.

The Mongols and Buddhism

The question also arose whether, in their progressive identification (up to a point) with their Chinese subjects, the Mongols would choose to abandon their ancestral Shamanism and embrace one or more of the religions of China. In fact Shamanism was probably never really abandoned. It was far from being a highly structured faith, and elements of its beliefs proved capable of co-existing in a tenacious fashion with almost anything. In any case, the Chinese did not necessarily regard religions as mutually exclusive. To take two eminent officials who served the Mongols as examples, Liu Ping-chung was 'a Buddhist-Taoist statesman', while Yeh-lü Ch'u-ts'ai was a 'Buddhist idealist and Confucian statesman'.[16] Confucianism, in so far as it should be regarded as a religion, seems to have held little personal appeal for Qubilai, though it was more favourably viewed by later Yüan emperors. Taoism had not succeeded in maintaining the initial advantage it had gained from the privileges extracted from Chingiz Khān by Ch'ang Ch'un.

There remained the theoretical possibility that the Mongols would turn away completely from the Chinese religious tradition, and adopt Islam, as they did in Persia and the lands of the Golden Horde, or Christianity, probably in its Nestorian form, as a number of influential individual Mongols did. Certainly the Mongols retained their traditional religious tolerance, except to some extent in the areas where they became Muslims. When particular religions were discriminated against, this usually had other than specifically religious causes.

In fact, however, Qubilai accorded his favour, and perhaps his personal allegiance, to one religion above all: to Buddhism. This was not of course an indigenous Chinese faith, though it had been naturalised over many centuries. But the form of Buddhism adopted by the Mongols was not a respectable Chinese variety. It was the Lamaistic, Tantric

---

[15]   Ibid., p. 6; see also *The Times* archaeological report, 21 August 1982.

[16]   Chan, 'Liu Ping-chung'; I. de Rachewiltz, 'Yeh-lü Ch'u-ts'ai (1189–1243): Buddhist idealist and Confucian statesman', in A. F. Wright and D. Twitchett (eds), *Confucian Personalities* (1962), pp. 189–216.

Buddhism of Tibet, which a purist would probably have regarded as a debasement of the original faith or its more elevated derivatives. It may be speculated that it was the elements in Lamaism that had been carried over into it from the pre-Buddhist religion of Bon that made it particularly attractive to those of a Shamanist background. We know that the magical skills of the Lamas were a great success at the Mongol court.

Tibet is counted as part of the Mongol Empire, though it was never thoroughly conquered. As Professor Franke observes, 'it seems to be a fact that most of Tibet proper remained outside the direct control of the Sino-Mongol bureaucracy and that even the borderlands were throughout the Yüan dynasty an unruly and troubled region'.[17] From the 1240s the Mongols had maintained relations with a number of Buddhist sects in Tibet, one of which was especially patronised by the Īlkhāns of Persia, who were as much Buddhist as anything until the conversion of Ghazan to Islam in 1295.[18] Particularly favoured was the Sa-skya sect, whose head the Mongols tried in the late 1240s to use as their agent in Tibet. It was this hierarch's nephew, 'Phags-pa, who was to become the most important Lamaist figure in Yüan China.

Like his uncle before him, 'Phags-pa was placed at the head of what passed for the Mongol secular government in Tibet, and in the 1260s the usual Mongol measures in subject territory – census, taxation, and the establishment of a *Yām* network – were duly implemented there.[19] But 'Phags-pa's real importance stemmed from the role he played in Yüan China. His position under Qubilai was one of great influence, though how great is in dispute. He was certainly granted the prestigious Chinese title of *ti-shih*, 'imperial preceptor', and was accorded the headship of the Buddhist church.

Franke maintains that 'Phags-pa's religious services to the Yüan emperors were twofold: he provided them with a pseudo-historical legitimation in Buddhist terms by incorporating them into the line of Buddhist universal emperors, the *chakravartin* kings, and he produced a Buddhist religio-political theory of world rule.[20] He must presumably be accorded the chief responsibility for inducing Qubilai to adopt Lamaist Buddhism as the dominant Mongol faith in China.

[17]   H. Franke, 'Tibetans in Yüan China', in Langlois, *China under Mongol Rule*, p. 301.
[18]   L. Petech, 'Tibetan relations with Sung China and with the Mongols', in M. Rossabi, *China among Equals*, p. 183.
[19]   Ibid., pp. 186–7.
[20]   Franke, 'Tibetans in Yüan China', pp. 306–10.

These politico-religious services were not all that 'Phags-pa provided at Qubilai's behest, however. He was also required to invent a new alphabet for the writing of Mongolian, which it was intended should replace the Uighur script that had been used since Mongolian had first become a written language in the time of Chingiz Khān. The 'Phags-pa script was declared official, and compulsory in government documents, in 1269.[21] Under imperial patronage it had some success, and a number of 'Phags-pa documents have survived.[22] But even if it was 'by far the best alphabet for writing preclassical Mongolian',[23] it did not ultimately oust the Uighur script, which is still used in the Chinese part of Mongolia, and in the Mongolian People's Republic was superseded by the Cyrillic script only during the last 40 years.

Mongol Rule in China

When the Chin Empire had been brought under Mongol control, much of its territory had been divided up into largely autonomous *apanages*, which were granted to the various Mongol princes and generals. It has been customary to assert that this system was not perpetuated when the Sung Empire was conquered by Qubilai, and that instead China was subjected to a rigorously centralised government based on a division of the country into 12 provinces in a rather modern fashion.[24] We have already seen how recent work suggests that this centralisation did not in fact occur.[25] According to Professor Farquhar's findings, the direct administrative competence of the Yüan government was felt only in the Metropolitan Province around Peking and in some thinly populated, largely non-Chinese adjoining regions.

The chief organ of Yüan government on the ground was not the traditional district magistrate, some of whose activities are so vividly portrayed in the Judge Dee detective stories of Robert van Gulik. Instead, government was by means of bureaux. The principal device for the

---

[21]   Petech, 'Tibetan relations with Sung China', p. 187.

[22]   See N. Poppe, *The Mongolian Monuments in hP'ags-pa Script*, ed. and tr. J. R. Krueger (1957).

[23]   Franke, 'Tibetans in Yüan China', p. 306.

[24]   See e.g. E. O. Reischauer and J. K. Fairbank, *East Asia: the Great Tradition* (1958), p. 274.

[25]   See D. M. Farquhar, 'Structure and function in the Yüan imperial government', in Langlois, *China under Mongol Rule*, pp. 25–55.

extension of administration outside the central area was the creation of replica bureau machinery in the various provinces. The provinces were therefore centralised internally, but their relationship with the government in Peking might be distinctly loose. The emperor retained the power of appointment and removal of officials and was the final court of appeal: he did have some weapons with which to fight the danger of local separatism. Further, the principle of reserving the highest posts to non-Chinese officials must have given him a powerful lever. The inhabitants of China were divided into four classes. In descending order of position and privilege, these were the Mongols themselves, the western and central Asians (se-mu-jen), the former subjects of the Chin Empire, largely Chinese (Han-jen), and the former Sung subjects (nan-jen), who as the latest comers to the benefits of Mongol rule ranked lowest.

The significance even of the Censorial system, whose officers had extensive roving powers of investigation and impeachment, has been downgraded by Farquhar, though it had previously been regarded as the acme of Yüan centralisation. Farquhar concedes, however, that since the Censorate divided China into only three parts, overriding the 12 provincial divisions, it may have helped to some extent to counter the worst effects of decentralisation.[26] Whether this radical reinterpretation of Yüan administrative history will be accepted remains to be seen. It certainly coincides more closely with the pragmatic, indeed frequently ramshackle and singularly unsystematic fashion in which the Mongols ran other parts of their empire than does the notion of a 'modern' centralised administration.

Living under Mongol rule cannot have been an especially agreeable experience at the best of times – and the reign of Qubilai probably was the best of times, provided one could avoid being in the path of the armies during the campaigns before 1279. But still, the tendency now among scholars who study Yüan China is to make a more positive assessment than was once usual, though there is much research to be done before a reliable general impression begins to emerge. Langlois says of the suggestive articles collected in *China under Mongol Rule* that 'we can and should draw conclusions from these essays, and it is likely that the verdict will be in the Mongols' favor, so to speak'.[27] Chinese civilisation and culture did not by any means go into deep freeze during the Yüan period. Indeed, for literary artists there may well have been

[26]   Farquhar, 'Structure and function', especially pp. 50–5, for the above.

[27]   Langlois, *China under Mongol Rule*, introduction, p. 21.

greater freedom of expression than under some more 'respectable' dynasties. There was nothing to match the eighteenth-century 'literary inquisition' if Ch'ien-lung; and the Ming emperors took a much closer, and far from benevolent, interest in what was being written than did their Yüan predecessors.

⌈Admittedly this apparent Mongol liberalism was partly the result of the fact that the Mongols in many ways maintained a considerable distance between themselves and their Chinese subjects.⌋ If sedition was being propagated in Chinese, few Mongols would have been able to read it. It is probable, then, that to the extent that literature flourished in Yüan times, it did so in the absence of governmental interference rather than because of official patronage. The policy of excluding Chinese from high administrative posts may also have had the side-effect of giving a boost to literary activity. For the mandarinate under the traditional system had been recruited from young men who had demonstrated the high level of their literary culture. In Yüan times such individuals, unless they were content with a fairly low-ranking position in the administration, were likely 'to pursue their scholarly energies in other careers'.[28] Private academies were set up in large numbers, and efforts were made to promote the continuance of education in the Confucian classics in a period during which the customary official encouragement was largely lacking. Other art forms also flourished. Landscape painting of the Yüan period is notably successful, and drama made great strides. Even if Qubilai and his successors can take only a limited amount of direct credit for such cultural achievements, it can at least be granted that in some senses they created the conditions that were necessary if cultural life was to flower.

⌈Most important of all, they provided China with a time of peace and, at first, of some economic prosperity.⌋ Hardly less important, they gave to China the political unity that it has never since lost.⌋ By the 1270s, when Qubilai conquered the Sung Empire, parts of north China had been under non-Chinese rule for 300 years, since the beginning of the Liao dynasty, whereas the south had never experienced alien government. The northern and southern Chinese had in many respects grown apart. Now they were to rediscover one another; and it has been suggested that the excitement of this opportunity is one of the reasons for the measure of support that the Chinese literati chose to give to the Yüan dynasty. The Yüan were also responsible for the re-establishment

[28]   Ibid., p. 15.

Plate 5.5 Kao K'o-kung, 'Clearing in the Mountains after a Spring Rain'. Chinese landscape of the late thirteenth century. National Palace Museum, Taipei, Taiwan, Republic of China

of a major economic link between north and south by their cutting of the Grand Canal, 1100 miles long, from Hang-chou to Peking. With the building of his new capital, Qubilai needed to be able to transport to it vast quantities of rice, and earlier experiments with coastal transportation had proved risky. The canal, though prodigiously expensive both to dig and to maintain, was a much safer route.

In the favourable commercial environment provided by the Mongols, contacts with other parts of the world prospered. Even the warfare that was endemic between the various khanates did not entirely disrupt them, though Marco Polo,[29] who had first gone to China by the overland route, was obliged to return by sea as far as Persia. How much of an impact visiting Europeans made on the Chinese is open to question. Marco Polo evidently learned no Chinese, which suggests that his contacts with the bulk of the population were very limited. No trace of him has ever been found in Chinese sources, despite a number of false alarms.[30] This may partly be because he seems to have exaggerated his own importance as a Yüan official in order to impress people at home in Venice. He claims that for three years he was governor of Yang-chou, but this was evidently not the case. Pelliot[31] thought that he probably held office in the administration of the government salt monopoly there, which would have been a position of considerable importance, though it might not have seemed so to his European readers had he admitted the truth.

The Polos are the earliest European visitors to China of whom we have any record, though they may not necessarily have been the first since the vast majority of merchant travellers will have left us no evidence of their journeys. They were followed by other ambassadors, missionaries and merchants of whom we do have some knowledge, notably John of Marignolli, papal envoy in the 1330s and 1340s, who achieved the unique distinction of having his presence in China recorded in the *Yüan-shih*. This was not because of the importance of his embassy as such, but solely as a result of the impression made on the Chinese by

---

[29]   The study of Marco Polo is something of an industry in itself. The best general book, full of fascinating material, is L. Olschki, *Marco Polo's Asia* (1960). An enormous amount of information is collected in Pelliot, *Notes on Marco Polo*.

[30]   H. Franke, 'Sino-western contacts under the Mongol Empire', *Journal of the Hong Kong Branch of the Royal Asiatic Society*, 6 (1966), p. 53.

[31]   Pelliot, *Notes on Marco Polo*, vol. 2, p. 834.

an enormous horse which he brought as a present for the emperor. It was painted by a court artist, and the picture was seen as late as 1815: it may have perished during the British burning of the summer palace at Peking in 1860. Of other travellers the most notable are the Franciscan Odoric of Pordenone, who was in China during the 1320s and who left an account of his experiences, and John of Monte Corvino, who was sent to China by the Pope as a missionary, was eventually made first Catholic archbishop of Khan-baliq, and died there. Apart from Marignolli's horse and a curious account in a court diary of 1261 which appears to refer to an embassy from northern Europe,[32] none of these visitors has so far as is known left any trace in Chinese sources. We would know little even of John of Monte Corvino's activities but for the survival in Europe of the missionaries' letters home, and the discovery of a Latin tombstone in Yang-chou.

Whether any quasi-racial anti-Mongol feeling was rife in China, as has sometimes been maintained, is questionable, at least in the long run. Some Chinese were prone to copying Mongol fashions in dress and choice of names, but although the first Ming emperor (who took the reign title Hung-wu) tried to suppress such imitation after he had seized power, he seems to have cherished no animus against the Mongols themselves. Indeed, he encouraged both them and other non-Chinese to remain in China, and he made extensive use of Mongol troops. The tone did not change until after the Oirat Mongols had captured the then Ming emperor in 1449: understandably, this did provoke anti-Mongol feeling in official circles.

As we have seen, Mongol government is likely to have appeared to the population at large as exploitative and, in the absence of strong central control, frequently corrupt. But claims have been made for the benevolence at least of the Mongol administration of justice. The Yüan dynasty was unique in Chinese history in that it did not promulgate a formal penal code. In fact it has been suggested that the very notion of such codes was meaningless to the Mongols, and that they preferred to rule through individual regulations and legislation.[33] This, if true, would tend to confirm the doubts expressed earlier about the existence of a written Great *Yāsā*. It appears that at any rate on paper, Mongol judicial administration was more humane than the system under the Sung or

---

[32] Franke, 'Sino-western contacts', pp. 54–5.
[33] Langlois, *China under Mongol Rule*, p. 10, n. 20, citing Uematsu Tadashi.

the Ming, and that it involved much less use of the death penalty.[34] We know little, however, of what actually happened in practice.

The Decline of Yüan Power

Yüan dynastic politics were fairly orderly for 30 years after the death of Qubilai. He was succeeded as Great Khān by his grandson Temür Öljeitü, who even managed for a time to achieve a state of peaceful co-existence between the Mongol khanates. But none of Qubilai's descendants was of his calibre, and the tradition of 'tanistry' was never far below the surface. Serious trouble began on the assassination of Shidebala in 1323. Ten years of factional struggle, civil war and murder followed, and during this period the imperial throne had four or five occupants.[35] In 1333 a boy of 13, Toghon Temür, ascended the throne. He was to be the last of the Yüan emperors and was to reign for as long as the first, though rather less successfully. For much of the last few decades of Yüan rule, Mongol energy was consumed in internal factional fighting, with the real power being in the hands of local Mongol warlords rather than of the emperor. This was no condition in which to face effectively a plethora of natural disasters, economic troubles and peasant revolts.

The natural disasters took the form of flood and pestilence. Extensive flooding of the Yellow River (which had changed its course as recently as 1194) did great damage and caused famine; and from the 1330s, but especially in the 1350s, China was devastated by outbreaks of disease. The first of these, in 1331, was locally confined, but in 1353–4 there was a major outbreak which would seem to have killed enormous numbers of the population and which may well be among the principal explanations for the demographic decline in Mongol China which was noted earlier. What the disease precisely was is not altogether clear from the sources. In view of the date of the epidemic the natural temptation is to assume that it was the Black Death, that is, bubonic plague, if the conventional identification of the nature of the Black Death in Europe is correct. In his fascinating *Plagues and Peoples* W. H. McNeill argues

[34]   P. Ch'en, *Chinese Legal Tradition under the Mongols: the Code of 1291 as Reconstructed* (1979).

[35]   See J. W. Dardess, *Conquerors and Confucians: Aspects of Political Change in Late Yüan China* (1973), chapter 2.

that it was indeed the Black Death, and that Europe has the existence of the Mongol Empire to thank for the disasters of the late 1340s.[36]

It is certainly true that the European Black Death originated in Mongol territory: it broke out in a Mongol force that was besieging Kaffa, in the Crimea. The disease infected the beleaguered garrison, who then carried it by sea to Europe. McNeill's argument, which is speculative but undoubtedly plausible, is that the opening up of the trade routes across Asia, and the network of communications created by the Mongols, made it possible as never before for the plague bacillus to travel vast distances in a very few years. If this theory is well founded, the massacres perpetrated by the armies of Chingiz Khān pale into insignificance by comparison with the loss of life for which the Mongols may unwittingly have been responsible. The case is reminiscent of that of the influenza epidemic of 1919, which killed so many more people than the First World War: there is no doubt that disease is a far more efficient way of reducing population than is warfare, even when conducted in the Mongol style. But so far McNeill's suggestion remains as much a speculation as does the reality of China's other possible gifts to Europe in the Mongol period and after: printing, gunpowder and the mariner's compass.

In addition to all this, the outbreak of revolts in the south disrupted the transportation of rice along the Grand Canal to Peking. A rise in prices followed, prompting the over-issue of paper currency and consequent inflation. But in the north the Mongols fiddled while the south burned. Throughout the troubles which led to the fall of the dynasty, the Mongol warlords showed themselves much more interested in fighting each other for control of the central government than in uniting to suppress the revolts in south China.

The rebels were not themselves much better at uniting against the common enemy. From the 1340s large-scale revolts against Mongol rule had raged in the south, a development in which a secret Buddhist society, the White Lotus, seems to have played a significant role. But each rebel leader was concerned at least as much to defeat his rivals as to drive out the Mongols. Ultimately one of the peasant leaders, the future Ming founder, achieved supremacy over the others and marched

---

[36]   W. H. McNeill, *Plagues and Peoples* (1976), chapter 4; the idea was previously suggested in E. Le Roy Ladurie, 'The "event" and the "long term" in social history: the case of the Chouan uprising', in his *The Territory of the Historian* (1979), pp. 112–13, an article first published in 1972.

north against the Yüan forces from his new capital at Nanking. The Mongols had insufficient, or insufficiently concentrated, military resources with which to deal effectively with the threat; and they had no policies to offer that might have saved Mongol rule. The bankruptcy of Mongol ideas in the last years of the Yüan is well illustrated by a story about one of Toghon Temür's ministers, Bayan. He saw the whole problem as one of excessive Sinicisation, and is said to have proposed (unsuccessfully) that it should be dealt with by the execution of all Chinese named Chang, Wang, Liu, Li, and Chao.[37] This, if effectively implemented, would have removed about nine-tenths of the population, and no doubt Toghon Temür's immediate problem as well.

Toghon Temür and his troops were driven from Peking in 1368, and the Yüan dynasty, after 96 years of official existence, was no more. The successful bandit rebel Chu Yüan-chang was installed as the first Ming emperor, and China was again ruled by a Chinese dynasty. The riders from the north had lost their greatest prize, and they were not to regain it until the Manchus entered Peking in 1644. Toghon Temür withdrew to Qaraqorum, the neglected former capital, where he died in 1370. Mongolia still had an independent future (see chapter 8), for the Ming emperors were not to become masters of the northern steppes. In the end they admitted that they could not hope to succeed to all the former Yüan territories, and in the sixteenth century marked that admission in the most conspicuous possible way by building, piecemeal, what we now know as the Great Wall of China.[38]

[37]   See I. de Rachewiltz, *Papal Envoys to the Great Khans* (1971), p. 190.
[38]   A. N. Waldron, 'The problem of the Great Wall of China', *Harvard Journal of Asiatic Studies*, 43/2 (1983), pp. 660–1.

6

Expansion to the West: The Mongols in Russia and Persia

The Invasion of Russia and Eastern Europe

It appears that the Mongols had always intended, in due time, to turn their attention to what is now Russia. The plains north of the Black Sea, the Qipchaq steppe, were ideal nomad's grassland, and doubtless they felt that something worth while could be extorted from the Russian principalities to the north, even if the forest land of those parts was not for its own sake attractive in Mongol eyes. The expedition that had been sent to pursue the Khwārazm-shāh had passed through southern Russia on its way back to Mongolia, and it had met and defeated an army sent by the Russian princes to oppose it. The Mongols for the moment went on their way, leaving the puzzled Novgorod Chronicler to record, under the year 1224, that 'the same year, for our sins, unknown tribes came, whom no one exactly knows, who they are, nor whence they came out, nor what their language is, nor of what race they are, nor what their faith is; but they call them Tartars.'[1] Within 15 years the answers to all these questions were to be known only too well.

In 1235, the year after the final conquest of the Chin, the Great Khān Ögedei convened a *quriltai* which decided on the great move westwards, to take possession of the lands granted by Chingiz Khān to his eldest son Jochi.[2] Batu, as Jochi's son and successor, was to be in at least

[1]   R. Michell and N. Forbes (trs), *The Chronicle of Novgorod* (1914), p. 64.
[2]   J. Chambers, *The Devil's Horsemen: the Mongol Invasion of Europe* (1979) is a good (*pace* C. J. Halperin, 'Russia in the Mongol Empire in comparative perspective', *Harvard Journal of Asiatic Studies*, 43/1 (1983), pp. 240–1) and readable popular account of the Mongol invasions of Russia and eastern Europe. J. L. I. Fennell, *The Crisis of Medieval Russia 1200–1304* (1983) is essential reading on the history of Russia in this period.

nominal command, and the other Mongol princes who joined the expeditionary force included two future Great Khāns, Güyük and Möngke. More important militarily, Chingiz Khān's great general Sübodei was also present.

The first stage of the assault, in 1237, was directed against the Volga Bulgars and the Bashkirs of 'Great Hungary', peoples to the east of the Russian principalities. There followed, between 1237 and 1240, a series of campaigns against the Russians, first north from Bulgar and then south to Kiev. The Russian defeat was total except in the case of Novgorod, from which the Mongols withdrew because of problems caused by the spring thaw. At best the Russians would probably not have proved a really formidable adversary, but they made matters much worse by their inability to join together effectively to oppose the invaders. The divisive tendencies of the Russian princes, exacerbated by their principle of lateral succession by seniority, were too deeply rooted to be set aside even in so serious an emergency.

The destruction inflicted on the Russian principalities by the Mongol invasion is traditionally said to have been very severe indeed. It has been almost common form to blame the Mongols for most of Russia's subsequent ills: they play a part in demonology that is not dissimilar to that which Cromwell plays in Ireland. Certainly it would be a mistake to minimise the horrors that occurred: what we know of the nature of Mongol warfare elsewhere at around this date allows few grounds for giving them the benefit of any doubt. But as in the case of Persia there is some reason for enquiring into the extent and universality of the disaster.

Professor Fennell has argued that although some Russian cities were captured and presumably damaged or destroyed, many others were probably bypassed by the Mongols and escaped sack. He points out that although John of Plano Carpini, who passed through Kiev a few years later on his way to Mongolia, says that the city was in ruins, the northern Russian chronicle that gives an account of the Mongol capture of Kiev does not speak of any destruction or massacre. One difficulty in assessing conditions is that from this date the northern chronicles have little material on the south of the country, probably because it had largely come under direct Mongol rule.

Fennell agrees that there was considerable destruction in places, but believes that the evidence points to speedy restoration and recovery. He suggests that the victories achieved by Alexander Nevsky, the later grand prince of Vladimir, against the Swedes and the German knights in 1240 and 1242 (celebrated in film and music by Eisenstein and Prokofiev)

Plate 6.1   A European view of fighting between Mongol and Hungarian troops. Austrian National Library, Picture Archives, Vienna: Cod. 2623, fol. 29r

show either that Russian resilience was remarkable or that Russia had not in fact been comprehensively devastated by the Mongols. 'So we are left', he concludes, 'with a picture of a Russia struck by yet another steppe invader, more formidable, more efficient both in war and peace and more enduring than the Pechenegs or the Polovtsians. But it was a Russia by no means as shattered, overwhelmed and dispirited as many modern historians would have us believe.'[3] While this is no doubt true with respect to the initial Mongol invasion, the problem for the Russians was perhaps more that, for centuries, the Mongols did not go away.

The Turkish inhabitants of the steppe bordering the Black Sea, called by the Russians the Polovtsians and otherwise known variously as the Cumans or the Qipchaqs, had behaved in a characteristically nomad way when faced with the Mongol menace. Most of them submitted, but a large group, headed by their khān, decamped to Hungary and asked

---

[3]   Fennell, *The Crisis of Medieval Russia*, p. 89.

for sanctuary from King Béla IV. They offered conversion to Christianity and their military services as the price they were prepared to pay. Against the advice of some, Béla accepted their offer and admitted them to his lands. Unfortunately for him, however, the Mongols were heading in the same direction. The failure of the Qipchaqs to make proper submission was one of the pretexts for invading the territories in which they had taken refuge. But as affairs turned out the Qipchaq princes were murdered and their khān killed himself to avoid the same fate. This was the work of some of those Hungarian nobles who had argued that the Qipchaqs ought not to be trusted. Certainly they could not be trusted after having suffered such an atrocity: they marched off towards Austria and then to Bulgaria, plundering as they went. Béla had been deprived of what might have proved a valuable military force.

Eastern Europe was invaded in 1241 in a carefully co-ordinated two-pronged attack after the classic Mongol fashion. The smaller force marched into Poland and headed towards eastern Germany. In April 1241 it met and defeated an army hastily collected together from Poles and Teutonic Knights, which was commanded by Duke Henry of Silesia (at that time part of Poland). The battle took place at Liegnitz. The larger Mongol detachment invaded Hungary and crushed King Béla's army in battle at the River Sajó, two days after Liegnitz. Hungary was occupied and the Mongols showed every sign of intending to incorporate it into their empire, evidently regarding the grassland of the Hungarian plain as suitable for settlement. They struck coins there,[4] presumably an earnest of their intention of remaining permanently, King Béla, unknowingly following the precedent set by the Khwārazm-shāh, fled to an island in the Adriatic. But unlike 'Alā' al-Dīn Muḥammad he was able in due course to return to his kingdom, and indeed to continue to rule it until his death in 1270.

The Mongol advance continued towards the west. The furthest point reached was Wiener Neustadt, where the defenders captured a mysterious Englishman who had been in Mongol service, so we learn from a document preserved by Matthew Paris. This is an intriguing incident which has given rise to some ill-judged speculation.[5] The Mongol army settled down to winter in Hungary.

---

[4]   B. Spuler, *The Muslim World: a Historical Survey* part II: *The Mongol Period* (1960), p. 13.

[5]   See G. Ronay, *The Tartar Khan's Englishman* (1978), and the comments in D. O. Morgan, 'The Mongol Empire: a review article', *Bulletin of the School of Oriental and African Studies*, 44/1 (1981), pp. 120–5.

No one can tell what plans the Mongols may have had for the campaign of 1242. For in December 1241 the Great Khān Ögedei died in Mongolia. Batu withdrew to the Qipchaq steppe, and the Mongol armies of conquest never returned in full force, though they continued to intervene in Hungary, especially during the period in the 1280s and 1290s when prince Nogai was virtual co-ruler of the Golden Horde: Nogai took an active interest in the affairs of eastern and south-eastern Europe. It has been usual to ascribe Batu's withdrawal directly to his perception of the implications of Ögedei's death. This is indeed entirely plausible. During the previous years' campaigning he had quarrelled with Büri, the grandson of Chaghatai; and more important, a irreconcilable breach had opened up between him and Ögedei's son and potential successor Güyük. The Mongol princes now had to agree on the selection of a new Great Khān, and if Güyük should obtain the nomination the Mongol world seemed likely to become full of hazards for Batu. He would be better able to safeguard his own interests if settled in the Qipchaq steppe than if he were to continue fighting in distant Europe. In fact, as we have seen in chapter 5, Güyük's enthronement as Great Khān was delayed until 1246, and his subsequent reign of only two years was not long enough to permit him to organise effective action against Batu. But no one could have predicted this in 1242.

Although concern over the possible consequences of Ögedei's death may largely explain Batu's withdrawal, this does not entirely account for the fact that the Mongols never again tried to include the supposedly very attractive Hungarian plain in their empire. Various solutions to this problem have been proposed, among them the excessive length of Mongol communications if campaigns were to be undertaken in Europe, and the series of political crises within the Mongol Empire, which may have made it difficult ever again to concentrate in Golden Horde territory a force adequate for so major an operation. The most attractive suggestion, however, is that of Professor Sinor. He maintains that although the Hungarian plain did indeed provide excellent pasture, it did not provide a large enough area of it to support permanently a Mongol force of sufficient size, bearing in mind the fact that each Mongol soldier would have possessed several horses. Sinor's figures have been criticised, and indeed they are improbably precise: he suggests that Hungary could have supported 68,640 men with three horses each.[6] But

---

[6] D. Sinor, 'Horse and pasture in Inner Asian history', *Oriens Extremus*, 19 (1972), pp. 181–2. See R. P. Lindner, 'Nomadism, horses and Huns', *Past and Present*, 92 (1981), p. 14, n. 43 for a rather different calculation.

in principle the theory seems sound, and provides a much more satisfactory explanation of the Mongols' precipitate and permanent withdrawal than any other that has been offered.

The Golden Horde

The rule of Batu in the Qipchaq steppe, however, was enduring. His khanate there is generally known as the Golden Horde,[7] possibly a reference to the Khān's tent. However, this is a name that was used only later, and by the Russians; in the east the usual term was 'the Khanate of Qipchaq', which serves to indicate the fact that most of the Qipchaq Turks who had inhabited the area before the arrival of the Mongols remained and were absorbed into the newly constituted Mongol state. It might even be said that in many respects the boot was on the other foot. There were a great many more Turks than Mongols in the lands of the Golden Horde, and evidence of the speed with which the Mongols were absorbed by the Turkish-speaking population is provided by the Golden Horde's coinage: Mongolian was replaced by Turkish on coins as early as the reign of Töde-Möngke (1280–7). By contrast, it is clear from surviving dual-language documents that Mongolian in Persia had a very long life ahead of it, at least as an official language.

Batu founded a capital city, at Sarai on the Volga. Its construction did not, however, imply that he took to a settled existence or abandoned the characteristic Mongol preference for living in tents. The capital was later transferred to another newly founded city, New Sarai, often called Sarai Berke because it is alleged to have been founded by Batu's brother Berke (ruled 1257–67). It seems, however, that in reality Batu's and Berke's Sarai were the same place, if the numismatic evidence is to be

---

[7]   On the Golden Horde the standard work is B. Spuler, *Die Goldene Horde: die Mongolen in Russland 1223–1502* (1965). In English there is G. Vernadsky, *The Mongols and Russia* (1953), part of a multi-volume history of Russia but the work of a scholar who also knew a great deal about the Mongols. Of contributions that bring out the integral nature of the relationship between the Golden Horde and the other parts of the empire, two may be especially recommended: T. T. Allsen, 'Mongol census taking in Rus', 1245–1275', *Harvard Ukrainian Studies*, 5/1 (1981), pp. 32–53, excellent on its specialised topic, and more generally Halperin, 'Russia in the Mongol Empire', which is full of stimulating ideas and has useful criticism, some of it unnecessarily captious, of the secondary literature.

believed, and that New Sarai was not built until the 1330s, the mistaken notion being derived from Persian sources.[8] Excavations have been carried out on the site of New Sarai, and have shown it to have been an extensive unwalled metropolis in which much evidence of prosperity had been buried under the ruins left after Tamerlane's sack of the city at the end of the fourteenth century.[9]

The Mongols remained in the south and allowed the Russians to continue to administer their own affairs, up to a point. Mongol residents (from whose activities the word *bāsqāq* entered the Russian language) were sent to supervise, and especially to ensure that taxes were paid promptly and in full to the Khān's government. A number of censuses were held of the Russian population in order to facilitate this[10] – an unpopular imposition, particularly in Novgorod, a rather independent-minded city. The more realistic of the Russian princes, such as Alexander Nevsky, appear to have concluded that there was no immediate prospect of driving the Mongols out, and that a *modus vivendi* had therefore better be reached. Alexander's view was that it was the Lithuanians, the Germans and the Swedes who could and should be opposed. Indeed, he made it his business to help in the suppression of resistance to the Mongols, even when it was led by members of his own family, and it is certainly possible to see him as something of a quisling. As Fennell puts it, 'the so-called "Tatar Yoke" began not so much with Baty's invasion of Russia as with Aleksandr's betrayal of his brothers' (in 1252).[11]

The rulers of the various principalities were obliged to seek their appointment from the Khān, and had to travel to Sarai, or wherever the Khān was, to receive their diplomas. They generally made their wills before setting off – not infrequently a necessary precaution. In the days of the Golden Horde's greatest strength Mongol supervision of Russian was close, and direct interference, whether military or otherwise, a regular occurrence. Control later slackened, however. Eventually the Khāns, for their own convenience, delegated the collection of taxes to the prince of Moscow, recognising him as Grand Prince of Russia and thus helping to create the instrument of the Khanate's ultimate downfall.

---

[8] I owe my knowledge of this to an unpublished lecture by Dr J. M. Rogers.

[9] See E. D. Phillips, *The Mongols* (1969), pp. 137–8.

[10] See Allsen, 'Mongol census taking in Rus'.

[11] Fennell, *The Crisis of Medieval Russia*, p. 108.

Batu was a major figure in the Mongol world. He was virtual king-maker at the time of Möngke's accession to the Great Khanate (see chapter 5), and in effect ruled the empire jointly with Möngke. As the Great Khān is reported by William of Rubruck as remarking: 'Just as the sun spreads its rays in all directions, so my power and the power of Baatu is spread everywhere.'[12] Once the Ögedeids and the Chaghataids had been dealt with, the Mongol Empire in the reign of Möngke was still a unity, albeit one in which different interests had to be rather care-fully balanced.

Batu died in 1255 and was followed on the throne of the Golden Horde by his son and grandson in quick succession. Then in 1257 Batu's brother Berke became Khān. He also became a Muslim, the first Mongol of importance to do so; and his disapproval of Hülegü's murder of the 'Abbasid Caliph (see later) is no doubt part of the reason for the out-break in 1262[13] of the first of a long series of wars between the Golden Horde and the Īlkhanate. But these continued after Berke's death in 1267, and his immediate successors were not Muslims. So another explanation of the enmity has to be sought. This is to be found in the wish of the Khāns of the Golden Horde to possess themselves of parts of north-west Persia and the Caucasus that had been occupied by the Īlkhāns. It has been shrewdly observed – and it enables us to see the history of the Golden Horde in a proper perspective – that 'Horde foreign policy focused overwhelmingly upon acquisition of the rich pastures and caravan routes of Azerbaijan. . . . Russia itself was periph-eral to the Horde, not only geographically but also politically and eco-nomically.'[14] The no doubt natural temptation for Europeans to see the Golden Horde as part of the history of Russia rather than as, in the first instance, part of the history of the Mongol Empire should be resisted.

The first of Berke's successors to follow him into the Muslim faith was Töde-Möngke, who was not only a Muslim but also an adherent of Sufism, the mystical side of Islam that in its popular form so fre-quently proved to appeal to the steppe nomads. But again this was a purely personal conversion, and not until the reign of Özbeg (1313–41) was the Golden Horde officially Muslim. Nevertheless the alliance

---

[12]   A. van Den Wyngaert (ed.), *Sinica Franciscana*, vol. 1 (1929), p. 251; tr. C. Dawson (ed.), *The Mongol Mission* (1955), p. 155.

[13]   Or 1261: see P. Jackson, 'The dissolution of the Mongol Empire', *Central Asiatic Journal*, 22 (1978), pp. 233–4.

[14]   Halperin, 'Russia in the Mongol Empire', pp. 250–1.

which Berke had created between the Golden Horde and the Mamlūks of Egypt against the Ilkhanate remained constant. By ultimately becoming Muslims the Mongols of the Golden Horde conspicuously identified themselves with their Turkish subjects and with the peoples to the south rather than with the Christian Russians to the north.

The Golden Horde continued to be an effective power far longer than any of the other Mongol khanates. But its decline, and the rise of Lithuania and Moscow, began in the mid fourteenth century. A brief revival under Tokhtamish (1376–95), who united for the first time the Golden Horde with the White Horde to the east, proved ephemeral, for Tokhtamish had originally been the protégé of Tamerlane, and that great conqueror ultimately threw down the Khān he had helped set up. During Tokhtamish's reign there occurred an event of some symbolic importance, the infliction at Kulikovo Pólye in 1380 of a defeat on the Mongol forces by the Muscovites. The defeat itself was reversed by Tokhtamish two years later, but it did at least give some indication of the shape of things to come.

In 1438 the Golden Horde was divided into two, the Khanates of Kazan and the 'Great Horde'. A further division in 1441 brought about the creation of the Khanates of Astrakhan and the Crimea. The destruction of the Great Horde by Mengli Girai of the Crimea in 1502 is usually taken as representing the 'official' end of the Golden Horde. Mengli Girai had himself accepted subordination to the Ottoman Turks around 1475. Kazan and Astrakhan fell to Ivan the Terrible in 1552 and 1554, leaving only the Crimea, which survived as the last vestige of the Eurasian empire of Chingiz Khān until its annexation by Catherine the Great in 1783. The Tatars of the Crimea themselves continued in existence as a community until Stalin's deportations at the end of the Second World War.

The Mongols and the Middle East

A limited kind of Mongol administration had been set up in parts of the Middle East during the 1230s and 1240s, under the headship of a series of viceroys appointed from Qaraqorum. There had also been some extension of Mongol power and influence in the region, notably the reduction to submission of the Seljük sultanate of Rūm in Anatolia as the result of the Mongol general Baiju's victory over the Seljüks at Köse Dagh in 1243. But there was still a long way to go before the eastern Islamic world as a whole could be said to form an integral part of the

Mongol Empire. In Persia there were a number of independent local dynasties, especially in the south. The 'Abbasid Caliphate in Baghdad had not surrendered its universalist claims, and in the absence of an effective central authority in the region it retained some of the local political influence it had accumulated during the long reign of the Caliph al-Nāṣir. In Syria the Ayyubid successors of Saladin still remained the dominant power, and had achieved a state of uneasy coexistence with the Crusader territories. Al-Nāṣir Yūsuf of Damascus was the most important Ayyubid; and there was no longer a family rival in Cairo after 1250, when the last Ayyubid sultan there was overthrown by the very military machine that had so long sustained the dynasty. A group of Mamlūks, military slaves, seized power and set up their own sultanate, in which succession (though often in practice hereditary) was in theory from master to slave rather than from father to son.[15] Most important in Mongol eyes of the enemies that still had to be dealt with in the Middle East were the Ismā'īlīs, the Assassins.

The Ismā'īlīs were a branch of the Shī'ī sect of Islam, one of the two main divisions of the Muslim faith (the Sunnī being the other). They are to be distinguished from the adherents of that variety of Shī'ī Islam which has been since the sixteenth century and remains to this day conspicuously the official religion of Persia. The Ismā'īlīs had provided Egypt with its Fatimid dynasty, suppressed by Saladin in 1171. In 1094 a schism developed within Fatimid Shī'ism over who ought rightfully to succeed the recently deceased Caliph in Cairo. The partisans of the defeated candidate, Nizār, removed themselves from Egypt to conduct their affairs elsewhere in the Islamic world. Already in 1090 a missionary sent from Egypt, Ḥasan-i Ṣabbāḥ, had established himself in the inaccessible castle of Alamūt, in the Alburz mountains of north Persia. This became the headquarters of the Nizārīs and Ḥasan became *de facto* head of the 'order'. They based their power on control of mountain castles and the surrounding countryside, the valleys of the Alburz remaining their chief centre. Strongholds were seized in various parts of Persia, but the principal centre other than parts of the Alburz was in Qūhistān in eastern Persia. A branch was also set up in the Lebanese mountains. It was as a result of the Crusaders' encounters with these Nizārīs that news of the sect found its way to Europe, together with the sinister reputation of the local Ismā'īlī chief, the 'Old Man of the

---

[15]   See P. M. Holt, s.v. 'Mamlūks', *EI*²; and R. Irwin, *The Middle East in the Middle Ages: the early Mamluk Sultanate 1250–1382* (1986).

Mountain' (possibly a literal translation of the Arabic *Shaykh al-jabal*). The Nizārīs were notorious for two of their activities: their practice of political murder, almost always with the dagger, rather than military confrontation, as their main means of securing their ends; and their indulgence – so it is, probably wrongly, alleged – in the drug hashish. From this the word 'assassin' was derived, and found its way into many European languages.[16]

Hülegü's Expedition

We have seen in chapter 5 that the Great Khān Möngke had resolved on two major military operations: the conquest of Sung China and an expedition to the Middle East. His brother Hülegü was to be in command of the latter. His primary objective was the destruction of the power of the Ismāʿīlīs. The reasons for this are said to have been two: an appeal from an Islamic judge (*qāḍī*) of Qazwīn, near Alamūt, who complained that he and his fellow citizens were obliged to wear armour permanently beneath their clothes for fear of the Assassins' daggers;[17] and, according to William of Rubruck, the exceedingly ill-advised despatch of 400 disguised Assassins to Qaraqorum to kill the Great Khān – a gesture that was not well received by that monarch.[18] For these reasons or others it was resolved that Hülegü's first duty should be to extirpate the Ismāʿīlīs once and for all.

Beyond that, Hülegü was to demand the submission of the ʿAbbasid Caliph, or to destroy him should he refuse to submit; and then Mongol power was to be extended further towards Syria and Egypt and perhaps beyond. To determine whether or not it was actually Möngke's intention that a result of the expedition should be the setting up of a Mongol

[16] See M. G. S. Hodgson, *The Order of Assassins* (1955) and 'The Ismāʿīlī state', in J. A. Boyle (ed.), *The Cambridge History of Iran*, vol. 5: *The Saljuq and Mongol Periods* (1968), pp. 422–82; B. Lewis, *The Assassins: a Radical Sect in Islam* (1967).
[17] E. Quatremère (ed. and tr.), Raschid Eldin, *Histoire des Mongols de la Perse* (1836), pp. 120–3; A. A. Alizade (ed.), Rashīd al-Dīn, *Jāmiʿ al-tawārīkh*, vol. 3 (1957), p. 20; ʿA. Nawāʾī (ed.), Ḥamd Allāh Mustawfī Qazwīnī, *Taʾrīkh-i guzīda* (1958–61), pp. 588–9.
[18] Van Den Wyngaert, *Sinica Franciscana*, vol. 1, p. 286; Dawson, *The Mongol Mission*, p. 184.

kingdom for Hülegü and his successors, as in fact happened, is something of a problem. Jūzjānī[19] certainly thought that this was what Möngke proposed. But writing as he was in Delhi, Jūzjānī is unlikely to have been privy to the details of discussions at a *quriltai* in Mongolia. Rashīd al-Dīn, on the other hand, was in a sense the court historian of the house of Hülegü, and must certainly have known, if not what was said and thought at the *quriltai*, at least what the official version of it subsequently became. He has a curious story to tell.[20] If he is to be believed, Möngke publicly told Hülegü to accomplish his various military operations as specified and then to return to Mongolia: but secretly Möngke intended him to remain and rule Persia as his own patrimony.

This suggests that there may well have been something irregular about the setting up of Hülegü's kingdom, the Ilkhanate, that it was impossible to conceal Möngke's overt instructions, presumably because they were well known, and that perhaps the 'secret intention' was concocted later to justify, *ex post facto*, what Hülegü had done. It was this oddity among other pieces of evidence that led Jackson to posit that the Ilkhanate's creation was a usurpation, in fact, of the rights (in Mongol eyes) to possession of Persia of the Jochids of the Golden Horde.[21] In my view this goes beyond what may reasonably be deduced from the evidence, the more so since the rulers of the Golden Horde themselves appear to have been unaware of all their supposed rights. But nevertheless a degree of suspicion is certainly in order. It might be legitimate to speculate that if the foundation of the Ilkhanate was not in Möngke's mind in 1251, it was the political turmoil into which the Mongol Empire was plunged after his death in 1259 that made it possible for Hülegü to look after his own dynastic interests with such conspicuous success. The embattled Qubilai would be unlikely to dispute the title of so potentially valuable an ally as his brother Hülegü. One final possibility, which ought not to be altogether discounted, remains: that what Rashīd al-Dīn tells us is in fact true.

Hülegü set off from Mongolia in 1253. He made elaborate preparations for the provisioning of his forces on the way, and at least by

[19]   'A. Ḥabībī (ed.), Minhāj al-Dīn Jūzjānī, *Ṭabaqāt-i Nāṣirī* (1964–5), vol. 2, pp. 188–9; tr. H. G. Raverty, *Ṭabakāt-i-Nāṣirī* (1881), vol. 2, pp. 1215, 1226.

[20]   Quatremère, *Histoire des Mongols*, p. 144; Alizade (ed.), *Jāmi' al-tawārīkh*, vol. 3, p. 24.

[21]   See Jackson, 'The dissolution of the Mongol Empire'.

Mongol standards he moved very slowly. He did not finally confront the Ismāʿīlīs until 1256. A young Grand Master had recently succeeded his murdered father and he, terrified by Mongol threats and by their military power, soon surrendered to Hülegü. At first he was well treated by his captor, who paraded him about the Assassin castles, requiring him to order their capitulation and thus save Mongol time, trouble and lives. Later the Grand Master expressed a wish to be sent to Möngke in Qaraqorum. According to Juwaynī, the Great Khān refused to see him (perhaps the memory of those 400 other uninvited Ismāʿīlī guests still rankled), and he began the journey back. On the way, he and his attendants were 'kicked to a pulp and then put to the sword' by their Mongol escort.[22] The Assassins of Persia were largely though not entirely wiped out after their surrender, and a menace whose suppression had eluded the efforts of Persia's orthodox Muslim rulers for a century and a half was no more. Gibbon, always ready to give the Mongols credit when it was due, expressed the view that this extirpation 'may be considered as a service to mankind'.[23] The Syrian branch, as events turned out, escaped Mongol wrath, only to fall victim a little later to the Mamlūk sultan Baybars. Some Ismāʿīlīs remained in Persia, however. In the nineteenth century their leader, a descendant of the Grand Masters of Alamūt, fled from Persia to India; and his ultimate successor, the Aga Khan, is still to this day at the head of the sect.

The Assassin question once definitively answered, Hülegü set off westwards to Hamadān, and from there marched into Iraq, approaching the Caliph's domain from the north in 1258. The summons to submit was refused. Confusion reigned in Baghdad, with the principal functionaries of the Caliphal government at odds with one another more than they were united against the Mongol threat. Treachery, we are told, was installed at the very heart of affairs: the Sunnī Caliph's wazīr, his chief minister, was a Shīʿī, and is alleged by Jūzjānī to have reduced the numbers and strength of the Baghdad garrison.[24] We may note that after the fall of Baghdad he was reappointed to his office by Hülegü.[25] The

[22]   M. M. Qazwīnī (ed.), ʿAṭā Malik Juwaynī, *Taʾrīkh-i Jahān Gushā*, vol. 3 (1937), p. 277; tr. J. A. Boyle, *The History of the World Conqueror* (1958), vol. 2, p. 724.

[23]   E. Gibbon, *The History of the Decline and Fall of the Roman Empire*, ed. J. B. Burry (1905–6), vol. 7, pp. 12–13.

[24]   See E. G. Browne, *A Literary History of Persia* (1982), vol. 2, p. 464.

[25]   J. A. Boyle, 'The death of the last ʿAbbāsid Caliph: a contemporary Muslim account', *Journal of Semitic Studies*, 6 (1961), p. 1600.

prospect of a negotiated peace was remote, but the Caliph could not realistically hope to drive off the Mongols by force. Baghdad was invested by Hülegü's army, and eventually the Caliph, at his wits' end and perhaps persuaded by his wazīr, surrendered. Baghdad was looted and many of the population killed. The later Persian historian Ḥamd Allāh Mustawfī Qazwīnī put the death toll at 800,000,[26] a figure that has often been quoted. But in the case of this massacre we for once have an estimate from someone who may have had a fairly accurate idea of the actual extent of the disaster – Hülegü himself. In his letter to Louis IX of France, written in 1262, he says that more than 200,000 were killed in Baghdad.[27] We do not of course know whether he was telling the truth.

The Caliph himself was also put to death. The manner of his end is variously reported, one of the favourite stories being that he was shut in a tower with his treasure and starved to death. This was intended to reinforce rather permanently the lesson that the treasure ought to have been spent on raising troops rather than being uselessly hoarded. The story is found in Marco Polo's narrative[28] and elsewhere. The account of the Caliph's death that is most generally credited, however, is that he was wrapped in a carpet and kicked or trampled to death.[29] Such an end would have been in accordance with Mongol custom. If the Mongols proposed to execute someone of royal or noble blood and wished to kill him honourably, they would inflict death by some method that did not involve the shedding of the victim's blood. This is what is said to have been done in the case of Chingiz Khān's old comrade and later adversary Jamuqa;[30] and such may well have been the motive behind the choice of the Caliph's mode of execution. He probably failed to appreciate the compliment.

So after five centuries ended the line of the 'Abbasid Caliphs as titular heads of the Sunnī Muslim community. Members of the family found their way to Egypt, where Sultan Baybars declared one of them to be the rightful Caliph. A line of puppet 'Abbasids was subsequently

[26]   Nawā'ī (ed.), *Ta'rīkh-i guzīda*, p. 589.
[27]   P. Meyvaert, 'An unknown letter of Hulagu, Il-Khan of Persia, to King Louis IX of France', *Viator*, 11 (1980), p. 256.
[28]   A. Ricci (tr.), *The Travels of Marco Polo* (1931), p. 27.
[29]   See Boyle, 'The death of the last 'Abbāsid Caliph'.
[30]   *Secret History*, para. 201: F. W. Cleaves (tr.), *The Secret History of the Mongols* (1982), pp. 140–1.

maintained by the Mamlūks,[31] but these Cairo Caliphs were never acknowledged outside Egypt and Syria except by one Persian local ruler and, for a time in the fourteenth century, in that other mamlūk empire, the sultanate of Delhi. The Sunnī community as a whole found, rather to its surprise, that it could now manage perfectly well without a Caliph at all; and so it remained until, very much later, the Ottoman sultans assumed the additional style of Caliph, a dignity which in the twentieth century survived for a brief time even Atatürk's abolition of the sultanate.

If there was general rejoicing in the Muslim world at the destruction of the perfidious Assassins, the fall of Baghdad gave it something of a shock, however nominal the Caliph's authority may have become. Not everyone bewailed what had happened, however. Some Christian writers saw it as divine judgement on the sink of infidel iniquity; and many Shīʿī Muslims, too, were delighted at this body blow to what they saw as a distorted version of the true faith, one which was also, normally, dominant politically. Sunnīs in Hülegü's entourage had warned of dreadful calamities if the Caliph were to be attacked. But a notable Shīʿī, the polymath Naṣīr al-Dīn Ṭūsī who had been acquired by Hülegü as part of the Ismāʿīlī booty, assured him that nothing of the sort would happen. Having thus established his reputation as a reliable prophet, Ṭūsī continued his distinguished career as a servant of the Īlkhāns. He produced for Hülegü or his son and successor Abaqa a treatise on government finance[32] and erected an astronomical observatory on the top of a hill outside Hülegü's capital, Marāgha. The excavated remains of the observatory can still be seen. He also pursued a wide variety of philosophical and other learned interests.

Hülegü's steamroller lumbered on, in 1260, towards Syria.[33] The Ayyubids were hardly more of an obstacle than the Caliph had been.

---

[31]   See P. M. Holt, 'Some observations on the 'Abbāsid caliphate of Cairo', *Bulletin of the School of Oriental and African Studies*, 47/3 (1984), pp. 501–7.

[32]   See V. Minorsky, 'Naṣīr al-Dīn Ṭūsī on finance', in his *Iranica* (1964), pp. 64–85.

[33]   Useful accounts of this phase of Mongol expansion are in C. Cahen, 'The Mongols and the Near East', in K. M. Setton (ed.), *A History of the Crusades* (1969), vol. 2, pp. 715–32, and R. S. Humphreys, *From Saladin to the Mongols* (1997), chapter 6. The important article by J. M. Smith Jr, 'ʿAyn Jālūt: Mamlūk success or Mongol failure?', *Harvard Journal of Asiatic Studies*, 44/2 (1984), pp. 307–45, appeared too late to be taken fully into account in this book.

Plate 6.2   Excavated remains of Naṣīr al-Dīn Ṭūsī's observatory at Marāgha,
Hülegü's capital

Al-Nāṣir Yūsuf was made prisoner and Aleppo and Damascus taken.
The Crusader ruler of Antioch and Tripoli hastened to make his submission and to join forces with the all-conquering Mongols. He earned
excommunication for this traffic with the infidel. But the famous scene
in which Damascus was entered by the Mongols and their allies, allegedly headed by three Christians – Bohemond of Antioch, King Hetʻum
of Cilician Armenia, and Hülegü's Nestorian general Kit-buqa – might
have seemed to herald a new era for the fortunes of Christianity in the
land of its foundation.[34]
It did not seem so to the Crusader authorities in Acre, when they had
to decide on their response to the Mamlūk sultan Quṭuz's request for
help in his forthcoming expedition against the Mongol invaders. After
much discussion the Crusaders decided not to participate actively in
the campaign, but to allow the Mamlūk army free passage through

[34]   See J. J. Saunders, *The History of the Mongol Conquests* (1971), p. 113.
The only source for this scene is the western *Gestes des Chiprois*.

Plate 6.3   Astronomical chart. From a book in Naṣīr al-Dīn Ṭūsī's own hand

Christian territory, and to provide it with supplies. This has long been seen as a 'missed opportunity' for the Crusaders. According to that opinion, most eloquently expressed by Grousset[35] and frequently repeated by other scholars, the Crusaders ought to have allied themselves with the pro-Christian, anti-Muslim Mongols against the Mamlūks. They might thus have prevented their own destruction by the Mamlūks in the succeeding decades, and possibly even have secured the return of Jerusalem by favour of the Mongols.

Dr Jackson's study of the events of 1260 has shown, however, that such a view is only reasonable if one has the historian's advantage of

[35]   R. Grousset, *Histoire des Croisades* (1934–6), vol. 3, pp. 525–30 and 580–606, and in other works.

hindsight. The Mongols had not in fact lavished particular benevolence on the Christians during their occupation of Syria. They had merely implemented their traditional even-handed approach towards all religions and their adherents. Nothing in Christendom's previous experience of the Mongols could have led anyone to regard them as other than barbarous, treacherous and thoroughly dangerous. In addition, the first ten years of Mamlūk rule in Egypt had apparently been extremely unstable: in 1260 there was no reason to suppose that the Mamlūk regime would become as enduring and formidable as proved to be the case. On the evidence available to them, the Crusaders' attitude was the only one possible: the Īlkhāns' more friendly posture towards Christendom after 1262–3 has tended to distort an accurate appreciation of the situation in 1260.[36]

In the meantime important events occurred elsewhere in the Mongol Empire. The Great Khān Möngke died in China, and dispute over the succession ensued between Hülegü's brothers Qubilai and Ariq-böke (see chapter 5). The situation was dangerous for Hülegü, and he withdrew with the bulk of his forces towards north-west Persia, leaving behind in Syria a part of his army under Kit-buqa. As the death of Ögedei in 1241 had perhaps saved Europe, so the death of Möngke was the salvation of the Mamlūks. Again, as the inadequacy of the grassland in Hungary may have been a further reason for Batu's withdrawal, Hülegü was similarly, according to his letter to Louis IX, obliged to take his army out of Syria because the greater part of the available fodder and grazing had been used up.[37] Kit-buqa met Quṭuz in battle at 'Ayn Jālūt (the 'Spring of Goliath') in Galilee, the supposed site of an earlier victory on the part of an apparently feeble combatant. The Mongols were defeated,[38] Kit-buqa was killed in the fighting or captured and then executed, and after a further defeat the Mongols were for the time being driven out of Syria. Hülegü rather ineffectively marked his vexation by having al-Nāṣir Yūsuf executed. Syria became a Mamlūk province.

---

[36] P. Jackon, 'The crisis in the Holy Land in 1260', *English Historical Review*, 95 (1980), pp. 481–513; see also J. Richard, 'The Mongols and the Franks', *Journal of Asian History*, 3 (1969), pp. 51–2 and n. 30.

[37] Meyvaert, 'An unknown letter of Hulagu', p. 258; see D. O. Morgan, 'The Mongols in Syria, 1260–1300', in P. W. Edbury (ed.), *Crusade and Settlement* (1985), p. 233.

[38] See Smith, ''Ayn Jālūt'; P. Thorau, 'The battle of 'Ayn Jālūt: a re-examination', in Edbury, *Crusade and Settlement*, pp. 236–41.

Quṭuz was not long to enjoy the fruits of victory: he was murdered after 'Ayn Jālūt by a group of Mamlūk amīrs, commanders, among them Baybars, who succeeded him as sultan and was to be the real founder of Mamlūk power.

'Ayn Jālūt can be said to have marked the putting of a term to Mongol expansion in the Middle East, but it would be going too far to say that that single battle in any real sense halted the Mongol advance. Certainly it must have given the Mamlūks a considerable psychological boost: it was now clear that the supposedly invincible Mongols could in fact be defeated, even if only when their forces were seriously depleted. While it is true that the Mongols frequently invaded Syria at intervals until the end of the century and a little beyond, and that on one occasion, in 1300, they occupied the whole country and drove out all the Mamlūk troops, they never stayed for long. Syria was not to form part of the Mongol Empire. There is a considerable body of evidence to support the view that the same difficulty that contributed to Hülegü's withdrawal in 1260, the inadequacy of the pasturelands, especially in southern Syria, was a major reason for these repeated Mongol failures.[39] But just as important was the nature of the Mongol Empire's internal politics after 1260. This made it certain that never again would it be possible to mount a major military expedition that had the full backing of Mongol imperial resources, as Hülegü's invasion had had.

We have seen that enmity developed between Hülegü and Berke of the Golden Horde, culminating in the outbreak of the first of a long series of wars between the two Mongol khanates in 1261 or 1262. It was for Baybars in Egypt to capitalise on this if he could. This was important both politically and economically: Baybars needed an ally against Hülegü, and the lands of the Golden Horde were the principal source for the new supplies of mamlūk soldiers on which the Egyptian regime depended. But there was a communications problem. The Ilkhanid enemy controlled Persia, Iraq, and most of Anatolia. The main route from Cairo to Sarai therefore had to be the sea route past Constantinople, which was controlled by the Latins, no friends to the Mamlūks. The recovery of Constantinople by the Byzantines of Nicaea in 1261 offered a possible solution.[40] Although the Emperor Michael Palaeologus was anxious as far as possible to avoid offending Hülegü,

---

[39]   Morgan, 'The Mongols in Syria'; and see Smith, ''Ayn Jālūt', pp. 331–45.

[40]   See J. J. Saunders, 'The Mongol defeat at Ain Jalut and the restoration of the Greek Empire', in his *Muslims and Mongols* (1997), pp. 67–76.

the route was opened and a long-standing alliance between the Mamlūks and the Golden Horde against the Mongols of Persia was forged. Mongol unity, already looking shaky because of events in the Far East, was irretrievably broken. The empire continued to expand in China until the final conquest of the Sung in 1279. But this was not a united Mongol effort: it could almost be described as Qubilai's private affair. With Qaidu and the Chaghataids in Central Asia opposed both to Qubilai and to his allies the Īlkhāns, and with the Golden Horde allied with a non-Mongol regime against fellow Mongols, it is with justice that Jackson characterises the events around the year 1260 as marking 'the dissolution of the Mongol Empire'.

The Īlkhāns of Persia

The period of the rule of the Ilkhanate by Hülegü and his immediate successors, from 1256 to 1295, has a certain unity in that during that time Muslim Persia and Iraq were dominated by pagans, and dominated, supposedly, in a singularly oppressive fashion.[41] Hülegü's own faith seems to have been little more than his ancestral Shamanism, though he is said to have favoured Buddhism. Since on his death in 1265 his funeral featured human sacrifices (it was the only Ilkhanid funeral to do so), we are entitled to doubt that his adherence to Buddhism went very deep. Nevertheless, if the early Īlkhāns had a religion other than Shamanism, it was Buddhism, in a form heavily influenced (as in Mongol China) by Tibetan Lamaism. Some of Hülegü's successors, notably Arghun (ruled 1284–91), seem to have taken their Buddhist beliefs seriously. But there are very few surviving traces of Persia's 40 years of officially patronised Buddhism because Ghazan Khān, on declaring his conversion to Islam in 1295, ordered that all Buddhist buildings should be razed to the ground. The Lamas were required either to become Muslims or to leave the Ilkhanate.

---

[41]   The best accounts of the individual Īlkhāns are the articles by P. Jackson appearing in the *Encyclopaedia Iranica*. This has only recently commenced publication, but since the Īlkhāns seem to have favoured the beginning of the alphabet we already have, or will soon have, Abaqa, Aḥmad Tegüder, Arghun, Abū Saʿīd, Arpa and Baidu. For general narratives of the period see B. Spuler, *Die Mongolen in Iran* (1968) and Boyle (ed.), *The Cambridge History of Iran*, vol. 5.

Of the handful of Buddhist remains of the Mongol period that still exist, the two complexes identified by Warwick Ball are of particular interest.[42] They were both later converted to Islamic use, but can be shown to have had Buddhist origins because of their strong structural similarities to known Buddhist temples in Central Asia. They are rock cut, and this explains their survival: series of caves were not susceptible of easy demolition. One is situated in the hill on top of which Naṣīr al-Dīn Ṭusī built his observatory. It had previously been argued that the caves were originally a Christian monastery church of the Jacobite sect, but Ball's identification seems more convincing. The hill is just outside Marāgha, and Ball's second cave complex is in a nearby village. Since Marāgha was the first of the Ilkhanid capitals, its vicinity is precisely where one would most expect to find traces of Mongol Buddhism.

In would not be accurate, however, to describe Buddhism as the 'official religion' of Persia in this period. All religions, in accordance with Chingiz Khān's reported precepts, were granted freedom. The difference from the immediate past lay in the fact that Islam was no longer in a privileged position; and the non-Muslims no longer had to pay their special poll-tax, the *jizya*. Christianity flourished, particularly in its local Oriental forms, Jacobite and Nestorian. The Jacobite prelate Bar Hebraeus wrote his vast chronicle, in both Syriac and Arabic versions, under the early Ilkhāns. The Nestorians were more numerous and influential than the Jacobites, and the period of Mongol rule saw an enormous extension of Nestorian activity throughout Asia, which may well have been more impressive than William of Rubruck, who only met Nestorian clerics of low rank, would have allowed.[43]

The most notable Nestorian hierarch of the time was the Catholicus Yaballāhā III, who presided over the whole Nestorian church in Asia from his seat in Iraq. He was originally a monk named Mark, an Önggüt Turk from inner Mongolia, who had set off on pilgrimage to Jerusalem as the disciple of another monk, Rabban Ṣaumā. They were able to travel no further than the Ilkhanate because of disorders in Syria; and

[42]   W. Ball, 'Two aspects of Iranian Buddhism', *Bulletin of the Asia Institute of Pahlavi University*, 1–4 (1976), pp. 103–63; 'The Imamzadeh Ma'sum at Vardjovi. A rock-cut Il-khanid complex near Maragheh', *Archaeologische Mitteilungen aus Iran*, 12 (1979), pp. 329–40.

[43]   See J. Dauvillier, 'Les provinces chaldéennes "de l'extérieur" au moyen âge', in *Mélanges F. Cavallera* (1948), pp. 261–316; 'Guillaume de Roubrouck et les communautés chaldéennes d'Asie centrale au moyen âge', *L'Orient syrien*, 2 (1957), pp. 223–42.

at that point, in 1281, the then reigning Nestorian Catholicus died. According to the extant Syriac life of Mark[44] he was promptly elected Catholicus, although he was very young and not notably learned, because he knew the Mongols' language and ways so intimately. He took the title of Yaballāhā. His master Rabban Ṣaumā was also given preferment, and indeed in 1287 was sent by Arghun on an embassy to Europe, of which his fascinating account was included in the biography of Yaballāhā III (see chapter 7). Yaballāhā himself acquired very considerable influence at the Ilkhanid court, and the fortunes of Christianity seemed to be prospering under Mongol patronage. Rabban Ṣaumā told the cardinals in Rome that 'many of our Fathers have gone into the countries of the Mongols, and Turks, and Chinese and have taught them the Gospel, and at the present time there are many Mongols who are Christians. For many of the sons of the Mongol kings and queens have been baptised and confess Christ.'[45] One of Arghun's sons, the future Īkhān Öljeitü (ruled 1304–16) was as a child a close intimate of the Catholicus, and was baptized Nicholas in honour of Pope Nicholas IV,[46] with whom Arghun had negotiated. There must have seemed, at least to the optimistic eye, a very real possibility that the ruling Mongols – at any rate in Persia – would adopt Nestorian Christianity and that the Ilkhanate, if not Mongol Asia as a whole, might become a Christian empire, united with Europe against the Muslim infidel. As Sir Richard Southern remarks, 'it was a noble prospect, and one which, if only a fraction of it had come true, would radically have altered the history of the world.'[47]

It was not to be. Already in the 1280s the Īlkhān Tegüder (ruled 1282–4) had declared his conversion to Islam, the faith of the majority of his subjects, and had taken the Muslim name of Aḥmad. Admittedly he was speedily overthrown, but this probably had more to do with his general incompetence and his unwisely merciful treatment of opponents than with Mongol objections to his religious proclivities.[48] In 1295 the

---

[44]   E. A. W. Budge (tr.), *The Monks of Ḳūblāi Khān, Emperor of China* (1928), pp. 152–3.

[45]   Budge, *The Monks of Ḳūblāi Khān*, p. 174.

[46]   J. Richard, *La Papauté et les missions d'Orient au moyen âge (XIII–XVe siècles)* (1997), p. 104.

[47]   R. W. Southern, *Western Views of Islam in the Middle Ages* (1962), p. 65.

[48]   See P. Jackson s.v. 'Aḥmad', *EIr*.

Īlkhān Ghazan, on the prompting of Nawrūz, the Mongol general who had done most to ensure his succession, became a Muslim. This time the rest of the Mongols of Persia followed suit.

In all probability this conversion was for many Mongols a fairly superficial affair. Ghazan's successor was his brother Öljeitü, who had once been Nicholas and who achieved the unusual distinction of belonging at one time or another to almost every currently available religion. Presumably a residual Shamanist, he had been a Buddhist as well as a baptised Christian, and he was later to oscillate between the Sunnī and Shī'ī forms of Islam. In his history of Öljeitü's reign Qāshānī gives an account of a dispute at court between the Ḥanafīs and the Shāfi'īs, two of the four major schools of Sunnī Islamic law. Losing patience with their wrangling, Öljeitü's commander-in-chief, Qutlugh-shāh, addressed his fellow Mongols, and said: 'What is this that we have done, abandoning the new *yāsāq* and *yūsūn* of Chingiz Khān, and taking up the ancient religion of the Arabs, which is divided into seventy-old parts? The choice of either of these two rites (i.e. Ḥanafī or Shāfi'ī) would be a disgrace and a dishonourable act, since in the one, marriage with a daughter is permitted, and in the other, relations with one's mother or sister. We seek refuge in God from both of them! Let us return to the *yāsāq* and *yūsūn* of Chingiz Khān.'[49] If Qutlugh-shāh was at all typical, the Mongols were taking some little time to acquire a knowledge or understanding of Islam that bore much relation to the faith as it is generally understood.

The rule of the pagan, or vaguely Buddhist, Īlkhāns would seem to have been characterised by ruthless and short-sighted exploitation, if Rashīd al-Dīn's testimony is to be credited. We have seen in chapter 1 that there are some grounds for reservation in that Rashīd al-Dīn was chief minister to the reforming Īlkhān Ghazan, and was thus to an extent writing as judge and jury in his own cause. But the details he offers are undoubtedly convincing circumstantially, and his picture in general term is confirmed by such other sources as the *Ta'rīkh-i Waṣṣāf*, especially through the data Waṣṣāf provides about conditions in his native province of Fārs. The administration was usually run by Persians from the capital, fixed by Abaqa (ruled 1265–82) at Tabrīz in the favoured grasslands of the north-west. It appears to have lurched from one financial crisis to another. Taxes were levied 20 or 30 times

[49]   M. Hambly (ed.), Qāshānī, *Ta'rīkh-i Ūljāytū* (1969), p. 98, with an omitted word from the unique MS, Aya Sofya 3019, f. 178a.

Plate 6.4   The Arg (citadel) at Tabrīz, Ilkhanid capital of Persia: in fact the remains of a mosque built by Tāj al-Dīn ʿAlī Shāh, colleague and rival of Rashīd al-Dīn

each year, and the methods of collection are well illustrated in the story of Arghun's Jewish minister Saʿd al-Dawla's expedition to Baghdad with the Mongol Orduqiya: Arghun sent them 'to collect the arrears and to demand the wealth due to the Treasury. They went there, and by using the bastinado and torture, they collected abundant wealth.' The result of such maladministration is said to have been 'a general flight from the land on the part of the peasants', and the reduction of nine-tenths of the cultivable land to waste.[50]

The first serious attempt at reform was made in Arghun's reign by Saʿd al-Dawla. By general consent he was very efficient, and he did succeed in balancing the books. But the Persians resented him because he was a Jew, and the Mongols saw their quick profits slipping away.

---

[50]   Alizade (ed.), *Jāmiʿ al-tawārīkh*, vol. 3, pp. 209, 457 and 558.

Plate 6.5　The Īlkhān Abaqa (reigned 1265–82) and his son Arghun (reigned 1284–91). From a Persian miniature. Bibliothèque Nationale de France MS. Persian Suppl. 1113, fol. 198v

As Bar Hebraeus puts it, 'to the nobles of the Camp he paid no heed, and he reduced the taking and giving of their hands, and he treated with contempt the principal Amīrs and the directors of general affairs'.[51] His

---

[51]　E. A. W. Budge (ed. and tr.), *The Chronography of Gregory Abū'l Faraj* (1932), vol. 1, p. 490.

position was entirely dependent on the monarch's favour, and advantage was taken of Arghun's terminal illness in 1291 to arrange the minister's fall and execution.

The accession of the amiable if dissolute Geikhatu did nothing to improve matters. His minister, Ṣadr al-Dīn, thought very hard about how to replenish a treasury emptied by royal extravagance, at a time when the Persian economy was also suffering from the effects of a great cattle plague. He decided that the answer was to issue paper money, called, after its Chinese model, *chao*.[52] Advice on how the Chinese system worked was obtained from Pulad Ching-sang, the Great Khān's resident in Tabrīz. The paper certificates followed the Chinese pattern even to the extent of having words in Chinese printed on them, though the Muslim confession of faith was also included, perhaps as a sop to local sentiment. The theory was that all precious metal would be driven into the hands of the government since its use as currency was forbidden on pain of the most fearsome penalties. The desired effect was not achieved: all commerce stopped dead and the *chao* had to be withdrawn. Ṣadr al-Dīn's stock was low, and Rashīd al-Dīn accuses him of being a Mazdakite. This was a reference to a standard Persian bogy man: Mazdak was the prophet of a curious quasi-communistic movement of pre-Islamic times in Persia. It is customary to suppose that the accusation of Mazdakism really means nothing more specific than to call someone a Communist or a Fascist often does today, i.e. that the speaker disapproves of the person concerned and wishes to blacken his character. It is worth noting, however, that Professor Yarshater has recently argued very persuasively that Mazdakism did in fact survive well into the Islamic period,[53] though it is perhaps doubtful whether it could still have been flourishing as late as Mongol times.

Ghazan, Arghun's son and the governor of Khurāsān, refused to have anything to do with the *chao* measure. Before long, conspirators had overthrown Geikhatu, but at their head was not Ghazan but another member of the house of Hülegü, Baidu. Within a few months he was himself forcibly displaced by Ghazan, and he remains a slightly mysterious figure.[54] His reign is not mentioned by Ghazan's near-panegyrist

[52]   See K. Jahn, 'Paper currency in Iran', *Journal of Asian History*, 4/2 (1970), pp. 101–35.

[53]   E. Yarshater, 'Mazdakism', in E. Yarshater (ed.), *The Cambridge History of Iran*, vol. 3: *The Seleucid, Parthian and Sasanian Periods* (1983), part 2, pp. 991–1024.

[54]   See P. Jackson s.v. 'Baidu', *EIr*.

Rashīd al-Dīn. With Ghazan's accession came the most sustained attempt to right the wrongs of the previous seven decades.

Ghazan and Reform

According to Rashīd al-Dīn Ghazan made a speech to the leading Mongols in which he justified his proposal to reform the administration of the Ilkhanate. 'I am not protecting the Persian peasantry', he is supposed to have said. 'If it is expedient, then let me pillage them all – there is no one with more power to do so than I. Let us rob them together. But if you expect to collect provisions and food in the future . . . I will be harsh with you. And you must consider: if you commit extortion against the peasants, take their oxen and seed, and cause their crops to be consumed – what will you do in the future?' Thus far we have a hard-headed appeal to common sense. But Ghazan continues: 'You must think, too, when you beat and torture their wives and children, that just as our wives and children are dear to our hearts, so are theirs to them. They are human beings, just as we are.'[55] The last may well have been a new thought to most of the Mongols, and even if Ghazan indeed uttered it we may think it unlikely that he will have made much of an impression.

Be that as it may, the reform programme was begun, and as we have seen, the reforming edicts, the texts of which Rashīd al-Dīn has preserved, were duly drafted and no doubt issued, with what practical result it is more difficult to say. I have already quoted (in chapter 1) A. H. M. Jones's very relevant comment on late Roman legislation. Closer to home if as far away in time, it has been suggested that Ghazan's reforms may well have had something in common with the late Shāh's 'White Revolution' – very fine on paper but with markedly limited effect on the ground. Still, the programme was certainly comprehensive, at least in intention.[56] Among many other decrees, the rates

---

[55]   Alizade (ed.), *Jāmiʿ al-tawārīkh*, vol. 3, p. 478.
[56]   On Ghazan's reforms see A. K. S. Lambton, *Landlord and Peasant in Persia* (1953), chapter 4; Spuler, *Die Mongolen in Iran*, pp. 314–22; I. P. Petrushevsky, 'The socio-economic condition of Iran under the Il-Khans', in Boyle (ed.), *The Cambridge History of Iran*, vol. 5, pp. 483–537, esp. pp. 494–500; also Petrushevsky, *Zemledelie i Agrarnie Otnosheniya v Irane XIII–XIVvv.* (1960), pp. 55–62, in Russian, of which there is a Persian translation in Petrushevsky, *Kishāwarzī wa munāsibāt-i arḍī dar Īrān* (1966), vol. 1, pp. 92–104.

and methods of payment of taxation were prescribed; the *Yām* system was reorganised; the coinage and weights and measures were reformed; the activities and payment of Islamic judges. *qāḍīs*, were regulated; incentives were offered to encourage the recultivation of land that had fallen out of use; and the problem of finding an appropriate way of paying the army was tackled.

No doubt there was some improvement in conditions, at least in the short term. Ḥamd Allāh Mustawfī Qazwīnī, writing in 1340, claimed that as a result of the reforms the government's annual revenue had increased from 17 million to 21 million currency *dīnārs*. This is a percentage increase which is not so large as to be implausible, and Ḥamd Allāh, a member of the financial bureaucracy, would have had good information.[57] But Ghazan's hand was not on the tiller for long, and 'the moment control was relaxed there was a tendency to relapse into the old habits, and thus it was a constant struggle to restrain the officials from committing extortion against those under their power'.[58] The Russian scholar Petrushevsky believed that there is evidence of a 'revival of agriculture', and concluded that 'in comparison with the previous system of pure club-law and unrestricted pillage, the new regime was an improvement from the point of view of the ra'iyyat' (i.e. the peasantry).[59] But it was not all benefit even for the peasants. One of the results of Ghazan's reforms was to tie them to the land, though admittedly this may have been no more than a regularisation of previous practice. Throughout the period more and more property appears to have been settled as *waqf*, supposedly inalienable religious endowment; it has been suggested that this may well be evidence of a lack both of real security of tenure, however hard Ghazan may have tried to improve matters, and of confidence in the justness of the Mongol government even after it had become Muslim.[60]

One result of the measures taken in Ghazan's reign may have been of far-reaching importance. There does seem within limits to have been an increasing sense of identification between the Mongols and their

[57]   G. le Strange (ed.), Ḥamd Allāh Mustawfī Qazwīnī, *The Geographical Part of the Nuzhat al-qulūb* (1915), p. 27.

[58]   Lambton, *Landlord and Peasant in Persia*, p. 92.

[59]   Petrushevsky, 'The socio-economic condition of Iran under the Il-Khans', p. 495.

[60]   A. K. S. Lambton, '*Awqāf* in Persia: 7th/13th and 8th/14th centuries' (forthcoming).

subjects in Persia. Conversion to Islam removed the most conspicuous difference between them, and there is some evidence of intermarriage between Mongols and Persian women, according to both Waṣṣāf and the Mamlūk writer al-'Umarī. I once argued that assimilation must have been materially helped by Ghazan's allocation of *iqṭāʿs* to his army, and that Rashīd al-Dīn's claim that most of the Mongols were anxious to settle down and engage in the very un-Mongol practice of agriculture was a significant pointer to changing attitudes.[61] There may be some truth in this, but it has to be remembered that the *iqṭāʿ* decree was issued only very shortly before Ghazan's early death, and we cannot say to what extent it was implemented. But one way or another the Mongols were in fact largely absorbed into at least the Turkish-speaking population of Persia: they were never driven out, as they were from China. It is probable that there were a great many more Turks than Mongols in Persia, so the process may ultimately have been inevitable. But if any credit is due for the non-violent disappearance of the Mongols of Persia, it may be that some of it ought justly to accrue to Ghazan.

The Last Īlkhāns

Ghazan's policies, as far as we can tell, were continued, if with less vigour, by his brother Öljeitü. Rashīd al-Dīn remained as chief minister, though he was not without rivals and detractors. Öljeitü is perhaps best remembered for his transfer of the capital from Tabrīz to Sulṭāniyya, where his magnificent tomb survives as the most eloquent testimony to the fact that the Mongols could build as well as demolish. His son Abū Saʿīd was to be the last of the direct line of Hülegü to rule the Ilkhanate.[62] He was very young at the time of his accession, and the early part of his reign was marked by factional struggles, an ominous pointer to future events.

But from 1327 to his death in 1335 he seems to have ruled with great competence, ably assisted by the (now dead) Rashīd al-Dīn's son Ghiyāth al-Dīn. We have some difficulty in discerning what was happening in

[61]　Alizade (ed.), *Jāmiʿ al-tawārīkh*, vol. 3, p. 509; D. O. Morgan, 'The Mongol armies in Persia', *Der Islam*, 56/1 (1979), pp. 91–6.

[62]　P. Jackson's *EIr* article on Abū Saʿīd is the only really adequate recent survey of his reign.

Plate 6.6   The funeral procession of the Īlkhān Ghazan. From a Persian miniature. Bibliothèque Nationale de France MS. Persian Suppl. 1113, fol. 245v

real detail, for we possess no authority for the reign that matches Juwaynī, Rashīd al-Dīn or Waṣṣāf for earlier periods. However, Abū Saʿīd seems to have been a successful ruler, and he was the first Īlkhān to negotiate peace with the Mamlūks, in 1322. Later writers saw his reign as something of a golden age. 'The time of his government', wrote one, 'was the best period of the domination of the Mongols.'[63] And yet the Ilkhanate collapsed on Abū Saʿīd's death: we appear to have here the perplexing phenomenon of an empire which fell without having previously declined, though apparently some degeneration can be seen in the quality of the coinage, which may (in the virtual absence of contemporary written sources) suggest that all was not well. The most obvious reason for what happened is that Abū Saʿīd, despite unremitting effort, left no son by any of his numerous wives. Factions had already begun to form during his minority. There was no readily acceptable candidate of the house of Hülegü available; if anyone had forgotten the good old tanistry of the steppe, they now remembered it, to judge from their actions. The Ilkhanate was there for whoever was strong enough to seize it. None was, and as a result it broke up. Persia had no effective central government again until it was conquered by Tamerlane, late in the century.

It may well have been the contrast between Abū Saʿīd's government, whatever its faults, and the chaos that came after that made his rule seem so benevolent in retrospect. Even the Mongols were better than nothing. But Ḥamd Allāh Mustawfī, writing just four years after the end of the Ilkhanate proper, was quite clear in his own mind about what the verdict should be on the century or more of Persia's Mongol experience: 'There is no doubt that the destruction which happened on the emergence of the Mongol state and the general massacre that occurred at that time will not be repaired in a thousand years, even if no other calamity occurs; and the world will not return to the condition in which it was before that event.'[64]

Fully fledged Mongol government, then, lasted for a shorter time in Persia than in China. Perhaps the Yüan rulers were right to resist China's notorious power of assimilating her barbarian conquerors, though they only postponed their eviction for 30 years after the disintegration of the Ilkhanate; and at least the Mongols of Persia were not obliged to make the great trek back to Mongolia. Much more striking is the long survival of the Golden Horde. One explanatory factor, no doubt, is that by

---

[63]   J. B. van Loon (ed. and tr.), Abū Bakr al-Quṭbī al-Aharī *Taʾrīkh-i Shaikh Uwais* (1954), text, p. 149, tr., p. 51; see also, *inter alia*, M. Sutūda (ed.), *Awliyā Allāh Āmulī, Taʾrīkh-i Rūyān* (1969), pp. 178–80.

[64]   Le Strange (ed.), *Nuzhat al-qulūb*, p. 27.

becoming Muslims the Mongols of the Horde ultimately averted whatever little chance there might have been of a *rapprochement* between them and their Christian Russian subjects. It could be argued that if the Khāns of the Golden Horde had followed the example of Batu's son and first successor, the Christian Sartaq, rather than that of the Muslim Berke, the subsequent history of Russia might have been very different.

But this is not really very persuasive. Perry Anderson's argument is more to the point: [The unique longevity of the Golden Horde's power was due essentially to its geographical fortune. Russia was the nearest European country to the Asian steppes, and the only one which could be subjected to tributary rule by nomad conquerors from the borderlands of pastoral territory itself. The Golden Horde's capital near the Caspian was poised for military intervention and control within agrarian Russia, while itself remaining within steppe country.[65] The Mongols of the Golden Horde survived, in fact, because they kept their distance from the conquered sedentary population to a far greater extent than was possible in China or Persia. They avoided 'contamination' by settled civilisation and maintained their traditional nomadic way of life. Hence they also, for a very long time, retained their military superiority over the conquered peoples. The Mongols forgot only at their dire peril that they had won their empire by military conquest.

[65] P. Anderson, *Passages from Antiquity to Feudalism* (1974), p. 227. See further Halperin, 'Russia in the Mongol Empire'.

7

The Mongols and Europe

Europe and Asia

In 1238, so Matthew Paris tells us, an embassy arrived in Europe from the Saracens, and more particularly from the Old Man of the Mountain. The purpose of this mission, sent in the first instance to the King of France, was to try to secure aid from the Franks against the Mongol menace.[1] One of the emissaries went on to England to make his plea for help to Henry III. Peter des Roches, bishop of Winchester, a formidable figure of wide reputation and a veteran of the Emperor Frederick II's crusade of 1227–9,[2] held strong views on the proper conduct of Middle Eastern affairs. He was present at the reception of the Saracen envoys, and declared: 'Let us leave these dogs to devour one another, that they may all be consumed, and perish; and we, when we proceed against the enemies of Christ who remain, will slay them, and cleanse the face of the earth, so that all the world will be subject to the one Catholic church, and there will be one shepherd and one fold.'

There was certainly Mongol activity in the Middle East in the 1230s, and it may well have seemed especially menacing in the neighbourhood of Alamūt, the Assassin headquarters from where this very surprising embassy would appear to have originated. The arrival of the mission, if indeed such a mission did in fact find its way to England, would be eloquent testimony to the desperation of the Ismāʿīlī leaders. The whole story does strike an improbable note, and its truth has often been doubted. But intriguing support has come from numismatic evidence.

---

[1] H. R. Luard (ed.), Matthew Paris, *Chronica Majora* (1872–84), vol. 3, pp. 488–9; J. A. Giles (tr.), *Matthew Paris's English History* (1852–4), vol. 1, pp. 131–2.
[2] J. B. Gillingham, *The Angevin Empire* (1984), p. 62.

The records show that in 1241 gold coins of ten pennyweights were in the possession of Henry III's government; and it appears that the only known coins of around that date that are of the right weight are certain coins of the Ghurid sultans, struck at Ghazna in Afghanistan in the early thirteenth century. There is no certain answer to the question of how such coins might have found their way to England, but one of Professor Grierson's suggestions is that they could possibly have come with the embassy of 1238.

This is only conjecture, but its plausibility is strengthened by the later discovery of evidence that the Assassins of Alamūt possessed considerable quantities of Ghurid gold coin, some of which may have been sent to them as tribute by the Assassins of Qūhistān. So the Ismāʿīlīs of Alamūt certainly had access to Ghurid gold, and could have brought some of it to England in 1238 – 'a fine example of the complicated paths that gold coin can take', and strong evidence of the panic that the Mongols were causing in the Muslim lands, even though the Ismāʿīlīs were still nearly 20 years away from their ultimate fate.[3]

As the bishop's remarks illustrate, few in western Europe, with the exception of the insatiably curious Matthew Paris, were disposed to bother their heads about the Mongols in 1238. But Batu's great campaign in Russia had begun in the previous year, and before long some cognisance would need to be taken of this alarming irruption from the unknown east.[4]

Before the thirteenth century not a great deal was known accurately in Europe about the remoter regions of Asia. Current concepts tended still to be those of classical times, heavily dependent on the wondrous tales found in the various versions of Alexander the Great's more fictional exploits. These were augmented by the further fantasies of the Prester John story (see chapter 2), which had become widely known and universally believed since the mid twelfth century. The Far East, it was confidently assumed, was a land of peace, wealth and good government, and thus it could be contrasted favourably with troubled and disordered Christendom. On the other hand it also seemed that much of the east

---

[3]   P. Grierson, 'Muslim coins in thirteenth century England', in D. K. Kouymjian (ed.), *Studies in Honor of George C. Miles* (1974), pp. 387–91. A. H. Morton, 'Ghūrid gold en route to England?', *Iran*, 16 (1978), pp. 167–70: quotation at p. 170.

[4]   On the whole question of European perceptions of and reactions to the Mongols before 1270, see the useful treatment in G. A. Bezzola, *Die Mongolen in abendländischer Sicht (1220–1270)* (1974).

was peopled by strange and physically deformed monsters: beings with no heads, or one foot, and the like. Oddly enough the Chinese had remarkably similar ideas about the Far West, and peopled it with much the same varieties of monsters.[5]

The vast expansion of European travel of various kinds that occurred in Mongol-ruled Asia did inflict some damage on these firmly held notions. But the monsters, at least, were not easily given up. The papal envoy John of Marignolli, who was in China in the mid fourteenth century, thought that he had found part of the explanation of the Asiatic monsters when he reached India. 'The truth', he suggested, 'is that no such people do exist as nations, though there may be an individual monster here and there. Nor is there any people at all such as has been invented, who have but one foot which they use to shade themselves withal. But as all the Indians commonly go naked, they are in the habit of carrying a thing like a little tent-roof on a cane handle, which they open out at will as a protection against sun or rain. . . . I brought one to Florence with me. And this it is which the poets have converted into a foot.'[6] Neither the attempted debunking of the monopods nor the umbrella appears to have caught on.

A century earlier, John of Plano Carpini had been told the usual stories. They were not peculiar to the Christians: Hamd Allāh Mustawfī Qazwīnī's geographical work, the *Nuzhat al-qulūb*, at one point offers the laconic information 'Here live the dog-headed men.' Of these old favourites, Carpini was given to understand that 'they would speak two words like human beings and the third they would bark like a dog, and they broke into barking in this way at intervals; however, they always came back to the matter in hand, so it was possible to understand what they were talking about'.[7] Asia had of course been found to be rather large, and no amount of travelling about it would really serve to disprove the possibility that the cherished monsters still existed in some unexplored corner of the continent.

Whatever the popularity of Prester John or the monsters, no one had heard of the Mongols. Chingiz Khān's conquests in Central Asia and China, unsurprisingly, went unnoticed. The Russians received their

---

[5]   See I. de Rachewiltz, *Papal Envoys to the Great Khans* (1971), chapter 1.

[6]   A. van Den Wyngaert, *Sinica Franciscana*, vol. 1 (1929), p. 546; H. Yule and H. Cordier (trs), *Cathay and the Way Thither* (1913–16), vol. 3, p. 256.

[7]   Van Den Wyngaert, *Sinica Franciscana*, p. 74; tr. C. Dawson (ed.), *The Mongol Mission* (1955), p. 31.

incomprehensible shock from Jebei and Sübodei, passing through on their way back to Mongolia in the 1220s, but apart from that the first news to reach Europe was another garbled story to be incorporated into the Prester John legend. In 1221 the Crusaders were encamped at Damietta in Egypt. News reached them there of a mysterious King David, Christian king of India. ('India' had geographical implications in the Middle Ages which were not entirely what we would expect: it included Ethiopia.[8]) King David was reported to be attacking the Muslims, so aid was clearly on the way to the Crusaders. In versions of the tale, David is variously identified with Prester John or (in view of the fact that the original priest-king would by now be at least 100 years old) his son or grandson.[9] Dr de Rachewiltz thinks that these encouraging tidings, which James of Vitry passed on to Rome in a letter to the Pope, may have played a part in persuading the Crusaders to refuse the sultan of Egypt's offer of peace and in inducing them to embark on their disastrous march towards Cairo.

King David did not come to the rescue; for the great Christian monarch, in this (possibly Nestorian) fabrication, must presumably have been based wishfully on Chingiz Khān, or conceivably on a conflation of Chingiz with Küchlüg the Naiman. David's attack on the Muslims would have been a reflection of Chingiz's campaign against the Khwārazm-shāh. The Mongols once again dropped out of Europe's sight.

The First Direct Contacts

The first European to have brought back accurate information about the Mongols was Friar Julian of Hungary, who travelled east as an emissary of King Béla IV of Hungary in 1234–5 and 1237. On the latter occasion his mission was interrupted by the beginnings of Batu's Russian campaign.[10] The invasion of eastern Europe woke Christendom up very sharply, as we can see from the quantity of letters from a number of

---

[8] See C. F. Beckingham, *The Achievements of Prester John* (1966), pp. 16–19; 'The quest for Prester John', *Bulletin of the John Rylands University Library of Manchester*, 62/2 (1980), pp. 299–300.

[9] See de Rachewiltz, *Papal Envoys to the Great Khans*, pp. 39–40.

[10] D. Sinor, 'Un voyageur du treizième siècle: le Dominicain Julien de Hongrie', *Bulletin of the School of Oriental and African Studies*, 14/3 (1952), pp. 589–602; de Rachewiltz, *Papal Envoys to the Great Khans*, pp. 41–2.

concerned clergy and princes that Matthew Paris reproduces in his *Chronica Majora*.[11] These include a circular letter from Frederick II to his fellow monarchs, urging them to assemble forces and to unite against this new peril. Matthew Paris also gives us some insight into the kinds of explanation for the sudden appearance of the Mongols that were being canvassed: they were the lost ten tribes of Israel, albeit lacking any knowledge of Hebrew; or it was a plot hatched by the Emperor Frederick, his object being to obtain the homage of the King of Hungary. The last allegation shocked the chronicler: 'God forbid' he exclaimed, 'that so much wickedness should be lurking in any one mortal body!'

But nothing was done. Pope and Emperor allowed no mere Mongol invasion to interrupt their bickerings, and if Batu had not turned back in 1242 he would not have had to encounter a formidable pan-European force. Fortunately he did turn back, and the Mongols never returned in full strength. No one, however, knew at the time that this would be so. The possibility of a renewed invasion of the part of this virtually unknown people had therefore to be faced.

It fell to Innocent IV, after his election to the papacy in 1243, to take effective action to clarify the situation.[12] The question of the Mongols was placed on the agenda of the Council of Lyons in 1245, and the result was the despatch of three embassies to Mongol territory. These were entrusted to members of the mendicant orders: both orders were already concerned with missionary work in the Middle East, and the Dominicans had been first in the field in the evangelisation of eastern Europe and the Qipchaq lands. Two Dominican missions were sent by the Middle Eastern route; they were to try to contact the Mongol

---

[11]   See J. J. Saunders, 'Matthew Paris and the Mongols', in T. A. Sandquist and M. R. Powicke (eds), *Essays in Medieval History presented to Bertie Wilkinson* (1969), pp. 124ff.

[12]   On the relations between the Papacy and the Mongols the two standard works are now de Rachewiltz, *Papal Envoys to the Great Khans* and Richard's masterly synthesis of work on the subject (J. Richard, *La Papauté et les missions d'Orient au moyen âge (XII–XVe siècles)* (1977). Richard's own other contributions are conveniently collected in three volumes of the Variorum Reprint series: *Orient et Occident au moyen âge: contacts et relations (XIIe–XVe s.)* (1976), *Les relations entre l'Orient et L'Occident au moyen âge: études et documents* (1977) and *Croisés, missionaires et voyageurs* (1983). On the early stages of the Papal-Mongol relationship, P. Pelliot, 'Les Mongols et la Papauté', *Revue de l'Orient chrétien*, 23 (1922–3), pp. 3–30, 24 (1924), pp. 225–335, 28 (1932), pp. 3–84, should still be consulted.

authorities and also to establish relations with the schismatic churches of the region, for the achievement of church union under papal leadership was also among Innocent's ambitions. The mission of Andrew of Longjumeau seems to have had little result apart from some encouraging discussions with the Nestorians in north-west Persia; but his fellow Dominican Ascelinus did succeed in reaching the camp of Baiju, the Mongol commander in western Asia, and indeed in grievously offending him. We know a good deal of Ascelinus's travels from his companion Simon of St Quentin's account.[13] Only the Franciscan mission of John of Plano Carpini, which travelled by the eastern European route, managed to penetrate as far as Mongolia.

The results of Innocent's initiative were useful rather than comforting. Christendom now possessed, particularly in the information contained in Carpini's report, a full and accurate idea of the Mongols' military strength and of what would be the necessary measures if the Mongols were to be resisted. But the prospects of persuading them to desist from their conquests and massacres or to become Christians did not appear good. The Pope's pleas for moderation in Mongol conduct fell on deaf ears, and the message that came back to Europe was an uncompromising one: the Pope, with the other European potentates, was required to present himself forthwith at the court of the Great Khān to make his submission. If he did not do so he could expect to have to take the unspecified but unmistakable consequences. This emerged clearly from the letter of the Great Khān Güyük to the Pope, which Carpini brought back. It exists in Latin translations,[14] and the 'original' Persian version, authenticated with Güyük's seal, still survives, though that is itself a translation of a Mongolian or Turkish original.[15]

Analysis of this letter and of others from the period has shown how clearly they reflect the Mongol view of the world.[16] As de Rachewiltz puts it, 'gradually they came to conceive the world as the Mongol

[13]   J. Richard (ed.), Simon de Saint-Quentin, *Histoire des Tartares* (1965).

[14]   K.-E. Lupprian (ed.), *Die Beziehungen der Päpste zu islamischen und mongolischen Herrschern im 13. Jahrhundert anhand ihres Briefwechsels* (1981), pp. 182–7, for the texts.

[15]   Translation of the Persian in de Rachewiltz, *Papal Envoys to the Great Khans*, pp. 213–14; French translation in Lupprian, *Die Beziehungen der Päpste*, pp. 186–9.

[16]   See E. Voegelin, 'The Mongol orders of submission to European powers, 1245–1255', *Byzantion*, 15 (1940–1), pp. 378–413.

empire-in-the-making, whose leaders by Heavenly appointment were Chingis Khan's successors. Even though many nations were still outside the Great Khan's control, they were nevertheless regarded as potential members of this universal Mongol empire.'[17] In these circumstances there was no possibility of negotiations of equal terms with the Mongols: in their opinion any ruler who had not submitted to them, whether or not he had ever heard of the Mongols, had the status of a rebel against the divinely ordained government of the world. In his account of the *quriltai* which decided on the invasion of Europe, Juwaynī says that 'they deliberated together concerning the extirpation and subjugation of all the remaining *rebels (ṭughāt)*.'[18] In this climate, Mongol–European relations were unlikely to prove fruitful.

For a time in the late 1240s it looked as though the situation might be showing signs of improvement. Louis IX of France, in Cyprus in 1248 to prepare for his crusade to Egypt, received two Nestorian ambassadors from Eljigidei, by that time the Mongol commander in the Middle East.[19] These ambassadors evidently hoped that the forthcoming crusade might be exploited to further Mongol designs against the Muslims: they gave St Louis a singularly (and presumably deliberately) misleading impression of the Mongols' goodwill towards Christianity, and in oral communications the envoys apparently said that both Eljigidei and Güyük had been converted to Christianity. It is perhaps worth noting that both Juwaynī and – probably repeating him – Bar Hebraeus say the same of Güyük: the Great Khān may at least have shown sympathy with the Christian faith. King Louis, much impressed, sent off the already experienced Andrew of Longjumeau with a richly ornamented portable chapel as a present for the royal convert.

But when Andrew arrived at Eljigidei's camp in 1249 he found that the political situation in the Mongol Empire had changed. Güyük had died in 1248, and pending the accession of a new Great Khān the empire was under the regency of his widow, Oghul-Qaimish. Eljigidei sent Louis's envoys on to Oghul-Qaimish's camp in Central Asia. There they

---

[17]   De Rachewiltz, *Papal Envoys to the Great Khans*, p. 104.

[18]   M. M. Qazwīnī (ed.), 'Aṭā Malik Juwaynī, *Ta'rīkh-i Jahān Gushā*, vol. 1 (1912), p. 224; tr. J. A. Boyle, *The History of the World Conqueror* (1958), vol. 1, pp. 268–9.

[19]   The part played by Louis IX in negotiations with the Mongols has now for the first time been done full justice in a biography of the king: J. Richard, *Saint-Louis, roi d'une France féodale, soutien de la Terre Sainte* (1983).

by no means received the friendly reception they must have expected. The regent chose to interpret their mission as an acknowledgement of Frankish submission, and sent them home with the usual message: bring tribute or face punishment. It has been suggested[20] that Oghul-Qaimish's attitude is to be explained as an attempt to buttress her own increasingly weak political position; and indeed she was executed after the descendants of Ögedei lost the struggle for power in 1251. This would have been small consolation to King Louis, who by the time that Andrew returned in 1251 had already endured the failure of his crusade and his own captivity in Egypt. His friend and biographer Joinville tells us that 'the King, you may be sure, repented of having sent him (the Great Khān) his ambassadors'.[21]

It is therefore hardly surprising that Louis set his face against sending any more envoys to the Mongols. When Friar William of Rubruck travelled to Mongolia in 1253–5 he did so on his own initiative, and as a missionary rather than as an ambassador. The King was not prepared to risk receiving any more rebuffs, though he was certainly interested in hearing William's report on his return. As we have seen, however, that report was given very little publicity until more recent times, even though it is arguably the most acute account of the Mongols to have come from any European pen.

The Īlkhāns and Western Christendom

A real change in the Mongol attitude towards Europe did come about, but not until after 1260. Events around that time marked the break-up of Mongol unity, and the Īlkhāns of Persia, faced with the hostility both of the Mamlūk regime in Egypt and of their cousins of the Golden Horde, speedily dropped the old hauteur and began to see the Christian powers as potentially useful allies. The basic idea behind such projects for alliance was a combined operation against the Mamlūks: a crusading force would be sent from Europe and its activities would be co-ordinated with an Ilkhanid invasion of Syria. Should Syria be conquered by the allies, the Crusaders would again take possession of Jerusalem; and

---

[20]   De Rachewiltz, *Papal Envoys to the Great Khans*, p. 123.
[21]   R. Hague (tr.), *The Life of St. Louis by John of Joinville* (1955), para. 492, p. 149.

there was always the tantalising possibility that the Mongols would themselves become Christian converts.[22]

These negotiations, as we now know, were initiated by Hülegü in 1262, when he sent his letter, recently discovered, to Louis IX. We cannot in fact be certain that Louis ever received the letter: Professor Richard's attempt to identify a Mongol embassy in Paris in 1262 with the delivery of the letter from Persia is interesting, but that particular embassy seems more likely to have been sent by Berke of the Golden Horde.[23] But from 1263 until well into the fourteenth century repeated attempts were made to arrange an alliance, and these appear to have been entered into in perfectly good faith by both sides. We possess the texts of numerous letters sent in both directions. The Popes were always enthusiastic, as much for evangelistic as for specifically crusading reasons, and several western monarchs also treated the idea of an alliance seriously. The letter of the Īlkhān Arghun to Philip the Fair of France, sent in 1289, illustrates well the change in the tone of Mongol communications with Christendom, compared with the years before 1260:

> We agree to your proposition which you conveyed to Us last year . . . 'If the armies of the Īlkhān go to war against Egypt, We too shall set out from here and go to war and to attack . . . in a common operation.' And We decided . . . after reporting to heaven, to mount our horses in the last month of winter [1290] . . . and to dismount outside Damascus on the 15th of the first month in spring [1291]. . . . If by the authority of heaven, We conquer those people, We shall give you Jerusalem. If . . . you should fail to meet the appropriate day, and thus lead our armies into an abortive action, would that be fitting? Even if you should later regret it, what use would that be to you?[24]

---

[22] Relation between the Īlkhāns and western Christendom are examined in J. A. Boyle, 'The Il-Khans of Persia and the princes of Europe', *Central Asiatic Journal*, 20/1–2 (1976), pp. 25–40, D. Sinor, 'The Mongols and Western Europe', in K. M. Setton (ed.), *A History of the Crusades*, vol. 3 (1975), pp. 513–44, and (briefly but perceptively) J. Richard, 'The Mongols and the Franks', *Journal of Asian History*, 3 (1969), pp. 45–57.

[23] P. Meyvaert, 'An unknown letter of Hulagu, Il-Khan of Persia, to King Louis IX of France', *Viator*, 11 (1980), pp. 245–59; J. Richard, 'Une ambassade mongole à Paris en 1262', *Journal des Savants*, 1979, pp. 295–303; P. Jackson, 'The dissolution of the Mongol Empire', *Central Asiatic Journal*, 22 (1978), p. 236, n. 228.

[24] B. Spuler (tr.), *History of the Mongols* (1972), pp. 141–2.

The fact that the Mongols of Persia had gone over to Islam in 1295 seems not to have registered in Europe. Admittedly the Īlkhāns did not go out of their way to force this information undiplomatically down Christian throats. Thus it was that when Edward II of England wrote to Öljeitü in 1307 – and by that date Öljeitü had definitely settled on Islam – he found it appropriate to include in his letter 'a venomous attack on "the abominable sect of Mohammed", which Öljeitü is asked to extirpate'.[25] The conversion of the Īlkhāns to Islam had made no difference to their political enmity towards the Mamlūks, and only the Mamlūk–Ilkhanid peace treaty of 1322 caused the Mongols of Persia to lose all interest in an alliance with the Christian powers.

By this time the Christians had been deprived of their last foothold in Syria: Acre had fallen to the forces of the Mamlūk sultan al-Ashraf Khalīl in 1291. No really effective joint action had ever been organised: in thirteenth-century conditions the problems of co-ordination appear to have been insuperable. The loss of Acre did not bring negotiations to an end. Indeed, at one point Europe was swept with rumours that the Mongols had actually taken Jerusalem from the Mamlūks and had returned it to Christian rule.[26] Although this had not in fact happened, the stories did reflect the reality of Ghazan's remarkable successes in 1299–1300, when he drove the Mamlūk forces completely out of Syria, only to withdraw again to Persia. In 1302 Ghazan wrote to Pope Boniface VIII, yet again proposing combined operations. His envoy on this occasion was a Genoese servant of the Īlkhāns, Buscarello Ghisolfi, who had played for many years an important part as a go-between in Ilkhanid–European relations.[27] In this he was by no means unusual. It was standard Mongol practice to make use as ambassadors of individuals in their service who had originally come from the lands to which they were sent as envoys. Italian merchants were especially prominent.[28] One Italian, known as Isol the Pisan (Zolo di Anastasio), even acted as Öljeitü's Christian godfather.[29]

[25]   Sinor, 'The Mongols and Western Europe', p. 538.

[26]   S. Schein, '*Gesta Dei per Mongolos 1300*. The genesis of a non-event', *English Historical Review*, 94 (1979), pp. 805–19.

[27]   J. A. Boyle, 'The Il-Khans of Persia and the princes of Europe', *Central Asiatic Journal*, 20/1–2 (1976), pp. 25–40.

[28]   See L. Petech, 'Les marchands italiens dans l'empire mongol', *Journal Asiatique*, 250 (1962), pp. 549–74.

[29]   J. Richard, 'Isol le Pisan: un aventurier franc gouverneur d'une province mongole?', *Central Asiatic Journal*, 14 (1970), pp. 186–94.

Contacts were maintained under Öljeitü; we have seen that he heard from Edward II of England, and a letter sent to Philip the Fair of France has survived.[30] But after Öljeitü's reign attempts at alliance at last ceased. Commercial relations continued to flourish, and missionary efforts were maintained. As late as 1318 the Pope created an archbishopric of Sulṭāniyya.[31] This was part of the process of rationalisation of the Asian missionary enterprise instituted by Pope John XXII: the Dominicans were given responsibility for the Ilkhanate, Central Asia and India, while the Franciscans were to take charge of the nearer east, the Golden Horde, Mongolia and China. The Franciscan mission was under the supervision of the Archbishop of Khan-baliq, i.e. Ta-tu, Peking. We have encountered the first Catholic archbishop in China, John of Monte Corvino (see chapter 5), who had arrived in China in 1294 and had been created archbishop in 1307. He had enjoyed some success, though not among the native Chinese. Three of his letters home survive, together with others written by members of his mission.[32] He died in China, and the Franciscan mission did not last beyond the fall of the Yüan Dynasty. The archdiocese of Sulṭāniyya, however, was still in existence at the beginning of the fifteenth century.

In the 1320s one William Adam was briefly Archbishop of Sulṭāniyya. In 1316 or 1317 he had produced perhaps the last major proposal for a workable alliance between Europe and the Īlkhāns. It is known as *De modo Sarracenos extirpandi*. This envisaged the construction of a naval squadron in the Indian Ocean, to be manned by the Genoese, which was to cut off the Mamlūk sultanate's vital trade lifeline with the east.[33] Nothing came of the scheme. The Īlkhān at the time of Adam's memorandum was Abū Saʿīd, who was to make peace with the Mamlūks a very few years later, and thus end all possibility of joint action against them.

---

[30]   A. Mostaert and F. W. Cleaves, *Les Lettres de 1289 et 1305 des ilkhans Arγun et Ölǰeitü à Philippe le Bel* (1962); Spuler, *History of the Mongols*, pp. 142–3.

[31]   See Richard, *La Papauté*, part 4.

[32]   Van Den Wyngaert, *Sinica Franciscana*, vol. 1, pp. 335–77; Dawson, *The Mongol Mission*, pp. 224–37.

[33]   See Beckingham, 'The quest for Prester John', pp. 295–9.

Eastern Images of Europe

The period of optimism, when the Popes and the European monarchs on the one side and the Īlkhāns on the other were genuinely hopeful of organising successful military action, did leave two interesting literary memorials. These are the travel narrative of Rabban Ṣaumā and the *History of the Franks* of Rashīd al-Dīn. It may well be that a study of these two documents will give us more insight into Mongol–European relations than any amount of detailed retailing of the comings and goings of ambassadors and the delivery of letters.

The Nestorian monk Rabban Ṣaumā was sent to Europe by Arghun in 1287. He wrote in Persian an account of his travels, which in an abridged Syriac translation ultimately found its way into the biography of his former companion and disciple Yaballāhā, whose fortunes were considered in the previous chapter. The Persian original of the travel narrative has not come to light.

Ṣaumā's route took him to Constantinople, by ship to Naples and from there to Rome, Genoa, Paris, Gascony and back to Rome. He had audiences with the Byzantine Emperor Andronicus II, the cardinals in Rome (Pope Honorius IV having died before his arrival), Philip the Fair of France, Edward I of England and, on his return to Rome, the newly elected Pope Nicholas IV who was to give his name to Arghun's son Öljeitü. Ṣaumā's account of these journeys is fascinating, and stands as the only known Asian equivalent to the narratives of Carpini, Rubruck and Marco Polo.

His picture of Europe is a very favourable one – much more so than one can imagine coming from the pen of a Muslim writer. He was a Christian priest, coming to what he was happy to acknowledge as the headquarters of Christianity. His chief passion in life was the cult of relics, and of these Rome in particular could offer him an unsurpassable feast. Before his final departure he badgered Nicholas IV for some to take back to Persia. The Pope gave in with an ill grace: 'If we had been in the habit of giving away these relics to the people (who come) in myriads, even though the relics were as large as mountains, they would have come to an end long ago. But since thou hast come from a far country, we will give thee a few.'[34]

---

[34] E. A. W. Budge (tr.), *The Monks of Ḳūblāi Khān, Emperor of China* (1928), p. 195.

Possibly the oddest feature of Ṣaumā's relations with cardinals and Pope is that they apparently failed to discover that he, as a Nestorian, was a heretic. He was asked to celebrate Mass before Edward I, and even before the assembled cardinals and Pope. According to Ṣaumā, 'they rejoiced, and said, "The language is different, but the use is the same."'[35] Lengthy theological disputation with the cardinals did not reveal significant doctrinal differences. They tried to catch him out on the 'filioque' clause in the Creed, but he seems to have given as good as he got, or so he says. Admittedly the cardinals would not necessarily have been on the look-out for specifically Nestorian errors since the Nestorians themselves never used the term, preferring the description 'Eastern Christians'. It may be that it was thought impolitic to charge an ambassador with heresy, especially since good relations with his Mongol master were so much desired. We have also to take into account the great enthusiasm in Rome for the union of churches, to which Ṣaumā's willingness to admit the Pope's supremacy over all Christians no doubt gave an encouraging boost. Lastly we may be inclined to question how thoroughly either the cardinals or indeed Ṣaumā himself were acquainted with the Christological controversies of the early centuries AD which had originally given rise to the Nestorian schism.

There was much in Europe besides the churches and relics of Rome that impressed Ṣaumā. In Naples, *en route* to Rome, he had a grandstand view of a sea battle between the Neapolitan and Aragonese fleets. While the battle was going on, 'Rabban Ṣaumā and his companions sat upon the roof of the mansion in which they lived, and they admired the way in which the Franks waged war, for they attacked none of the people except those who were actually combatants.'[36] Ṣaumā's experience of living in the Mongol Empire had evidently accustomed him to a rather different style of warfare.

In Paris, apart from the local stocks of relics it was the learned community that most captured Ṣaumā's attention. To anyone who taught in a modern university before the 1980s his remarks must have a curiously familiar ring: 'There were in it thirty thousand scholars . . . and they engaged constantly in writing (theses), and all these pupils received money for subsistence from the king.'[37]

Europe, then, is presented to Ṣaumā's readers (whoever he may have intended that they should be) as a land steeped in Christian traditions and relics, ruled by mighty and gracious potentates. But this book of

[35]   Ibid., p. 190.
[36]   Ibid., p. 171.
[37]   Ibid., p. 183–4.

Ṣaumā's is unique, an isolated document; and it is written, in the version that has been passed down, in Syriac, a minority language. It is a Christian minority report, and it derives its interest from its uniqueness, the vivid nature of its observation, and the fact that it does represent the point of view of a part of Persian society which, for a brief time, was enjoying a degree of influence and royal favour that it had never known before and was never to see again. It offers us some understanding of the mind of at least one of those who worked with enthusiasm for a Mongol–European *rapprochement* in the thirteenth century. But the views it puts forward were very far from representing the standpoint of Muslim Persian society. For that we must turn as so often before to the works of Rashīd al-Dīn.

His *History of the Franks*[38] formed part of the second instalment of his great historical encyclopaedia, the *Jāmi' al-tawārīkh*, the section that had been commissioned by Öljeitü as a memorial to his brother Ghazan. It has been said that it is apparently 'the only attempt made by a mediaeval Muslim historian at an outline of the history of the Christian West',[39] and it is this rather than any new information it gives that makes it of interest. It consists of two parts: the first a survey of Europe, country by country; the second an annalistic account of European history from the birth of Christ to the time of writing, with events tabulated under the headings of the reigns of popes and emperors – western emperors after Charlemagne.

Its chief literary source appears to be the late-thirteenth-century chronicle of Martin of Troppau, otherwise known as Martinus Polonus. Martin was a Dominican who died in 1279 as bishop of Gnesen. His work was not apparently of any great merit, but it was extraordinarily popular, still surviving in numerous manuscripts and having inspired, it seems, more continuations than any other medieval chronicle.[40] Presumably it is this that explains how a copy of it found its way to Persia:

---

[38]   There are two editions of the *History of the Franks*: K. Jahn (ed. and tr.), *Histoire universelle de Rašīd al-Dīn Faḍl Allāh Abul Khair. 1. Histoire des Francs* (1951), and K. Jahn (ed. and tr.), *Die Frankengeschichte des Rašīd ad-Dīn* (1977). The former gives a printed Persian text and a French translation; the latter, facsimiles of early MSS (containing interesting illustrations) and a German translation. The 1977 edition is slightly but not significantly more complete. I have given references to the 1951 edition.

[39]   B. Lewis, 'The Muslim discovery of Europe', in his *Islam in History* (1973), p. 98.

[40]   See Jahn, *Histoire universelle*, introduction; D. Hay, *Annalists and Historians* (1977), pp. 64 and 49.

it may very well have been brought by one of Martin's fellow Dominicans. Rashīd al-Dīn supplemented his Martin of Troppau material with other gleanings, no doubt including what could be learned from western envoys and merchants, though he names none.

The *History of the Franks* contains strong reminders that it was based on a work by a former official at the papal court. A striking example of this is Rashīd al-Dīn's listing of the principal rulers of Europe. There is no doubt about which of them has priority: 'First is the Pope, which means father of fathers; and he is considered the caliph (i.e. representative) of the Messiah; and then the Emperor . . . and then the King of France.'[41] The title of Emperor is defined as *sulṭān-i salāṭīn*, sultan of sultans; the King of France, *raydāfrans* (which he seems to suppose to be a single word, like Emperor) is interpreted as meaning *pādishāh-i pādishāhān*, king of kings. He remarks that the Empire is elective while the kingdom of France is hereditary – a fair distinction even if the Capetians never precisely defined their throne as hereditary.[42] It is a distinction that is carefully brought out in the Arabic-Persian terminology used: for a sultan, at least in theory, was elected while a pādishāh, a king, succeeded by hereditary right. Similarly it would have been hard to translate 'Vicar of Christ' more exactly than by *khalīfa-i masīḥ*.

We are also given a surprising account of the part played by the Pope in crowning the Emperor. It appears that the Pope uses the bent head and neck of the Emperor as a step from which to mount his horse: only after this ritual has been performed can the Emperor be proclaimed. Curiously, Rabban Ṣaumā relates what appears to be a cognate story which he heard in Rome. According to him, at an imperial coronation the Pope 'takes up the crown with his feet, and clothes the Emperor with it . . . [to show], as they say, that priesthood reigneth over sovereignty'.[43] Throughout, then, Rashīd al-Dīn exhibits a markedly papal bias – the struggle between the papacy and the Emperor Frederick II is represented as an imperial revolt – but this merely shows the extent to which he was at the mercy of his sources.

Rashīd al-Dīn sometimes for one reason or another surprises us with his information. He outdoes Rabban Ṣaumā by ascribing 100,000 students to the city of Paris; he knows that there are no 'poisonous reptiles' in Ireland; he understands very well the activities of the Teutonic Knights

---

[41]   Jahn, *Histoire universelle*, text, p. 2; tr., p. 15.
[42]   R. Fawtier, *The Capetian Kings of France* (1960), pp. 49–50.
[43]   Jahn, *Histoire universelle*, text, p. 3; tr., p. 16; Budge, *The Monks of Kūblāi Khān*, pp. 178–9.

Plate 7.1 Popes (on the left) and Emperors (on the right). From a manuscript of Rashīd al-Dīn's *History of the Franks*. Topkapi Palace Museum, Istanbul, MS. H. 2154 fol. 303

in Prussia.[44] But overall the reader of this section of the *Jāmiʿ al-tawārīkh* is likely to feel that the author was performing here more a duty than a labour of love. The second part of his history was to contain accounts of the peoples with whom the Mongols had come into contact, so for the sake of completeness the Franks had to be included. The description of Europe is certainly interesting, but the annalistic section is bare and lifeless in a way that is not true of any other part of the *Jami' al-tawārīkh*.

We have to search very hard to find references to the Franks in other parts of Rashīd al-Dīn's work. While there are lists in his main chronicle of Muslim and Chinese rulers, and references to his separate *History of China*, there are none to Frankish kings or to his Frankish chronicle. It is in no way integrated into the work as a whole. Indeed there seems almost to have been a deliberate suppression of information on the Franks. Not once is there so much as a hint of the comings and goings of European ambassadors to the Ilkhanate, and this was a traffic in which it is hard to believe that Rashīd al-Dīn, as chief minister, was not personally involved.

There is a very revealing reference to the embassy with which Marco Polo came back from China. In Polo's account, Qubilai unwillingly permitted Marco, with his father and uncle, to return to Venice because he needed envoys to accompany a Mongol princess who was being sent from China as a bride for the Īlkhān Arghun. The Polos therefore travelled, according to Marco, as official emissaries of the Great Khan with the princess and three ambassadors who had been sent to China by Arghun and were now returning. Rashīd al-Dīn gives an account of the party's arrival in Persia. It confirms the Polo version in every way – the one survivor of Arghun's ambassadors is named in effect identically, the princess is married to Ghazan because Arghun is dead, and so on – but with one difference. Neither here nor anywhere else are the Polos named, nor is the very existence of such people so much as mentioned.[45]

It might be argued that the significance of this is that Marco Polo was once again exaggerating his own importance as a servant of the Mongols. This is possible, but it is more likely to be evidence that Rashīd al-Dīn shared the traditional Muslim prejudices about the Franks. Throughout the Middle Ages Muslims regarded Europe as a remote and

[44]   Jahn, *Histoire universelle*, text, p. 5; tr., pp. 18–19.
[45]   A. Ricci (tr.), *The Travels of Marco Polo* (1931), pp. 15–17; A. A. Alizade (ed.), Rashīd al-Dīn, *Jāmiʿ al-tawārīkh*, vol. 3 (1957), p. 280. See J. A. Boyle, 'Rashīd al-Dīn and the Franks', *Central Asiatic Journal*, 14 (1970), pp. 62–7.

Plate 7.2   A European view of the Great Khān Qubilai (reigned 1260–94) with Niccolò and Maffeo Polo (Marco's father and uncle). From an English manuscript of *c.* 1400. The Bodleian Library, University of Oxford, MS. Bodl. 264, fol. 219r

barbarous area, hardly worthy of the attention of a civilised man. Even the twelfth-century Syrian nobleman Usāma ibn Munqidh, who knew the Crusading variety of Frank well, could write in his justly celebrated autobiography such words as these: 'Mysterious are the works of the Creator, the author of all things! When one comes to recount cases regarding the Franks, he cannot but glorify Allāh (exalted is He!) and sanctify Him, for he sees them as animals possessing the virtues of courage and fighting, but nothing else; just as animals have only the virtues of strength and carrying loads.'[46]

---

[46]   P. K. Hitti (tr.), *An Arab-Syrian Gentleman and Warrior in the Period of the Crusades* (1929), p. 161.

The Mongol conquests had changed much for the Islamic world, but they had not changed its attitude towards Christendom. It has been suggested that Rashīd al-Dīn might have suppressed material about the Franks in order to avoid possible discredit to his sovereigns, since they were now converts to Islam but were also in negotiation with the infidel against their fellow Muslims in Egypt. But this seems unduly conspiracy minded. No prejudice against non-Muslims as such prevented Rashīd al-Dīn from giving full accounts of India and China, or from frankly acknowledging the excellent relations that existed between the Īlkhāns and the Great Khān in Peking, who was certainly not a Muslim. The very uniqueness of the *History of the Franks* speaks for itself, and the more eloquently when we see that Rashīd al-Dīn's view of Christendom, the view even of the man whom Boyle called 'the first world historian', remained the end product of centuries of prejudice and contempt. The Islamic world had seen Europe, not without reason, as an inferior civilisation which need not be taken seriously. By the fourteenth century this perspective was beginning to be out of date. But it was not until the Ottoman period that what Lewis calls 'the Muslim discovery of Europe' really came to anything; and even then. Muslim curiosity about the west never matched European interest in the east.[47]

The Mongol Legacy

The impact of the Mongol conquests on Asian knowledge or understanding of Europe seems, then, to have been slight. Muslim attitudes remained essentially unchanged, and the presence of Europeans in China, whether as merchants, missionaries or Mongol government servants, appears to have made little impression on the Chinese consciousness. For many more centuries China remained the most self-sufficient culturally of all the great civilisations. Even within the Mongol Empire there was a marked difference between Middle Eastern and Chinese attitudes. The Muslims of western Asia may have despised the Europeans, but they were prepared to learn from the Chinese. The most visually striking example of this is to be found in Persian miniature painting of the period. The rocks, the trees and the clouds frequently have a very Chinese look about them. But in this as in other fields 'cultural inter-

---

[47]   See Lewis, 'The Muslim discovery of Europe' and *The Muslim Discovery of Europe* (1982).

change' 'was a one-way traffic under the Mongols'.[48] There are no Persian motifs in the Chinese art of the Yüan Dynasty. The many Middle Easterners who found their way to China were valued by the Chinese only for whatever technical skills they might possess.

European knowledge of Asia, by contrast, did undeniably expand enormously, even if the full realisation of this knowledge's potential had to await the great Age of Discovery. Marco Polo was regarded with some incredulity, but his book did influence European notions of geography. From the fourteenth century Polo was greatly exceeded in popularity by the *Travels* of Sir John Mandeville, a fictional work full of monsters and marvels. The fact that Mandeville and the Alexander Romance seem to have been regarded as at least as 'true' as Marco Polo should caution us against over-estimating the transformation in Europe's knowledge of the east.

Yet even Mandeville drew on sources better than himself, and a good deal of accurate information is buried among the tall stories. The commercial traffic with Mongol Asia in the fourteenth century was sufficiently important to justify the inclusion of a detailed discussion of Asian trade routes in a merchant's handbook by Francesco Pegolotti.[49] Even if Pegolotti's most often quoted sentence – 'the road you travel from Tana [at the mouth of the Don] to Cathay is perfectly safe, according to what the merchants say who have used it'[50] – may make us wonder about the reliability of his informants, the existence of the book is an important fact in itself. There were a great many European merchants in the Mongol Empire, a considerable number of missionaries, and some ambassadors. Most of these have left no record of their Asiatic travels, or at least none that has survived to the present day. But this does not necessarily mean that what they told people when they came home had no effect on contemporary notions of the world. Marco Polo received his due in the end: 200 years after his return to Venice his book 'was still the best account of the Far East available to Europeans'.[51] When Christopher Columbus set sail from Spain in 1492 he was heading for Cathay, the land of the Great Khān. His copy of the 1485 edition of

[48]   H. Franke, 'Sino-western contacts under the Mongol Empire', *Journal of the Hong Kong Branch of the Royal Asiatic Society*, 6 (1966), p. 69.

[49]   A. Evans (ed.), Francesco Pegolotti, *La Pratica della Mercatura* (1936).

[50]   H. Yule and H. Cordier (trs), *Cathay and the Way Thither* (1913–16), vol. 3, p. 152.

[51]   J. H. Parry, *The Age of Reconnaissance* (1964), p. 24.

Plate 7.3 Part of the Catalan Atlas of 1375, based on the information in Marco Polo's *Travels*. Bibliothèque Nationale de France Map Esp. 30, fol. 3v and 4

Marco Polo's *Travels* is still extant in Seville,[52] and his proposals for his voyage were based partly on miscalculations founded upon his reading of Marco. This was not an asset when it came to convincing potential backers of the soundness of his ideas, since 'most learned men at that era regarded *The Book of Ser Marco Polo* as pure fiction.'[53] Columbus's experience is some indication both of the limits to the expansion of European knowledge of the world which resulted from the Mongol conquests and of the curtain which dropped when the empire collapsed, and Asia was no longer under the political dominance of one remarkable family.

[52]   S. E. Morison, *The Great Explorers: the European Discovery of America* (1978), p. 370.
[53]   Ibid., p. 371.

8

What Became of the Mongols?

The Mongol khanates in the lands of ancient sedentary civilisation, Persia and China, were the first to collapse. It was easier for the Mongols to retain control where, as in the Golden Horde and the Chaghatai Khanate, they were also able to maintain their ancestral nomadic way of life and hence their military supremacy over the subject populations. Many Mongols did indeed remain in China after the fall of the Yüan Dynasty in 1368: the new Ming rulers were not so xenophobic as to be blind to the advantages of having Mongol cavalrymen available to them. The spectre of a new Mongol conquest of China was always before the eyes of the Ming emperors, and it was sound policy to be prepared to fight Mongols with Mongols to some extent. In Persia there was no eviction of Mongols when the Ilkhanate dissolved in the 1330s. The Mongols of Persia, probably always fairly small in number, were in due course absorbed into the Turkish tribal population which, apart from a brief interlude in the eighteenth century, provided Persia with its rulers until 1925.[1]

But in the mid fourteenth century the Chaghatai Khanate in Central Asia still had a long, though singularly obscure, life ahead of it. In the course of that century it fell into two parts. In the west, Transoxania, with its great cities of Samarqand and Bukhārā, had a population that was in large part sedentary and Muslim. It was progressively alienated

---

[1] On Central Asia generally in the post-imperial period see the convenient account in G. Hambly (ed.), *Central Asia* (1969). For Mongolia proper the standard work is C. R. Bawden, *The Modern History of Mongolia* (1968). For relations between the Mongols and China see M. Rossabi, *China and Inner Asia from 1368 to the Present Day* (1975) and, more briefly, J. F. Fletcher, 'China and Central Asia, 1368–1884', in J. K. Fairbank (ed.), *The Chinese World Order: Traditional China's Foreign Relations* (1968), pp. 206–24 and 337–68.

Plate 8.1   The head of Tīmūr (Tamerlane), reconstructed from his exhumed
skull by Gerasimov. John Massey Stewart Picture Library

from the eastern, nomadic and still largely pagan half, which was
known as Mughulistān, 'the land of the Mongols', and whose people
the Transoxanians knew as 'Jete', robbers. The career of Tīmūr the
Lame, Tamerlane in western literature,[2] had as its basis his ability to
capitalise on the hostility between Transoxania and Mughulistān. Born

---

[2]   The best account of Tīmūr at present available is H. Hookham, *Tamburlaine the Conqueror* (1962). On the Timurids see W. Barthold, *Ulugh Beg* (*Four
Studies on the History of Central Asia*, vol. 2, tr. V. and T. Minorsky)
(1958).

Plate 8.2 The Gūr-i Mīr, Tamerlane's tomb in Samarqand. John Massey Stewart Picture Library

near Samarqand at around the time of the Ilkhanate's dissolution, he was of Mongol descent though Muslim by religion and Turkish in speech and culture. His career, from bandit to conqueror, bears some resemblance to that of Chingiz Khān, though the differences are perhaps more striking than the similarities. His army was organised in much the same way as his predecessor's, and he was undeniably a highly gifted and successful general. But he indulged in destruction and wanton cruelty to an extent that Chingiz would have considered pointless; and it may be felt that as a man who had been brought up as a Muslim and in a highly 'civilised' society, he had less excuse.

His power base in Transoxania was secured by his defence of that land from the incursions of the nomads of Mughulistān. The world was despoiled for the greater glory of Transoxania and in particular of Samarqand, Tīmūr's capital. Suburbs were erected there, named after the great cities of the Islamic world that Tīmūr had ruined. So the people of his native land had no reason for complaint about their treatment at his hands, though he was himself a nomad as were his troops. But Tīmūr's career was really a series of plundering expeditions on a massive scale. He did not have the statesmanlike qualities of Chingiz Khān, and he did not leave behind him an empire as large or as enduring. China was fortunate in escaping his attentions: he had planned to invade it, perhaps dreaming of re-establishing the empire of Chingiz Khān. But he died on the way there, in 1405. He had succeeded in fending off the predatory incursions of the people to the east of Transoxania, but Mughulistān did not become part of the Timurid Empire.

The Chaghatai Khanate therefore survived. In the years that followed, most of the Khāns were Muslims, but many of their followers remained loyal to Shamanism. Not until the seventeenth and eighteenth centuries did Mughulistān become a firmly Islamic land. Political dissolution set in from the middle of the sixteenth century, though it was long before the house of Chaghatai ceased to exercise at least nominal authority. The prestige that attached itself to the house of Chingiz Khān was enormous: even Tīmūr, not a Chingizid, had for much of his reign felt it necessary to maintain a member of the imperial family as puppet Khān of the Timurid Empire; his successors eventually dispensed with this fiction. Transoxania was never restored to the Chaghataids. It remained under Timurid control until the end of the fifteenth century, when it fell to the Özbeg Turks who still give their name to the modern Soviet republic of Uzbekistan. One Timurid prince, Bābur, fled from the Özbegs to Afghanistan and then to India, where in the early sixteenth century he became the founder of the Moghul Empire. He left a fascinating autobiography[3] which reveals a personality whose attractiveness is remarkable in a man who was descended from both Tamerlane and Chingiz Khān. The last Chaghataids were reduced to their lands in the east around the city of Kāshghar, now in the Chinese province of Sinkiang. There they survived until the middle of the seventeenth century. In the eighteenth century their former territories were incorporated by the Manchus into the Chinese Empire.

The last Yüan Emperor had been forced back on the original Mongol homeland after 1368. The period of Ming rule in China (1368–1644) saw a series of attempts to revive Mongol power under the leadership of different tribal confederacies. Mongolia at this time, like the Chaghatai Khanate, tended to fall into eastern and western halves. The peoples of eastern Mongolia, of whom the most important were the Khalkhas, were ruled by the descendants of the Chingizid Great Khāns.

[3]   See A. S. Beveridge (tr.), *The Bābur-nāma in English* (1922).

The leading tribe of the western Mongols was the Oirats (who later appear under the names Kalmuck or Kalmyk and Jungar). The western Mongols had not played a prominent part in the great imperial adventure, but they now entered into rivalry with the eastern Mongols for what was left of the Yüan inheritance. In the first half of the fifteenth century the Oirats were the dominant power in Mongolia, and they were a serious threat to Ming China. In 1449, under their ruler Esen, they captured the Ming Emperor and might have taken Peking had they acted more decisively. Later in the century, and for much of the sixteenth, the eastern Mongols managed to reassert themselves, especially under the Chingizid Dayan Khān (1470–1543) and his grandson Altan Khān (1543–83), though Altan's power was based more on the support of tribes near the Chinese frontier than on that of the Khalkhas.

Altan Khān was responsible for a momentous innovation – the reintroduction of Tibetan Buddhism. Buddhism appears to have died out among the Mongols after the fall of the Yüan Dynasty, and Shamanism recovered its old position. But now, Professor Bawden writes, 'growing dissatisfaction was making itself felt with the barbaric notions of shamanism, its bloody sacrifices, its primitive cosmology, its unattractive revelations of the world beyond, and its complete lack of organization which made it useless as an instrument of political power and did not provide the careers and dignities offered by a hierarchical church'.[4] The Buddhism which was now to become the religion of Mongolia was a reformed variety of Lamaism promoted by what is known in the west as the 'Yellow Hat' sect. Sonam Gyatso, the head of sect, travelled to Mongolia in 1578 and converted Altan Khān. It soon transpired, to general satisfaction, that Altan was a reincarnation of Qubilai and Sonam Gyatso of 'Phagspa. Altan conferred on Sonam Gyatso the title of Dalai Lama, deeming him to be the third incarnation: the title was granted posthumously to his two predecessors as head of the Yellow Hats.

The new Lamaism spread rapidly, and Mongolia was soon dotted with Buddhist monasteries as well as exalted incarnations called *khutukhtus* or 'living Buddhas'. Some historians have tried to explain the fact that after the sixteenth century Mongol history became less bloodthirsty than hitherto as the result of the influence of Buddhism. But it is not easy to demonstrate that the Mongols, except for the increasingly large proportion of the population that became monks,

[4]   Bawden, *The Modern History of Mongolia*, p. 28.

were much less warlike than their ancestors. They were certainly less effective militarily, but this probably has more to do with political developments and changes in military technology than with religion.

In the seventeenth century the Khalkhas submitted to the new Manchu rulers of China, and the lands of the eastern Mongols remained a part of the Chinese Empire, though held on a loose rein, until 1911. The Khalkhas seem to have considered the rule of the Manchus more acceptable than that of the Oirats, who again became prominent in the early Manchu period. Under Galdan Khān (died 1697) the Oirats controlled much of Central Asia and were a menace to China until their defeat by the Emperor K'ang-hsi in 1696. Checked by the Manchus, they turned their attention westwards, and remained a major power until their final destruction by the Manchu Emperor Ch'ien-lung in 1758.

Thereafter, what had been Mongol territory was gradually divided between the expanding empires of Russia and China. Some Mongols, notably the Buriats in the Lake Baikal area, to the north of Mongolia proper, came under direct Russian rule, as the Mongols of Inner Mongolia, the lands south of the Gobi desert, were under close Chinese supervision. During the late nineteenth and early twentieth centuries, as the Manchu Dynasty declined and its control over its dependencies relaxed, there was heavy Chinese settlement in Inner Mongolia. This resulted in the loss to agriculture of much of the Mongols' pasture land, and the numerical swamping of the Mongol population. Nevertheless an Inner Mongolian Autonomous Region was created after the Communist takeover in China, and there are to this day more Mongols inside the Chinese frontier than in the Mongolian republic to the north. The death of reputed last Inner Mongolian descendant of Chingiz Khān, an official of the government of the People's Republic of China, was reported in 1984.

Perhaps influenced by what they knew of the effects of Chinese policies, or the lack of them, in Inner Mongolia, the Khalkhas of the north declared their independence of China when the Manchus fell in 1911 and China became a republic. Sovereignty was vested in the chief 'living Buddha', the Jebtsundamba Khutukhtu of Urga (now Ulan Bator). Outer Mongolia came increasingly under the influence of the Russians, whom the Mongol princes appear to have preferred to the Chinese. There was a brief attempt to re-establish Chinese control, which was frustrated largely through the efforts of a bizarre White Russian adventurer, Baron Ungern-Sternberg. After this episode Russian influence came to mean Soviet Communism. The eighth Jebtsundamba Khutukhtu died in 1924, and it was not permitted that any further incarnation should be discovered; Mongolia became a People's Republic as a Russian satellite, but nevertheless 'a state run by Mongols, for Mongols'.[5] China was extremely reluctant to recognise permanently the independence of any land that had formed part of the Manchu Empire, as the Tibetans found to their cost in 1950; but Mongolia had the advantage of powerful patron in the Soviet Union. China recognised the Mongolian People's Republic in 1946. In 1961 Mongolia became a member state of the United Nations. Much of the old nomadic way of life still survives; and in spite of official disapproval the Mongols do not seem to have forgotten entirely the time when their ancestors were the rulers of most of the then known world.

[5]   Hambly, *Central Asia*, p. 291.

9

The Mongol Empire since 1985

This book, as originally published, represented to the best of its author's ability a snapshot of what the history of the Mongol Empire looked like around 1985. The two decades since then have been, perhaps, more productive historiographically than any comparable period, and the subject now has a distinctly different feel to it. This is not, for the most part, because startlingly revealing new primary sources have been discovered and published, though there has been some progress along that front; and a number of important sources have either appeared in better editions or have been made more accessible by having been translated into English or other European languages. It is more that perspectives have changed: historians have begun to look at different issues. They have dug deeper into Mongol history, and their emphasis has shifted away from purely military aspects, away from the death and destruction which, while it undeniably did characterise the initial Mongol imperial expansion, is now seen as very far from being all, or even what is most important, that there is to say about the extraordinary Mongol phenomenon.[1] The results of this new research are to be found in specialised monographs, collective volumes and journal articles. There has not as yet been any attempt at an overall scholarly synthesis, though Robert

[1] Discussions of work published since the first edition of this book include D. Sinor, 'Notes on Inner Asian bibliography IV: history of the Mongols in the 13th century', *Journal of Asian History*, 23/1 (1989), pp. 26–79; P. Jackson, 'The state of research: the Mongol Empire, 1986–1999', *Journal of Medieval History*, 26/2 (2000), pp. 189–210, which is explicitly an account – and a very comprehensive and judicious one – of what has happened since *The Mongols* appeared; and, more narrowly on the western part of the empire, D. O. Morgan, 'The Mongols in Iran: a reappraisal', *Iran*, 42 (2004), pp. 131–6. Essays 1–6 (pp. 1–99) in P. D. Buell, *Historical Dictionary of the Mongol World Empire* (2003) are also very helpful, especially on the eastern parts of the empire.

Marshall's splendidly illustrated *Storm from the East*,[2] written to accompany a television documentary series of the same name, by its producer, is an admirable survey which is in some ways more up to date than *The Mongols*. The fifth and last section of the first volume of David Christian's history of Russia, Central Asia and Mongolia also provides an excellent account of the Mongol Empire.[3] More recent is Hugh Kennedy's contribution to a series on military history.[4] The Mongol section of this book is well informed and level-headed, and the book, like Marshall's, has excellent illustrations. It should be added that at least for the eastern parts of the empire we do have a fairly recent collective synthesis in the shape of the relevant chapters of the sixth volume of the *Cambridge History of China*.[5] Among several valuable chapters, that on the rise of the Mongols by Thomas Allsen – of whom more later – is particularly notable. I have not tried to update the main text of this book to take account of what has been published since it was written: what follows here is intended as an introduction – by no means an exhaustive nor, I hope, an exhausting one – to some of the more interesting and important developments of recent years.

Sources

The basic and essential source for the early history of the empire, *The Secret History of the Mongols*, has continued to attract a good deal of attention. In particular, there have been two new translations into English of this often perplexing document. Urgunge Onon is the first Mongol to have tried his hand at the task, and his version has appeared in two successive editions.[6] Compared with the translations cited in 1985, these are a great deal more readable than Cleaves and much more

---

[2]   R. Marshall, *Storm from the East. From Genghis Khan to Khubilai Khan* (1993). See the review article by T. N. Haining in *JRAS*, 3rd series, 4/2 (1994), pp. 251–4.

[3]   D. Christian, *A History of Russia, Central Asia and Mongolia I. Inner Asia from Prehistory to the Mongol Empire* (1998), pp. 385–429.

[4]   H. Kennedy, *Mongols, Huns and Vikings* (2002), pp. 108–71.

[5]   H. Franke and D. Twitchett (eds), *The Cambridge History of China 6. Alien Regimes and Border States 907–1368* (1994).

[6]   *The History and the Life of Chinggis Khan* (1990) and *The Secret History of the Mongols. The Life and Times of Chinggis Khan* (2001).

accessible than de Rachewiltz's articles. But the real landmark has been the publication in book form, revised and expanded, of de Rachewiltz's translation.[7] The translation, both readable and accurate, occupies only a fairly small proportion of the two volumes' 1,300 pages. Most of the rest is a detailed commentary: the most formidable and indispensable collection of material on the prehistory and early history of the Mongol Empire ever assembled. This is undoubtedly one of the handful of outstanding works of scholarship in Mongol studies.

Nothing of equal significance has appeared so far as the Persian sources are concerned, though Boyle's translation of Juwaynī has been republished in one volume, with a slightly different title and a certain amount of updating.[8] But we have lost what we once thought was a collection of major importance: Rashīd al-Dīn's *Letters*. Alexander Morton has shown these to be a forgery, probably of the Timurid period.[9] On the other hand, a work of Rashīd al-Dīn's on agronomy, of which only the title was previously known, has been discovered, published and discussed.[10] This reveals yet another aspect of that many-sided man. Possibly of more general interest, it is no longer true that, as I said above (p. 22), the non-Persian reader needs Russian for Rashīd al-Dīn. Wheeler Thackston has published a complete translation of the Mongol history parts of the *Jāmiʿ al-tawārīkh*,[11] so now, for the first time, the whole of the greatest work of Mongol-period historical writing (apart from its world-history sections) can be read through in clear and

[7] I. de Rachewiltz, *The Secret History of the Mongols. A Mongolian Epic Chronicle of the Thirteenth Century*, 2 vols (2004).

[8] *Genghis Khan. The History of the World-Conqueror*, with introduction and additional bibliography by D. O. Morgan (1997).

[9] A. H. Morton, 'The Letters of Rashīd al-Dīn: Īlkhānid fact or Timurid fiction?', in R. Amitai-Preiss and D. O. Morgan, *The Mongol Empire and its Legacy* (1999), pp. 155–99. The attempt to defend the letters' authenticity in A. Soudavar, 'In defense of Rašīd-od-dīn and his Letters', *Studia Iranica*, 32 (2003), pp. 77–122, does not strike me as persuasive.

[10] Rashīd al-Dīn, *Āthār wa Aḥyāʾ*, ed. M. Sotoodeh and I. Afshar (1989). For discussion see A. K. S. Lambton, 'The *Āthār wa āḥyā* of Rashīd al-Dīn Faḍl Allāh Hamadānī and his contribution as an agronomist, arboriculturist and horticulturist', in Amitai-Preiss and Morgan, *The Mongol Empire and its Legacy*, pp. 126–54.

[11] Rashiduddin Fazlullah's *Jamiʿuʾt-tawarikh. Compendium of Chronicles*, 3 vols (1998–9).

comprehensible English. One particular benefit is that it is now possible for the English reader to compare Rashīd al-Dīn's account of the early history of the Mongols and the career of Chinggis Khan with the independent version to be found in *The Secret History of the Mongols*. This is important because, as remarked above (pp. 11–12), Rashīd al-Dīn used the now lost Mongolian chronicle the *Altan Debter* as his principal source. It is now clear that Rashīd al-Dīn's Mongol informant and intermediary was the Great Khan Qubilai's representative at the Ilkhanid court, Bolad Chingsang, about whom we know a good deal as a result of Allsen's research.[12] As de Rachewiltz remarks at various points in his *Secret History* commentary, there can be little doubt that Rashīd al-Dīn's account is often more reliable, factually, than the *Secret History*. Unfortunately, no comparable translations from the hardly less important Chinese sources, such as the *Yüan-shih*, have appeared.

Nor have there been major new discoveries in respect of European sources, though the new Hakluyt version of William of Rubruck may be found useful, and there is also an excellent French translation which appeared just too late to be used in the first edition of this book.[13] The most famous of the European travellers, Marco Polo, continues to receive attention, scholarly and otherwise. The current situation is admirably summed up in an article by Peter Jackson.[14] A good deal of interest was inspired by Frances Wood's book,[15] in which she engagingly argued that Marco never went further east than the Black Sea. Few scholars have been convinced; and the book provoked de Rachewiltz to a magisterial demolition.[16] Her arguments tended to depend on alleged

---

[12]   In chapters 10 and 11 of his *Culture and Conquest in Mongol Eurasia* (2001 – discussed further below), and in several articles.

[13]   *The Mission of Friar William of Rubruck. His Journey to the Court of the Great Khan Möngke, 1253–1255*, tr. P. Jackson, ed. P. Jackson with D. O. Morgan (1990); C. and R. Kappler, *Guillaume de Rubrouck. Voyage dans l'Empire Mongol (1253–1255)* (1985).

[14]   P. Jackson, 'Marco Polo and his "Travels"', *BSOAS*, 61/1 (1998), pp. 82–101, reprinted in G. R. Hawting (ed.), *Mamluks, Mongols and Crusaders* (2005), pp. 263–82.

[15]   *Did Marco Polo go to China?* (1995).

[16]   I. de Rachewiltz, 'Marco Polo went to China', *Zentralasiatische Studien*, 27 (1997), pp. 34–92. For a review on similar lines that is both much shorter and a great deal less learned, see D. O. Morgan, 'Marco Polo in China – or not', *JRAS*, 3rd series, 6 (1996), pp. 221–5.

omissions, such as that Marco failed to mention the Great Wall of China. However, it was already clear when this book was published that Marco could hardly have seen the Great Wall, since it was not there at the time (above, p. 58). I based this conclusion on an article by A. N. Waldron. His wide-ranging later book[17] left very little room for any remaining doubts. The best recent book on Marco, by John Larner, has no qualms about authenticity. On a different tack, a book by John Critchley is very interesting on what a study of Marco Polo tells us not so much about Asia as about Europe.[18]

So far as the history of the Mongols in western Asia is concerned, the principal change has not been the result of the discovery of new sources as the bringing into play of material previously largely ignored. In particular, historical material written in the Mamlūk sultanate in Egypt and Syria has increasingly been used to shed light, not just on Mamlūk–Mongol relations, but also on the internal history of the Ilkhanate. Two notable exponents of this are Reuven Amitai and Charles Melville. Amitai has given us a far more detailed and comprehensive understanding of the first phase of Mamlūk–Ilkhanid relations than we had before; but he has also shown how Mamlūk sources can add to our knowledge of internal Ilkhanid affairs.[19] So has Melville, for example in his study of the conversion of Ghazan Khan to Islam; a study which shows, from Mamlūk sources, that Ghazan was following other Mongols, not, as we had thought, leading them, in deciding to become a Muslim.[20]

[17]   A. N. Waldron, *The Great Wall of China. From History to Myth* (1990). The author of the most recent study, J. Lovell, *The Great Wall. China against the World 1000 BC – AD 2000* (2006), pp. 176–7, agrees.

[18]   J. Larner, *Marco Polo and the Discovery of the World* (1999); J. Critchley, *Marco Polo's Book* (1992).

[19]   R. Amitai-Preiss, *Mongols and Mamluks. The Mamluk–Īlkhānid War, 1260–1281* (1995), supplemented by his 'The resolution of the Mongol–Mamluk war', in R. Amitai and M. Biran (eds), *Mongols, Turks and Others. Eurasian Nomads and the Sedentary World*, pp. 359–90; and many articles, e.g. 'New material from the Mamluk sources for the biography of Rashid al-Din', in J. Raby and T. Fitzherbert (eds), *The Court of the Il-khans 1290–1340* (1996), pp. 23–37.

[20]   'Pādshāh-i Islām: the conversion of Sultan Maḥmūd Ghāzān Khān', in C. P. Melville (ed.), *Pembroke Papers I. Persian and Islamic Studies in Honour of P. W. Avery* (1990), pp. 159–77.

Studies

It would seem natural to begin with the Mongol Empire's founder, Chinggis Khan.[21] The Preface to the 1990 reprint of this book mentioned the biography by Leo de Hartog,[22] a clear and reliable narrative. But far and away the best biography when this book was written was Paul Ratchnevsky's of 1983, at that time available only in German. That situation has not changed, except that Ratchnevsky can now be read in English translation. That version, by the late Thomas Haining,[23] achieves the remarkable feat of being a substantial improvement on the excellent original. This is because Haining edited as well as translated. He incorporated many of the (sometimes very long) footnotes into the text, and did some judicious updating where necessary. As Jackson remarks,[24] 'the conqueror who emerges from the pages of this important study is a more lifelike figure, with weaknesses as well as strengths writ large, and the assessment of his achievements and his legacy is grounded on a painstaking examination of the sources'. No historical work is ever 'definitive', unless the field of study it deals with is stone dead: but Ratchnevsky's book, in its Haining recension, is likely to remain standard for a good many years.

That fact, very widely admitted though it may be, has not, however, prevented other writers from offering their own particular perspective on the great conqueror's life. There are two admirable short introductions, by James Chambers and Jean-Paul Roux, the latter being lavishly illustrated.[25] 2004 was a particularly bumper year. An

---

[21] 'Chinggis' is the Mongolists' preferred spelling. As I explained (above, p. 4), the Persian spelling, 'Chingiz' was used in this book. I got into trouble for this (see D. Sinor's 'Notes', cited above, n. 1, p. 34, and in his otherwise extremely generous *EHR* review of the book, mentioned above, p. xiii). In this chapter I have therefore recanted, though I cannot say I feel very strongly about the matter: even if we call the great man 'Genghis', we do know who it is we are talking about, which is what matters.

[22] *Genghis Khan, Conqueror of the World* (1989). I wrote an introduction and a bibliographical note for the 2005 Folio Society edition.

[23] *Genghis Khan. His Life and Legacy* (1991).

[24] 'The state of research', p. 194.

[25] J. Chambers, *Genghis Khan* (1999); J-P. Roux, *Genghis Khan and the Mongol Empire* (2003).

American anthropologist, Jack Weatherford, published *Genghis Khan and the Making of the Modern World*, which, as its title indicates, made rather substantial claims for its hero, and was distinctly more favourably inclined towards the Mongols than more traditionally minded western historians have tended to be. His extensive on-the-ground acquaintance-ship with Mongolia, and his anthropological background, enabled him to offer many shrewd insights, even if some of the book, considered as history, is open to dispute. In some ways similar is John Man's *Genghis Khan. Life, Death and Resurrection*. Man is a traveller and writer who has long been fascinated by the Mongols, and, like Weatherford, he knows the country well. He is especially informative (this is the 'Resurrection' of the book's title) on the contemporary cult of Chinggis Khan in a Mongolian Republic which is now, since the collapse of the USSR, fully independent. Both of these books are readable and interesting, though they do not displace Ratchnevsky from his throne. The third 2004 book, George Lane's *Genghis Khan and Mongol Rule*, is more of a handbook and introduction to the Mongol imperial phenomenon generally – as well as a narrative of events, it includes a number of bio-graphical sketches of important individuals, documents in translation, and a helpfully annotated bibliography.

Biographies of Chinggis Khan, as of almost any other historical figure of the medieval period, cannot be biographies in the modern sense. We do not have the material which would allow us to reconstruct a life to such a degree of detail and penetration. In particular, we can say very little with certainty, or even plausibility, about motivation. Why did Chinggis set out on his career of conquest, and why did that career follow the course it did? Our sources cannot tell us: what we have are records of the events, from which we can, if we wish, attempt to extrapolate explanation. Nevertheless, an accumulation of biographical data is of immense value if we are to understand what the Mongol Empire was and how it worked. A notable example of the results of such research is a formidable volume edited by de Rachewiltz and others.[26] This contains short biographical studies of 37 notable figures of the early Mongol Empire, by a wide array of leading scholars, and is a quite invaluable resource.

After Chinggis, the Mongol ruler about whom we have most material for a biography is probably his grandson Qubilai. This major

[26] *In the Service of the Khan. Eminent Personalities of the Early Mongol–Yüan Period* (1993).

historiographical gap was illuminatingly filled in 1988 by Morris Rossabi.[27] We are given a fully rounded picture of a remarkable and many-sided ruler, a picture which emphasises Qubilai's Mongol identity while recognising the striking degree of sympathy towards his Chinese subjects which he managed to achieve. One conclusion one might draw from the book is that the verdict on Qubilai as a military leader found above (p. 107) was probably something of an underestimate, despite the disasters in Japan and elsewhere. It should be added that Rossabi has also written an interesting study of Rabban Ṣaumā, the Nestorian monk who, with his disciple Mark, later the Nestorian Catholicus Yaballāhā III (above, p. 140), travelled from Qubilai's China to Persia, and then on to Europe as the Ilkhanid ambassador.[28]

In this book, as elsewhere, it has been customary to describe the political evolution of the Mongol Empire in terms of its dissolution into four more or less independent (and by no means necessarily friendly) khanates, ruled by different branches of the Mongol royal house: the Great Khanate in China and Mongolia, the Chaghatai Khanate in Central Asia, the Ilkhanate in Persia and Iraq, and the Golden Horde in the Pontic steppes. Jackson has shown[29] that the process was a good deal more complex than that schema implies; and a major example of this was the fate of Central Asia. One feature of this book was the almost total dearth of information it offered on the Chaghatai Khanate (a deficiency generously not remarked on by the book's reviewers – no doubt they appreciated the difficulties involved because of the absence of indigenous sources). The significance of Qaidu, a descendant of the Great Khan Ögedei who ruled for decades in Central Asia, who dominated the Chaghatai Khanate though himself a member of a different branch of the imperial family, and who was unremittingly hostile to Qubilai, was briefly mentioned (pp. 105, 139), but at the time there was little more that could have been said. Michal Biran had changed all that. Her book,[30] as its title implies more a study of the emergence of a state

---

[27]   *Khubilai Khan. His Life and Times.* In subsequent reprints, including the Folio Society edition of 2005, Rossabi incorporated various revisions into his text.

[28]   *Voyager from Xanadu. Rabban Sauma and the First Journey from China to the West* (1992).

[29]   'From *Ulus* to Khanate: the making of the Mongol states, c.1220–c.1290', in Amitai-Preiss and Morgan, *The Mongol Empire and its Legacy*, pp. 12–38.

[30]   *Qaidu and the Rise of the Independent Mongol State in Central Asia* (1997).

than a personal biography of Qaidu, has gone a long way towards filling a considerable gap in our knowledge.

Another study which is, inevitably, more about a reign than about the individual who reigned is Thomas Allsen's book on the Great Khan Möngke[31] – though as it happens we do have more of a 'personal' impression of Möngke and his character than of most of his contemporaries, thanks to William of Rubruck's account of his visit. Allsen demonstrated very convincingly how military expansion during Möngke's reign – which included the beginnings of the final assault on Sung China as well as Hülegü's expedition to the Middle East – was based on reforms in administration and taxation, which made possible a much more effective mobilisation of resources.

The questions of how the Mongol Empire worked; whether there was more to it than military expansion (and, ultimately, contraction); what part, if any, the Mongols themselves played beyond their role of maintaining their military supremacy, are the kinds of issues that Allsen began to address in that first book, and they have subsequently been prominent among the concerns of other historians of the Mongol Empire. The background to Mongol expansion has received some attention: did the Mongol Empire arise from a total vacuum? It seems inherently improbable, but if that is so, where did the most significant influences come from?

One fascinating book that puts the Mongols into a long-term context of nomads and their relations with their biggest and most formidable neighbour, China, is Thomas Barfield's study.[32] This surveys two millennia, from the point of view of an anthropologist who is exceedingly well informed historically. Two of his arguments may be mentioned here. He suggests that on the whole, successful conquerors from the north tended to come not from Mongolia, but from the north-east, what is now Manchuria. Such invaders had the military advantages typical of nomad warrior cavalrymen, while also being better acquainted than were invaders from Mongolia with sedentary civilization, which made it easier for them to establish stable rule in China. Two examples would be the Chin dynasty who ruled northern China immediately before the Mongol invasions, and China's last dynasty, the Ch'ing. So far as relations between China and nomadic confederations centred in Mongolia

---

[31]   *Mongol Imperialism: The Policies of the Grand Qan Möngke in China, Russia and the Islamic Lands, 1251–1259* (1987).

[32]   T. J. Barfield, *The Perilous Frontier. Nomadic Empires and China 221 BC to AD 1757* (1989).

are concerned, Barfield contends that historians have perceived them quite wrongly. The normal situation was not 'strong nomads/weak Chinese', or indeed its opposite. According to him, nomadic and Chinese polities rose and fell together. A strong nomadic confederation saw it as being in its interests for the government of China also to be strong, since such a government would be well placed to provide the nomads with what they wanted, in terms of trade goods or (however disguised) tribute. Hence we find instances of nomadic rulers attempting to prop up Chinese regimes which looked in danger of falling: little could be expected from the south if there was not an effective government there to provide it. It was, Barfield says, only in such dire circumstances that nomadic rulers from Mongolia would resort to the desperate expedient of invading and conquering north China – only then, when they could not obtain what they required by any other means.

If Barfield is right – and for the most part, though possibly not in every instance, it seems to me that he is – then a phrase like '[t]he conquest of China, especially north China, had always been every steppe ruler's dream, and Chingiz was no exception' (above, p. 13) must be regarded as seriously misleading. That said, however, Barfield is well aware that the Mongols of the thirteenth century were an exception to all his rules of normal nomad behaviour. After all, they did conquer China – and, uniquely up to that time, the whole of it, not just the north. But Barfield's view of things does make sense of a characteristic of the Mongol invasions of China which I noted (p. 58): that the early Mongol incursions look more like predatory raids than an attempt at conquest and occupation. According to the Barfield schema, it may be that these raids turned into permanent conquest just because the Mongols found there was no alternative, if they were to get what they wanted from the rich lands that lay to their south.

Thanks to several chapters in volume 6 of the *Cambridge History of China* (above, n. 4), non-Sinologists now have access to able accounts of the pre-Mongol regimes in north China, notably Liao, Chin and Hsi-Hsia. Many of the big questions continue to revolve around the importance, if any, of the sub-Liao empire of Qara-Khitai in Central Asia. I remarked, perhaps a little adventurously (above, p. 44), that the Mongol Empire might be seen as 'a successor state, on a much grander scale, to the Qara-Khitai empire'. The problem in 1985 was that although there were some suggestive articles, notably by Paul Buell, Qara-Khitai was 'still very little known and understood: the study of its history requires a knowledge of Arabic, Persian and Chinese' (p. 43). I could not have suspected that that sentence would turn out to be possibly the most influential in the book, since apparently it inspired Michal Biran to take up the subject. The results are enormously impressive and illuminating.[33] At last we have a full account, from a scholar who does know all the sources in their disparate languages, and who has the acumen to interpret them with skill and lucidity. Biran has shed a flood of light on a place that was very dark indeed: it will be some time before the full implications of her research have been worked out.

To mention one possible instance of Khitan or Qara-Khitai influence on the Mongols, already in 1985 it was clear (above, p. 107) that there was a suspicious similarity between the Mongol postal courier system, the *Yām*, and its Khitan Liao precursor – perhaps antecedent. The *Yām* is often regarded as the most successful and essential of Mongol imperial institutions: for example, Sinor[34] remarks that '[i]f there was one single Mongol innovation instrumental in the creation and the maintenance of their imperium, it was the *Jam*'. Yet it has still not attracted very much scholarly attention. There is a recent book in French,[35] whose author also contributed a short article on the subject to the *Encyclopaedia of Islam*; and I wrote an article which expanded somewhat on what was to be found in this book.[36]

A more controversial topic, the alleged 'Great *Yāsā* of Chinggis Khan', has, however, been the subject of rather more investigation, perhaps in part provoked by the somewhat iconoclastic view presented in this book (pp. 96–9) and, at greater length, in an article published in the same year.[37] I have surveyed and assessed the later literature in another article.[38] Suffice it to say that while I think I may have slightly overstated my case here and there, it still seems to me to be essentially valid. However, no less a scholar than de Rachewiltz disagrees: he argues in

---

[33] *The Empire of the Qara Khitai in Eurasian History. Between China and the Islamic World* (2005). See also, *inter alia*, her ' "Like a mighty wall": the armies of the Qara Khitai', *Jerusalem Studies in Arabic and Islam*, 25 (2001), pp. 44–91.

[34] 'Notes on Inner Asian bibliography', p. 56.

[35] D. Gazagnadou, *La poste à relais. La diffusion d'une technique de pouvoir à travers l'Eurasie, Chine–Islam–Europe* (1994).

[36] 'Reflections on Mongol communications in the Ilkhanate', in C. Hillenbrand (ed.), *The Sultan's Turret* (1999), pp. 375–85.

[37] This has been reprinted in Hawting, *Mamluks, Mongols and Crusaders*.

[38] 'The "Great *Yasa* of Chinggis Khan" revisited', in R. Amitai and M. Biran (eds), *Mongols, Turks and Others* (2005), pp. 291–308.

Plate 9.1 *Paiza* (tablet of authority, or passport) in 'Phags-pa script, iron inlaid with silver, Yüan dynasty (1271–1368), China, 18.1 cm × 11.4 cm. The Metropolitan Museum of Art, purchase, bequest of Dorothy Graham Bennett, 1993 (1993.256), image © The Metropolitan Museum of Art, New York

favour of the likelihood of a written Great *Yāsā*, and his arguments should be carefully considered.[39]

The significance of some of the other peoples of Mongolia at the time of Chinggis's rise to power has also been examined. Gumilev's book[40] was described above (p. xiv) as 'highly eccentric but enjoyable'. It is a book that at times is only loosely anchored to the historical realities,[41] but it does provide some useful material on the Naimans. Much more valuable is Isenbike Togan's sometimes difficult but rewarding study.[42] She makes out a carefully argued and convincing case for the formative influence of the Keraits (whose ruler, Toghril, was of course the young Chinggis's patron and later enemy). It does seem that the Kerait Khanate provided Chinggis, up to a point, with a model in terms of state formation. Incidentally, she also provides supporting evidence for a suggestion I made (above, p. 79): that Chinggis Khan's decimal military reorganisation created what might be called 'an artificial tribal system'. Professor Togan calls this process 'detribalization'.

What kind of an empire was the Mongol Empire? The traditional view was that it was a conquest empire, predicated on Mongol military supremacy over all likely enemies, on continual expansion, and on loot: an empire which would tend towards decay and collapse once expansion ceased and the supply of booty dried up. So far as government and administration were concerned, the Mongols were not interested in the details, only in the proceeds which came their way in terms of goods and wealth. If they found a competent bureaucracy in place in, say, Persia or China, they would leave its experienced members in office, and expect them to get on with the job: especially with the collection of taxes. They were well aware of the financial benefits of trade, and encouraged it; but they had little or no interest in cross-cultural contacts for other than purely materialistic reasons. The Mongols were, in fact, no more than barbarian exploiters of such of their non-Mongol subjects

---

[39] 'Some reflections on Činggis Qan's *J̌asaγ*', *East Asian History*, 6 (December 1993), pp. 91–104.

[40] L. N. Gumilev, *Searches for an Imaginary Kingdom. The Legend of the Kingdom of Prester John* (1987).

[41] One of its reviewers – Robert Irwin – commented that '[i]t is exciting, but it would be more exciting if it was right' (*Times Literary Supplement*, 15–21 April 1988, p. 429).

[42] I. Togan, *Flexibility and Limitation in Steppe Formations. The Kerait Khanate and Chinggis Khan* (1998).

as had had the good fortune to escape being massacred during the initial invasions.

On the whole, this was with some qualifications the point of view presented in the first edition of *The Mongols*. In particular, having in the 1970s written a PhD thesis on Mongol government, I tended to present the Mongols – both in the book and in an article published a few years previously[43] – as not much involved in the administration of their empire. However, I soon began to have my doubts over whether it was plausible to imagine the Mongols as so supremely indifferent to how their empire was run; and indeed over whether the evidence really supported such an interpretation. In 1996 I published another article,[44] in which I argued that I had been wrong: there is in fact a good deal of evidence which suggests that the Mongols were much more involved in the minutiae of imperial administration, at least in the Ilkhanate, than I (and others) had supposed. This was a small step towards putting the Mongols back where they belonged: into their own history.

Other scholars have taken much larger steps in a similar direction. Of these, the most influential has been Thomas Allsen, in a series of articles and two important books. His first book, *Mongol Imperialism*, mentioned above, had already caused us to re-evaluate the reign of Möngke and the mechanics of Mongol expansion during his reign. Then came *Commodity and Exchange in the Mongol Empire* (1997), a short book centred on the fate of Muslim textile workers who were shipped east by their new Mongol masters for the sake of their professional skills, and in particular to help satisfy the Mongols' vast appetite for gold brocade. As Jackson remarks,[45] the book is of much wider significance than if it were merely a treatise on 'the economic or even the political significance of luxury textiles to the steppe-dwellers'. More importantly, 'it highlights the positive impulses deriving from the tastes and needs of the nomadic Mongols in the interchange of goods between sedentary societies, as opposed to the passive, facilitating role represented by some notional *Pax Mongolica*'.

Two years after Jackson made that assessment, Allsen published his much longer and more wide-ranging *Culture and Conquest in Mongol Eurasia* (2001). The main sections of this are on 'political–economic

[43]   'Who ran the Mongol Empire?', *JRAS*, 1982/2, pp. 124–36.
[44]   'Mongol or Persian: the government of Ilkhanid Iran', *Harvard Middle Eastern and Islamic Review*, 3, 1/2 (1996), pp. 62–76.
[45]   'The state of research', p. 202.

relations,' 'intermediaries' and 'cultural exchange'. This carried much further the revisionist view of the Mongols and their role in their empire that had been evident in the earlier book. Among many other matters, it discussed such cultural intermediary figures as Marco Polo, Rashīd al-Dīn and Bolad Chingsang (Pulad Ching-sang), and it showed that the Mongols were actively involved in a wide range of cultural exchange across the length and breadth of Eurasia: historiography, geography and cartography, astronomy, agriculture, cuisine, medicine, printing. It is an extraordinarily enlightening book: no one who reads it is likely ever to envisage the Mongol Empire in quite the same way again, or to think of the Mongols themselves as nothing more than a brutal and licentious soldiery. A major explanation for the innovative importance of the book, as well as of Allsen's other publications, is his linguistic range. I commented above (p. 5) that a historian of the Mongols should ideally know a large number of languages so as to read his primary sources: I mentioned some ten, which was by no means an exhaustive list. I am not sure whether Allsen, like the late Joseph Fletcher (see above, p. 28, n. 31), knows all of them. But what is important in this context is that, unusually, he does know both Persian and Chinese, and has a deep knowledge of the sources in both languages: and those are far and away the two most important source languages. What he does is to bring together these two bodies of material, and make them illuminate each other. The results are revolutionary, and the book is in my judgement the most significant to be published on the Mongol Empire since I first became interested in the subject more than forty years ago.

Such a reassessment should not be thought to imply that the first Mongol invasions were any the less appalling than traditional scholarship has led us to believe. There is something of a tendency to argue that since there were, as is now established, many positive aspects to Mongol rule, their original conquests could not possibly have been as destructive of life and property as we thought: no doubt people were killed, but the Mongols were no worse than anyone else in their day. But there is no good reason to take such a view. As Kennedy justly writes,[46] '[r]evisionist historians have questioned the extent of Mongol ferocity and destructiveness, suggesting that such accounts are largely rhetoric and hyperbole. However, the weight of contemporary evidence is very strong and it is backed up by the archaeology.' The Mongols themselves would have been baffled by their apologists, having no

[46]   *Mongols, Huns and Vikings*, p. 138.

notion that their conquests and massacres were in any way discreditable, or indeed anything less than the fulfilment of the will of Tengri.

It has long been clear that Hülegü's invasion of Persia and Iraq in the 1250s was nothing like as destructive as his grandfather's campaign a generation earlier had been: why, after all, should he have wished to destroy his own potential property and future taxpaying subjects? It should, however, be mentioned that when writing to Louis IX of France in 1262, Hülegü in fact claimed (if implausibly) that two million people were killed during his sack of Baghdad, not the mere 200,000 that was alleged in the first edition of this book to be the figure.[47] Nonetheless, Hülegü has not himself, until recently, found many apologists. The prevalent tendency has been to assume that life in Ilkhanid Iran was all downhill, until the accession of Ghazan Khan in 1295, and his attempt at reforms which were designed to undo the damage caused by seven decades of Mongol rule. But now both Hülegü and his immediate successors have found a sturdy defender in George Lane.[48] Lane draws on a wide range of sources (not all of them Persian) to support his contention that the early Ilkhans have been sorely misrepresented and misunderstood; that they were in fact remarkably enlightened rulers. I am not myself sure that this is one hundred per cent convincing, but Lane certainly makes an eloquent case. And it would unquestionably be fair to agree that our view of the superiority of the reformer Ghazan over his allegedly benighted predecessors owes rather too much to the testimony of Rashīd al-Dīn, who was not only Ghazan's historian but also his joint chief minister, and hence not perhaps the most objective of witnesses.[49] Charles Melville has suggested[50] that the average Mongol of the Ilkhanate, if asked, might well have seen Ghazan not so much as a great and admirable reformer as the ruler who had, unfortunately, brought the Good Old Days to a premature end.

One of the features of this book which prompted comment at the time of its publication was the fact that it somewhat improbably

---

[47]   See above, p. 133, and n. 27. The Latin text of the letter is quite clear: I was misled by the editor's translation, and consequently misled my readers.

[48]   *Early Mongol Rule in Thirteenth-Century Iran. A Persian Renaissance* (2003).

[49]   On these issues see my 'Rašīd al-dīn and Ġazan Khan', in D. Aigle (ed.), *L'Iran face à la domination mongole* (1997), pp. 179–88.

[50]   C. P. Melville, 'Abū Sā'id and the revolt of the amirs in 1319', in Aigle, *L'Iran*, p. 115.

inaugurated (together with, rather more plausibly, Roger Collins's volume on *The Basques*) a series on 'The Peoples of Europe'. The series has since spawned numerous offspring: Peoples of Africa, South-East Asia, America, Asia; and no doubt if *The Mongols* were to be published now for the first time, they would be deemed to be a people of Asia. But the book's presence in its series did provide a pretext for giving the European dimension to the Mongol phenomenon a fair amount of attention. That aspect of the subject has been extensively studied since, and several new books of considerable importance have appeared. Most significant are two books in German and two in English.[51] Of the two books in English, Ruotsala deals essentially with only a decade of contacts (1245–55), whereas Jackson's book is much more comprehensive, stretching as it does from the first Mongol–European contacts down to the aftermath of the death of Tamerlane. This is a remarkable book, based on research in sources from many parts of Europe as well as Asia. It sets the study of this aspect of Mongol history on a vastly more detailed and secure foundation, including thematic as well as chronologically organised chapters. Incidentally, its first chapters provide, as background, a convenient, short and up-to-date introduction to the rise of the Mongol Empire. This is certainly one of the outstanding books on Mongol history to be published in recent times. Jackson's book follows on from his earlier chapter in the *New Cambridge Medieval History*.[52] As he points out,[53] the fact that such a chapter was commissioned (there was no such attention paid to the subject in the original 1929 volume) is a significant indication of the extent to which the Mongols have come 'to loom larger within the framework of orthodox medieval European history'. Even before then, an admirable account of European contacts with the Mongols formed part two of J. R. S. Phillips's *The Medieval Expansion of Europe*.[54]

---

[51]   A. Klopprogge, *Ursprung und Ausprägung des abendländischen Mongolenbildes im 13. Jahrhundert* (1993); F. Schmieder, *Europa und die Fremden. Die Mongolen im Urteil des Abendlandes vom 13. bis in das 15. Jahrhundert* (1994); A. Ruotsala, *Europeans and Mongols in the Middle of the Thirteenth Century. Encountering the Other* (2001); P. Jackson, *The Mongols and the West, 1221–1410* (2005).

[52]   'The Mongols and Europe', in D. Abulafia (ed.), *The New Cambridge Medieval History V: c.1198–1300* (1999), pp. 703–19.

[53]   'The state of research', p. 190.

[54]   2nd ed., 1998.

Inevitably, the most extensive contacts were with the two Mongol khanates nearest to Europe: the Golden Horde and the Ilkhanate. The standard general study of the Golden Horde remains that of Spuler, of which the second (and last) edition was published in 1965: it has never been translated into English. A useful and straightforward narrative was provided by Leo de Hartog, as a sequel to his biography of Chinggis Khan.[55] De Hartog followed the conventional date for the end of the Golden Horde – 1502 – but he took note of an article by Leslie Collins which argued that this is a misreading of the events.[56] Collins contended that all that happened in 1502 was that the Tatars of the Crimea, in defeating the Great Horde, had in effect taken over, not destroyed, the Golden Horde, which duly continued under their leadership. There is much food for thought on what the effect of Mongol rule and domination was on Russia in Charles Halperin's two books: *Russia and the Golden Horde. The Mongol Impact on Medieval Russian History* (mentioned above, p. xiv) and his later *The Tatar Yoke* (1986). Halperin interestingly discusses what he calls 'the ideology of silence', in accordance with which Russian bookmen, in effect, showed themselves as being in denial about the very fact of the Mongol conquest: though this did not hinder the Mongols' being blamed as the root cause of everything bad that ever subsequently happened in Russia. What influence the Mongols actually had on the development of society and government in Russia is persuasively examined by Donald Ostrowski.[57] The results of his enquiries suggest only a limited degree of such influence, mostly in the sphere of administration. He finds little evidence of Mongol influence on the development of Russian military tactics or the evolution of its autocratic form of government.

One startling suggestion regarding the long-term influence of the Golden Horde on subsequent history is so remarkable that it must be mentioned. This is to be found in an article by Colin Heywood.[58] What

---

[55]   *Russia and the Mongol Yoke. The History of the Russian Principalities and the Golden Horde, 1221–1502* (1996).

[56]   'On the alleged "destruction" of the Great Horde in 1502', in A. Bryer and M. Ursinus (eds), *Manzikert to Lepanto. The Byzantine World and the Turks 1071–1571*, special issue of *Byzantinische Forschungen*, 1991, pp. 361–99.

[57]   *Muscovy and the Mongols. Cross-Cultural Influences on the Steppe Frontier, 1304–1589* (1998).

[58]   'Filling the Black Hole: the emergence of the Bithynian Atamanates', in K. Çiçek at al (eds), *The Great Ottoman-Turkish Civilisation*, 1 (2000), pp. 107–15.

he was attempting to do was to find an explanation for the mysterious appearance, around the year 1300, of the Ottoman emirate in north-west Anatolia. His suggestion is that that explanation lies in the turbulent events which followed the defeat and death of the powerful Golden Horde prince Nogai (on whom see above, p. 124), in 1299. There was, it would seem, large-scale displacement of Turko-Mongol peoples from north of the Black Sea at this time: and it is this movement of peoples which Heywood contends accounts for the foundation of the initially small Ottoman emirate. It is a persuasive theory, even if the evidence is less than overwhelming in bulk. And if there is indeed anything in it, the Mongols would then, if inadvertently, be ultimately responsible for the beginnings of what was later, and for many centuries, the Ottoman Empire: a major legacy indeed.

One of the striking differences between the Mongols of the Golden Horde and those of the other khanates is that they did not ultimately adopt the religion of their conquered subjects: in this case that would have been Orthodox Christianity.[59] Instead, like their cousins in the Ilkhanate and the Chaghatai Khanate, they eventually became Muslims. Indeed, as has been noted (above, p. 127), the second Khan of the Golden Horde, Berke, was the first important Mongol to be converted to Islam. It was, however, many decades before the Golden Horde as a whole followed his example. What this process may have been like is the subject of a difficult but extremely rewarding book by Devin DeWeese.[60] What DeWeese does is to look at a sixteenth-century account of the conversion of Özbeg, the khan under whom the Golden Horde became officially Muslim, and to examine what this can tell us about the blending of Islamic belief and values with those indigenous to Central Asia. Hence this is not specifically a study of the conversion of the Golden Horde; but there is nevertheless much that can be learnt about that transformation from the book.

---

[59]   On Mongol attitudes towards their subjects' religions, see the important paper by Peter Jackson, 'The Mongols and the faith of the conquered', in Amitai and Biran (eds), *Mongols, Turks and Others*, pp. 245–90. Jackson argues that the Mongols' religious tolerance has been overstated (e.g., perhaps, above, p. 37): in his opinion what has been taken for tolerance was in fact mostly *Realpolitik*. The same volume contains a discussion by Michal Biran (pp. 175–99) of a singularly intriguing question: 'True to their ways. Why the Qara Khitai did not convert to Islam'.

[60]   *Islamization and Native Religion in the Golden Horde. Baba Tükles and Conversion to Islam in Historical and Epic Tradition* (1994).

As we have seen, it has been argued, notably by George Lane, that even the first Ilkhans have conventionally been unjustly condemned. Not everyone who has written about the Ilkhanate in recent years, however, has returned an entirely favourable verdict. A. K. S. Lambton's *Continuity and Change in Medieval Persia. Aspects of Administrative, Economic and Social History, 11th–14th Century* (1988 – above, p. xiv) studies both the Seljuk and the Mongol periods; and it cannot be said that the Mongols come particularly well out of the comparison, particularly in respect of the Persian economy. An especially striking feature of this book is the extensive use its author makes of Waṣṣāf, a major source who has tended to be neglected because of the extreme difficulty of his Persian style (see above, pp. 21–2). Consequently we learn a great deal, in illuminating detail, about Waṣṣāf's home province, Fārs, and what conditions there were like during the period of Mongol rule. On the workings of the central bureaucracy, and relations between Persian bureaucrats and their Mongol masters, we now have a remarkable short book by the late Jean Aubin.[61] This sheds much light on the manoeuvrings of various factions – factions which included both Persians and Mongols – and thus shows how acculturation could well be a two-way process.

As with the Golden Horde, we have no synthesis of recent work on the Ilkhanate. New findings tend to appear as articles or as collective volumes. An exception to this – and a most welcome one, concentrating for once, as it does, on what went on away from the Mongol political centre – is Denise Aigle's book-length study of Fārs in the thirteenth and fourteenth centuries.[62] One of the more notable collective volumes is what appears, on the face of it, to be a book of art history, edited by Julian Raby and Teresa Fitzherbert.[63] Some of the contributions are indeed concerned with painting and with artistic patronage; but the articles – by such scholars as Allsen, Amitai and Melville – have much wider implications. A more wide-ranging collection – it contains 15 contributions, mostly but not entirely in French – is that edited by Denise Aigle.[64] These all repay careful study. Here I single out just three.

---

[61]   *Emirs Mongols et vizirs persans dans les remous de l'acculturation* (1995).

[62]   *Le Fārs sous la domination mongole. Politique et fiscalité (XIIIe–XIVe S.)* (2005).

[63]   *The Court of the Il-khans 1290–1340* (Oxford Studies in Islamic Art, XII, 1996): see above, n. 19.

[64]   *L'Iran face à la domination mongole*: see above, nn. 48, 49.

First there are Bert Fragner's ruminations on 'Iran under Ilkhanid rule in a world history perspective'.[65] This is a consideration of the Mongol legacy to Iran; and Fragner's verdict is strikingly positive. For him, as I have remarked elsewhere, 'the Mongol legacy was in fact modern Iran which, he says, is an Ilkhanid creation in terms of nomenclature ("Iran" not having been much used since pre-Islamic times), language (the final triumph of New Persian over Arabic), geographical boundaries and political geography (the definition of Iran's eastern frontier on the Oxus; the importance of Tabriz), and the population and ethnic composition of the country (a large influx of Turks under Mongol auspices; the continued importance of the tribal population as compared with most other parts of the Middle East)'.[66] At the opposite pole from these wide-ranging thoughts is Birgitt Hoffmann's discussion (pp. 189–201) of 'The gates of piety and charity. Rašīd al-dīn Faḍl Allāh as founder of pious endowments'. This is one of the results of her work on the *waqf-nāma*, the deed of endowment for Rashīd al-Dīn's quarter in Tabriz (see above, p. 19). Since then she has published a detailed examination of the document,[67] which throws a flood of light on many of the details of the social, economic and religious history of Mongol Persia.

Then there is Charles Melville's examination (pp. 89–120 – see above, n. 49) of the revolt of the amirs in 1319. This is one of a number of studies which Melville has published on the 'decline and fall' of the Ilkhanate: they culminated in a short but tightly packed book.[68] According to Melville, the seeds of dissolution had long been visible when the Ilkhanate collapsed on the death of Abū Sāʿid in 1316. This is a very different picture from the one presented in the first edition of this book (above, pp. 170–4): that of an empire which, in defiance of what I have elsewhere termed 'Gibbon's Law',[69] contrived to fall without having previously declined. It was argued above that some later chroniclers' characterisation of the reign of Abū Sāʿid as a kind of Golden Age,

[65] Pp. 121–31. He continues these reflections in a contribution to L. Komaroff (ed.), *Beyond the Legacy of Genghis Khan* (2006).

[66] Morgan, 'The Mongols in Iran: a reappraisal', p. 135.

[67] *Waqf im mongolischen Iran. Rašīduddīns Sorge um Nachrum und Seelenheil* (2000).

[68] *The Fall of Amir Chupan and the Decline of the Ilkhanate, 1327–37. A Decade of Discord in Mongol Iran* (1999). See my review in *BSOAS*, 63/3 (2000), pp. 430–2.

[69] E.g. in Morgan, 'The decline and fall of the Mongol Empire', in S. Cummings and H. Kennedy, *Empire and After* (forthcoming).

Figure 9.2 *Firmān* (edict) of the Īlkhān Geikhatu, Iran, 1292, ink on paper, 105.4 × 33.6 cm. Lent by the Art and History Collection, photo courtesy of the Arthur M. Sackler Gallery, Smithsonian Institution, Washington, DC, LTS1995.2.9

however much that may have been influenced by contrast with the anarchy that followed the collapse of the Ilkhanate, was at least to some extent justified. As a caveat, I suggested (p. 150) that the apparent decline in the quality of Ilkhanid coinage might suggest that all was not entirely well: but John Masson Smith, in his review of this book (above, p. xiv), pointed out that no such decline occurred. My argument was that the Ilkhanate collapsed, above all, because Abū Saʿīd left no sons, and hence contention for the throne was inevitable: had there been an unchallenged heir of the house of Hülegü, there seemed to me no obvious reason why the Ilkhanate should not have successfully survived the 1330s.

Melville's unprecedentedly detailed examination of the years from 1327 to 1337 leads him to quite other conclusions. For him, the rot had set in at least by the beginning of Abū Saʿīd's reign. Thereafter he sees a pattern of factional struggles, decay and disintegration – an impression based in part on his use of several sources, notably two Persian verse chronicles, which have previously been virtually ignored. If this interpretation is right, it solves my 'fall without decline' conundrum at a stroke. However, I am not entirely convinced. Some contemporary observers – notably the singularly acute North African traveller Ibn Baṭṭūṭa[70] – while being well aware of the factional struggles that were going on, nevertheless seem to subscribe to something very like the 'Golden Age' view of Abū Saʿīd's reign. Nor is it clear to me that in terms of general turbulence, Abū Saʿīd's reign was very much worse than those of some of his predecessors – even that of Ghazan, generally thought of (rightly or wrongly) as the strongest and most decisive of the Ilkhans. We do not, on the whole, have very good sources for the Abū Saʿīd period: there is no equivalent to Juwaynī, Rashīd al-Dīn or Waṣ-ṣāf. It is indeed true that the sources on which Melville has, perforce, to rely, depict, as he puts it, a 'maze of alliances, uprisings, vendettas and betrayals', but that may tell us more about the sources, and their limitations, than it does about the reality of a stark contrast between Abū Saʿīd's and earlier reigns. As far as I can see, the abrupt collapse of Mongol rule in Persia still has an element of the mysterious about it.

For all the interest of the Ilkhanate and the Golden Horde, and the continuing comparative obscurity of the Chaghatai Khanate, there is no escaping the fact that the wealthiest, most powerful, and in almost all

---

[70] His account is found in ch. 6, pp. 271–359, of *The Travels of Ibn Baṭṭūṭa A. D. 1325–1354*, vol. II, tr. H. A. R. Gibb, Hakluyt Society, 1962.

respects, most significant part of the Mongol Empire was what was, after the success of Qubilai in the succession struggle of 1260–4, the realm of the Great Khan: China and Mongolia. As we have seen, scholarly interest in the Yüan period, once conspicuous by its absence, had begun to revive at the time when the first edition of this book was being written. This has continued. Notable landmarks – Rossabi's biography of Qubilai, volume 6 of the *Cambridge History of China*, the collection of biographies under the title of *In the Service of the Khan* – have already been mentioned. It should be added that the Mongol period is treated at considerable length in F. W. Mote's history of pre-1800 China.[71]

One conspicuous area of advance has been the administrative and governmental history of Mongol China. Elizabeth Endicott published a valuable study of local government.[72] She concentrates on the office of *darughachi*, on which she has much that is illuminating to say. Incidentally, she dismisses Paul Buell's view, followed in this book, that the office probably had Khitan antecedents.[73] On this point her reasoning does not seem to me to be persuasive. In the place of the Khitans, she offers a far more remote and, to my mind, vastly less plausible candidate: the late T'ang office *ya-ya*.[74] But that is very minor compared with the book's contribution in helping us to know what was going on away from the imperial centre – always an elusive area for the historian of premodern times. The leading historian of Yüan government, until his early death in 1985, was David Farquhar. For fifteen years he had worked on his *magnum opus* on the subject, and it eventually appeared, five years after his death.[75] What Farquhar did was to describe the government of Mongol China as it was in 1332, at which point a lengthy treatise was produced which, though it is now lost, formed the basis of the treatment of the system in the *Yüan-shih*. Essentially what Farquhar does is to

[71]   F. W. Mote, *Imperial China 900–1800* (1999), Part 3, 'China and the Mongol World' (chs 17–20), pp. 403–513, with notes on pp. 1003–1010.

[72]   E. Endicott-West, *Mongolian Rule in China. Local Administration in the Yuan Dynasty* (1989).

[73]   *Ibid.*, p. 151, n. 55: see above, p. 95.

[74]   *Ibid.*, p. 6 and p. 139, n. 18. It should be noted that Michal Biran accepts the Khitan origins of the Mongol period offices of *darughachi/shaḥna/bāsqāq* (Biran, *The Empire of the Qara Khitai*, pp. 121–3, 203).

[75]   *The Government of China under Mongolian Rule. A Reference Guide* (1990).

provide an annotated list of offices, with vast explanatory apparatus. This does not make for easy reading, but it does enable the determined student to learn a great deal about how Mongol government actually worked. As he remarks, the Mongols 'were able to preserve and incorporate into the Yüan government an amazing amount of their early political culture', especially in terms of replicating in China the structure of the greater empire, with 'a powerful imperial state at the center in North China surrounded by a cluster of dependent states (the other provinces) . . . similar in government and structure to the emperor's own domain, and to a great extent, administratively independent'.[76] In his preface to the book, Professor Herbert Franke described it as 'a monumental work' which 'embodies a lifetime of research on the Yüan dynasty in all its aspects'. And no scholar was better qualified to commend the book than Franke, some of whose own very important articles in English on Mongol China have been usefully collected together.[77]

If the predominant overall message that emerges from the scholarship on the Mongol Empire that was published in the 20 years after this book first appeared is, as I suggested at the beginning of this chapter, that there is a great deal more that is positive to say about the Mongols than used to be supposed, this would come as no surprise to historians of art, who have long seen the Mongol period as one of constructive innovation, in which artistic influences flowed across Asia to an extent hardly before dreamed of. The rest of us, prompted by the work of Allsen and others, are now catching up with the art specialists.

This is not, of course, to suggest that art historians of the period have now shot their bolt. That field continues in full vigour. One important collective volume (see above, n. 60) has already been mentioned. Most spectacularly, 2002/3 saw the most stunning exhibition of Mongol-period art ever to have been assembled. This was shown in both New York and Los Angeles. The catalogue of the exhibition,[78] a magnificent achievement in itself, contains a number of valuable articles, by such historians as Rossabi and Melville, and art historians of the stature of Sheila Blair and Robert Hillenbrand, as well as illustrations and discussion of the exhibits. The proceedings of a symposium held while the

---

[76]   *Ibid.*, p. 8.

[77]   *China under Mongol Rule* (1994).

[78]   L. Komaroff and S. Carboni (eds), *The Legacy of Genghis Khan. Courtly Art and Culture in Western Asia, 1256–1353* (2002).

exhibition was in Los Angeles have been published:[79] many of these papers are concerned with aspects of the art history of the period. It may be that, on occasion, art historians will tend towards speculation, on the basis of what to historians looks like thin or even nonexistent evidence.[80] But overall, the contribution made by such scholars as Blair and Hillenbrand – who know a great deal more history than most historians know art – has been massive and extraordinarily illuminating. The bibliography of *The Legacy of Genghis Khan*, for example, lists 15 relevant articles by Sheila Blair, perhaps the leading Mongol-period art historian, as well as several books by her or written jointly with her husband, Jonathan Bloom.[81] She and her colleagues have shown eloquently – particularly as regards the western parts of the Mongol Empire – how much creativity there was, creativity which was not only tolerated but actively encouraged by the Mongols. It would hardly have been possible to walk attentively around the great exhibition, or even to read through the catalogue, and to come away still thinking that the Mongol era was solely about killing and devastation.

At the end of my essay in *Beyond the Legacy of Genghis Khan*, I mentioned a remarkable article by Dr C. Tyler-Smith and others, which was published electronically in 2003 and entitled 'The genetic legacy of the Mongols'.[82] This purported to demonstrate, on the basis of research into the DNA of the Y chromosome, that something of the order of one per cent of the male population of the entire world (that is, around sixteen million men) are descended either from Chinggis Khan himself or from one of his fairly immediate ancestors. If I may quote myself by way of conclusion, 'it marks something of a change in perception if Chinggis Khan should now be remembered for peopling the world, rather than for depopulating large parts of it'.

---

[79]   L. Komaroff (ed.), *Beyond the Legacy of Genghis Khan* (2006). My own paper in the collection, 'The Mongol Empire in world history' (pp. 425–37), includes brief comments on each of the other papers in the volume.

[80]   See e.g. O. Grabar and S. Blair, *Epic Images and Contemporary History. The Illustrations of the Great Mongol Shahnama* (1980), and my review in *BSOAS*, 65/2 (1982), pp. 364–5; and A. Soudavar, 'The Saga of Abu-Saʿid Bahador Khan', in Raby and Fitzherbert, *The Court of the Il-khans*, pp. 95–218.

[81]   To give just one or two examples: Blair, 'The Mongol capital of Sulṭāniyya, "the Imperial"', *Iran*, 24 (1986), pp. 139–51; *A Compendium of Chronicles: Rashid al-Din's Illustrated History of the World* (1995); Blair and Bloom, *The Art and Architecture of Islam, 1250–1800* (1994).

[82]   *American Journal of Human Genetics*, 72 (17 January 2003).

References

Introductory Note

The best modern introduction to the subject is J. J. Saunders, *The History of the Mongol Conquests* (1971). P. Brent, *The Mongol Empire* (1976) is a straight-forward and well-illustrated narrative, without notes or references. E. D. Phillips, *The Mongols* (1969) is useful for the scant archaeological material and his excellent black and white illustrations, but unlike Saunders's book it tends to degenerate into a catalogue of khāns and battles. B. Spuler, *The Muslim World: a Historical Survey. Part II: The Mongol Period* (1960) and *The Mongols in History* (1971) pack a great deal of information into a small space. They are in large part virtually identical. S. Jagchid and P. Hyer, *Mongolia's Culture and Society* (1979) is an extremely interesting and informative general book about the Mongols. R. Grousset, *The Empire of the Steppes* (1970: translated from the French of 1939) and G. Hambly (ed.), *Central Asia* (1969) are the best approaches to the wider chronological context. Some of these and other recent books are discussed in D. O. Morgan, 'The Mongol Empire: a review article', *Bulletin of the School of Oriental and African Studies* 44/1 (1981), pp. 120–5. B. Spuler, *History of the Mongols* (1972) and E. Bretschneider, *Medieval Researches from Eastern Asiatic Sources* (1888) are valuable collections of source material in English translation.

Adams, R. M. *Land behind Baghdad* (Chicago and London, 1965).
Alizade, A. A. (ed.) Rashīd al-Dīn, *Jāmiʿ al-tawārīkh* vol. 3 (Baku, 1957).
— (ed.) Muḥammad ibn Hindūshāh Nakhjawānī, *Dastūr al-kātib fī taʿyīn al-marātib* vol. 2 (Moscow, 1976).
— (ed.) Rashīd al-Dīn, *Jāmiʿ al-tawārīkh* vol. 2 part 1 (Moscow, 1980).
Allsen, T. T. Mongol census taking in Rus', 1245–1275. *Harvard Ukrainian Studies* 5/1 (1981), 32–53.
— The Yüan Dynastry and the Uighurs of Turfan in the 13th century. In Rossabi, *China among Equals* (1983), 243–80.
Anderson, P. *Passages from Antiquity to Feudalism* (London, 1974).
Aubin, J. L'ethnogénèse des Qaraunas. *Turcica* 1 (1969), 65–94.

Ayalon, D. The great *Yāsa* of Chingiz Khān: a re-examination. A. *Studia Islamica* 33 (1971), 97–140.

— On one of the works of Jean Sauvaget. *Israel Oriental Studies* 1 (1971), 298–302.

Balazs, E. Marco Polo in the capital of China. In his *Chinese Civilization and Bureaucracy* (New Haven and London, 1964), 79–100.

Ball, W. Two aspects of Iranian Buddhism. *Bulletin of the Asia Institute of Pahlavi University* 1–4 (1976), 103–63.

— The Imamzadeh Ma'sum at Vardjovi. A rock-cut Il-khanid complex near Maragheh. *Archaeologische Mitteilungen aus Iran* 12 (1979), 329–40.

Barbier de Meynard, C. (tr.) *Dictionnaire géographique, historique et littéraire de la Perse* (Paris, 1861).

Barthold, W. *Ulugh Beg* (*Four Studies on the History of Central Asia* vol. 2, tr. V. and T. Minorsky) (Leiden, 1958).

— *Turkestan down to the Mongol Invasion*, 4th edn (London, 1977).

Bawden, C. R. *The Modern History of Mongolia* (London, 1968).

— Riding with the Khans. (A review of Cleaves, *Secret History*). *Times Literary Supplement*, 24 June 1983, 669.

Beazley, E. and Harverson, M. *Living with the Desert* (Warminster, 1982).

Beckingham, C. F. *The Achievements of Prester John* (London, 1966). Reprinted in Beckingham, *Between Islam and Christendom*.

— The quest for Prester John. *Bulletin of the John Rylands University Library of Manchester* 62/2 (1980), 291–310. Reprinted in Beckingham, *Between Islam and Christendom*.

— *Between Islam and Christendom* (London, 1983).

Berezin, I. N. (ed. and tr.) Rashīd al-Dīn, *Sbornik Letopisei*. In *Trudy vostočnago otdêlenija Imperatorskskago Russkago Arkheologičeskago Obščestva* 13 (1868), 15 (1888).

Beveridge, A. S. (tr.) *The Bābur-nāma in English* (London, 1922).

Bezzola, G. A. *Die Mongolen in abendländischer Sicht (1220–1270)* (Berne and Munich, 1974).

Boyle, J. A. (tr.) 'Atā Malik Juvainī, *The History of the World Conqueror*, 2 vols (Manchester, 1958).

— The death of the last 'Abbāsid Caliph: a contemporary Muslim account. *Journal of Semitic Studies* 6 (1961), 145–61. Reprinted in Boyle, *The Mongol World Empire*.

— A form of horse sacrifice amongst the 13th- and 14th-century Mongols. *Central Asiatic Journal* 10 (1965), 1450–50. Reprinted in Boyle, *The Mongol World Empire*.

— (ed.) *The Cambridge History of Iran* vol. 5, *The Saljuq and Mongol Periods* (Cambridge, 1968).

— Dynastic and political history of the Īl-Khāns. In Boyle, *The Cambridge History of Iran*, 303–421.

— Rashīd al-Dīn and the Franks. *Central Asiatic Journal* 14 (1970), 62–7. Reprinted in Boyle, *The Mongol World Empire.*

— The burial place of the Great Khan Ögedei. *Acta Orientalia* 22 (1970), 45–50. Reprinted in Boyle, *The Mongol World Empire.*

— (tr.) Rashīd al-Dīn, *The Successors of Genghis Khan* (New York and London, 1971).

— Turkish and Mongol Shamanism in the Middle Ages. *Folklore* 83 (1972), 177–93. Reprinted in Boyle, *The Mongol World Empire.*

— The thirteenth-century Mongols' conception of the after-life: the evidence of their funerary practices. *Mongoliam Studies* 1 (1974), 5–14. Reprinted in Boyle, *The Mongol World Empire.*

— The Il-Khans of Persia and the princes of Europe. *Central Asiatic Journal* 20/1–2 (1976), 25–40.

— *The Mongol World Empire 1206–1370* (London, 1977).

Brent, P. *The Mongol Empire* (London, 1976).

Bretschneider, E. *Medieval Researches from Eastern Asiatic Sources*, 2 vols (London, 1888).

Browne, E. G. *A Literary History of Persia*, 4 vols (Cambridge, 1928).

Budge, E. A. W. (tr.) *The Monks of Ḳūblāi Khān, Emperor of China* (London, 1928).

— (ed. and tr.) *The Chronography of Gregory Abū'l Faraj . . . Commonly Known as Bar Hebraeus*, 2 vols (London, 1932).

Buell, P. D. Sino-Khitan administration ion Mongol Bukhare. *Journal of Asian History* 13/2 (1979), 121–51.

— The role of the Sino-Mongolian frontier zone in the rise of Cinggis-Qan. In Schwarz, H. G. (ed.) *Studies on Mongolia: Proceedings of the First North American Conference on Mongolian Studies* (Bellingham, Washington, 1979), 63–76.

— Kalmyk Tanggaci people: thoughts on the mechanics and impact of Mongol expansion. *Mongolian Studies* 6 (1980), 41–59.

Cahen, C. *Pre-Ottoman Turkey* (London, 1968).

— The Mongols and the near East. In Setton, K. M. (ed.) *A History of the Crusades* vol. 2 (Madison, 1969), 715–32.

Chambers, J. *The Devil's Horsemen: the Mongol Invasion of Europe* (London, 1979).

Chan, H. Liu Ping-chung; a Buddhist-Taoist statesman at the court of Khubilai Khan. *T'oung-pao* 53 (1967), 98–146.

Ch'en, P. *Chinese Legal Tradition under the Mongols: the Code of 1291 as Reconstructed* (Princeton, 1979).

Clauson, G. *An Etymological Dictionary of pre-Thirteenth Century Turkish* (Oxford, 1972).

Cleaves, F. W. The historicity of the Baljuna covenant. *Harvard Journal of Asiatic Studies* 18 (1955), 357–421.

— (tr.) *The Secret History of the Mongols* (Cambridge, Mass., 1982).

Collins, L. J. D. The military organisation and tactics of the Crimean Tatars during the sixteenth and seventeenth centuries. In Parry, V. J. and Yapp, M. E. (eds) *War, Technology and Society in the Middle East* (London, 1975), 256–76.

Coulton, G. G. *From St. Francis to Dante* (Philadelphia, 1972).

Crone, P. *Slaves on Horses: the Evolution of the Islamic Polity* (Cambridge, 1980).

Dardess, J. W. From Mongol Empire to Yüan Dynasty: changing forms of imperial rule in Mongolia and Central Asia. *Monumenta Serica* 30 (1972–3), 117–65.

— *Conquerors and Confucians: Aspects of Political Change in Late Yüan China* (New York, 1973).

Dauvillier, J. Les provinces chaldéennes 'de l'extérieur' au moyen âge. In *Mélanges F. Cavallera* (Toulouse, 1948), 261–316. Reprinted in Dauvillier, *Historire et institutions.*

— Guillaume de Roubrouck et les communautés chaldéennes d'Asie centrale au moyen âge. *L'Orient syrien* 2 (1957), 223–42. Reprinted in Dauvillier, *Histoire et institutions.*

— *Histoire et institutions des églises orientales au moyen âge* (London, 1983).

Dawson, C. (ed.) *The Mongol Mission* (London and New York, 1995).

De Rachewiltz, I. Yeh-lü Ch'u-ts'ai (1189–1243): Buddhist idealist and Confucian statesman. In Wright, A. F. and Twitchett, D. (eds) *Confucian Personalities* (Standford, 1962), 189–216.

— Some remarks on the dating of the *Secret History of the Mongols. Monumenta Serical* 24 (1965), 185–206.

— Personnel and personalities in north China in the early Mongol Period. *Journal of the Economic and social History of the Orient* 9 (1996), 88–144.

— *The Secret History of the Mongols. Papers in Far Eastern History* 4 (1971), 5 (1972), 10 (1974), 13 (1976), 16 (1977), 18 (1978), 21 (1980), 23 (1981).

— *Papal Envoys to the Great Khans* (London, 1971).

— Some remarks on the ideological foundations of Chinggis Khan's empire. *Papers in Far Eastern History* 7 (1973), 21–36.

— Turks in China under the Mongols: a preliminary investigation of Turco–Mongol relations in the 13th and 14th centuries. In Rossabi, *China among Equals*, 281–310.

Dvornik, F. *Origins of Intelligence Services* (New Brunswick, 1974).

EI²: Encyclopaedia of Islam, 2nd edn (in progress).

EIr: Encyclopaedia Iranica (in progress).

Eliade, M. *Shamanism* (New York, 1964).

Ellis Davidson, H. R. *The Viking Road to Byzantium* (London, 1976).

Evans, A. (ed.) Francesco Pegolotti, *La Pratica della Mercatura* (Cambridge, Mass., 1936).

Farquhar, D. M. Stucture and function in Yüan imperial government. In Langlois, *China under Mongol Rule*, 25–55.

Fawtier, R. *The Capetian Kings of France* (London, 1960).

Fennell, J. L. I. *The Crisis of Medieval Russia 1200–1304* (London, 1983).

Fischer, K. From the Mongols to the Mughals. In Allchin, F. R. and Hammond, N. (eds) *The Archaeology of Afghanistan from the Earliest Times to the Timurid Period* (London, New York and San Francisco, 1978), 357–404.

Fletcher, J. F. China and Central Asia, 1368–1884. In Fairbank, J. K. (ed.) *The Chinese World Order: Traditional China's Foreign Relations* (Cambridge, Mass., 1968), 206–24, 337–68.

— Turco-Mongolian monarchic tradition in the Ottoman Empire. *Harvard Ukrainian Studies* 3–4 (1979–80), 236–51.

Fox, R. *Genghis Khan* (London, 1936).

Franke, H. Sino-western contacts under the Mongol Empire. *Journal of the Hong Kong Branch of the Royal Asiatic Society* 6 (1966), 49–72.

— Tibetans in Yüan China. In Langlois, *China under Mongol Rule* (1981), 296–328.

Franke, O. *Geschichte des chinesischen Reiches*, 5 vols (Berlin, 1930–52).

Gernet, J. *Daily Life in China on the Eve of the Mongol Invasion* (London, 1962).

Gibb, H. A. R. (tr.) *The Travels of Ibn Baṭṭūṭa*, 3 vols, Hakluyt Society (Cambridge, 1958, 1962, 1971).

Gibbon, E. *The History of the Decline and Fall of the Roman Empire*, ed. J. B. Bury, 7 vols (London, 1905–6).

Giles, J. A. (tr.) *Matthew Paris's English History*, 3 vols (London, 1852–4).

Gillingham, J. B. *The Angevin Empire* (London, 1984).

Grierson, P. Muslim coins in thirteenth century England. In Kouymjian, D. K. (ed.) *Studies in Honor of George C. Miles* (Beirut, 1974), 387–91.

Grousset, R. *Histoire des Croisades*, 3 vols (Paris, 1934–6).

— *Conqueror of the World*, tr. Sinor, D. and MacKellar, M. (Edinburgh and London, 1967).

— *The Empire of the Steppes*, tr. Walford, N. (New Brunswick, 1970).

Ḥabībī, 'A. (ed.) Minhāj al-Dīn Jūzjānī, *Ṭabaqāt-i Nāṣirī*, 2 vols, 2nd edn (Kabul, 1964–5).

Hague, R. (tr.) *The Life of St. Louis by John of Joinville* (London, 1955).

Halperin, C. J. Russia in the Mongol Empire in comparative perspective. *Harvard Journal of Asiatic Studies* 43/1 (1983), 239–61.

Hambis, L. *Gengis-Khan* (Paris, 1973).

Hambly, G. (ed.) *Central Asia* (London, 1969).

Hambly, M. (ed.) Qāshānī, *Ta'rīkh-i Ūljāytū* (Tehran, 1969).

Hay, D. *Annalists and Historians* (London, 1977).

Heissig, W. *A Lost Civilisation: the Mongols Rediscovered* (London, 1966).

— *The Religions of Mongolia* (London, 1980).

Hitti, P. K. (tr.) *An Arab-Syrian Gentleman and Warrior in the Period of the Crusades* (New York, 1929).

Hodgson, M. G. S. *The Order of Assassins* (The Hague, 1955).
— The Ismā'īlī state. In Boyle, *The Cambridge History of Iran*, vol. 5, 422–82.
Holt, P. M. Some observations on the 'Abbāsid caliphate of Cairo. *Bulletin of the School of Oriental and African Studies* 47/3 (1984), 501–7.
Hookham, H. *Tamburlaine the Conqueror* (London, 1962).
Hsiao, C. *The Military Establishment of the Yuan Dynasty* (Cambridge, Mass., 1978).
Humphreys, R. S. *From Saladin to the Mongols* (Albany, 1977).
Hung, C. China and the nomads: misconceptions in western historiography on Inner Asia. *Harvard Journal of Asiatic Studies* 41/2 (1981), 597–628.
Irwin, R. *The Middle East in the Middle Ages: the Early Mamluk Sultanate 1250–1382* (London, 1986).
Jackson, P. The accession of Qubilai Qa'an: a re-examination. *Journal of the Anglo-Mongolian Society* 2/1 (1975), 1–10.
— The dissolution of the Mongol Empire. *Central Asiatic Journal* 22 (1978), 186–244.
— The crisis in the Holy Land in 1260. *English Historical Review* 95 (1980), 481–513.
Jagchid, S. and Hyer, P. *Mongolia's Culture and Society* (Boulder and Folkestone, 1979).
Jahn, K. (ed. and tr.) *Histoire universelle de Rašīd al-Dīn Faḍl Allāh Abul Khair. 1. Histoire des Francs* (Leiden, 1951).
— Paper currency in Iran. *Journal of Asian History* 4/2 (1970), 101–35.
— (ed. and tr.) *Die Frankengeschichte des Rašīd al-Dīn* (Vienna, 1977).
Jones, A. H. M. *The Later Roman Empire*, 3 vols (Oxford, 1964).
Karīmī, B. (ed.) Rashīd al-Dīn, *Jāmi' al-tawārīkh*, 2 vols (Tehran, 1970).
Krueger, J. R. (tr.) Sagang Sechen, *A History of the Eastern Mongols to 1662*, part 1. Mongolia Society Occasional Papers no. 2 (Bloomington, 1964).
Kwanten, L. *Imperial Nomads: a History of Central Asia, 500–1500* (Leicester, 1979).
Lambton, A. K. S. *Landlord and Peasant in Persia* (London, 1953).
— *Awqāf* in Persia: 7th/13th and 8th/14th centuries (forthcoming).
— Mongol fiscal administration in Persia (forthcoming).
Langlois, J. D., Jr (ed.) *China under Mongol Rule* (Princeton, 1981).
Latham, R. E. (tr.) *The Travels of Marco Polo* (Harmondsworth, 1958).
Lattimore, O. Inner Asian frontiers – defensive empires and conquest empires. In his *Studies in Frontier History* (London, 1962), 501–13.
— The geography of Chingis Khan. *Geographical Journal* 129/1 (1963), 1–7.
Le Roy Laduire, E. The 'event' and the 'long term' in social history: the case of the Chouan uprising. In his *The Territory of the Historian* (Brighton, 1979), 111–31.
Le Strange, G. (ed.) Ḥamd Allāh Mustawfī Qazwīnī, *The Geographical Part of the Nuzhat al-qulūb* (Leiden and London, 1915).

Lewis, B. *The Assassins: a Radical Sect in Islam* (London, 1967).
— The Muslim discovery of Europe. In his *Islam in History* (London, 1973), 92–100 and 311–12.
— The Mongols, the Turks and the Muslim polity. In his *Islam in History* (London, 1973), 179–98 and 324–5.
— *The Muslim Discovery of Europe* (London, 1982).
Liddell Hart, B. H. *Great Captains Unveiled* (London, 1927).
Lindner, R. P. Nomadism, horses and Huns. *Past and Present* 92 (1981), 3–19.
— What was a nomadic tribe? *Comparative Studies in Society and History* 24/4 (1982), 689–711.
— *Nomads and Ottomans in Medieval Anatolia* (Bloomington, 1983).
Luard, H. R. (ed.) Matthew Paris, *Chronica Majora*, 7 vols, Rolls Series (London, 1872–84).
Lupprian, K.-E. (ed.) *Die Beziehungen der Päpste zu islamischen und mongolischen Herrschern im 13. Jahrhundert anhand ihres Briefwechsels* (Vatican City, 1981).
McGovern, W. M. *The Early Empires of Central Asia* (Chapel Hill, 1939).
McNeill, W. H. *Plagues and Peoples* (Oxford, 1976).
Martin, H. D. The Mongol army. *Journal of the Royal Asiatic Society* 1943/1–2, 46–85.
— *The Rise of Chingis Khan and his Conquest of North China* (Baltimore, 1950).
Meyvaert, P. An unknown letter of Hulagu, Il-Khan of Persia, to King Louis IX of France. *Viator* 11 (1980), 245–59.
Michell, R., and Forbes, N. (trs) *The Chronicle of Novgorod*, Camden Society (London, 1914).
Minorsky, V. Naṣīr al-Dīn Ṭūsī on finance. In his *Iranica* (Tehran, 1964), 64–85.
— Pūr-i Bahā and his poems. In his *Iranica* (Tehran, 1964), 292–305.
Morgan, D. O. Cassiodorus and Rashīd al-Dīn on barbarian rule in Italy and Persia. *Bulletin of the School of Oriental and African Studies* 40/2 (1977), 302–20.
— The Mongol armies in Persia. *Der Islam* 56/1 (1979), 81–96.
— The Mongol Empire: a review article. *Bulletin of the School of Oriental and African Studies* 44/1 (1981), 120–5.
— Who ran the Mongol Empire? *Journal of the Royal Asiatic Society* 1982/2, 127–36.
— Persian historians and the Mongols. In Morgan, D. O. (ed.) *Medieval Historical Writing in the Christian and Islamic Worlds* (London, 1982), 109–24.
— The Mongols in Syria, 1260–1300. In Edbury, P. W. (ed.) *Crusade and Settlement* (Cardiff, 1985), 231–5.
— The 'Great *Yāsā* of Chingiz Khān' and Mongol law in the Īlkhānate. *Bulletin of the School of Oriental and African Studies* 49/1 (1986), 163–76.

Morison, S. E. *The Great Explorers: the European Discovery of America* (New York, 1978).

Morton, A. H. Ghūrid gold en route to England? *Iran* 16 (1978), 167–70.

Mostaert, A. and Cleaves, F. W. *Les Lettres de 1289 et 1305 des ilkhans Arγun et Ölǰeitü à Philippe le Bel* (Cambridge, Mass., 1962).

Moule, A. C. *Quinsai, with other notes on Marco Polo* (Cambridge, 1957).

— and Pelliot, P. (trs) *Marco Polo: the Description of the World*, 2 vols (London, 1938).

Nawā'ī, 'A. (ed.) Ḥamd Allāh Mustawfī Qazwīnī, *Ta'rīkh-i guzīda* (Tehran, 1958–61).

Olbricht, P. *Das Postwesen in China unter der Mongolenherrschaft im 13 und 14 Jahrhundert* (Wiesbaden, 1954).

— and Pinks, E. (trs) *Meng-Ta pei-lu und Hei-Ta shih-lüeh* (Wies-baden, 1980).

Olschki, L. *Marco Polo's Asia* (Berkeley and Los Angeles, 1960).

Önnerfore, A. (ed.) *Hystoria Tartarorum C. de Bridia Monachi* (Berlin, 1967).

Parry, J. H. *The Age of Reconnaissance* (New York, 1964).

Pelliot, P. Les Mongols et la Papauté. *Revue de l'Orient chrétien* 23 (1922–3), 3–30, 24 (1924), 225–335; 28 (1932), 3–84.

— *Notes on Marco Polo*, 3 vols (Paris, 1959–73).

— and Hambis, L. *Histoire des campagnes de Gengis Khan*, vol. 1 (Leiden, 1951).

Petech, L. Les Marchands italiens dans l'empire mongol. *Journal Asiatique* 250 (1962), 549–74.

— Tibetan relations with Sung China and with the Mongols. In Rossabi, *China among Equals* (1983), 173–203.

Petrushevsky, I. P. *Zemledelie i Agrarnie Otnosheniya v Irane XIII–XIVvv.* (Moscow and Leningrad, 1960).

— *Kishāwarzī wa Munāsibāt-i arḍī dar Īrān*, 2 vols, tr. K. Kishāwarz (Tehran, 1966).

— The socio-economic condition of Iran under the Īl-Khāns. In Boyle, *The Cambridge History of Iran*, 483–537.

— Rashīd al-Dīn's conception of the state. *Central Asiatic Journal* 14 (1970), 148–62.

Phillips, E. D. *The Mongols* (London, 1969).

Poppe, N. *The Mongolian Monuments in ḫP'ags-pa Script*, 2nd edn, ed. and tr. J. R. Krueger (Wiesbaden, 1957).

Pritsak, O. Two migratory movements in the Eurasian steppe in the 9th–11th centuries. *Proceedings of the 26th International Congress of Orientalists, New Delhi 1964* vol. 2 (New Delhi, 1968), 157–63. Reprinted in Pritsak, O., *Studies in Medieval Eurasian History* (London, 1981).

Qazwīnī, M. M. (ed.) 'Aṭā Malik Juwaynī, *Ta'rīkh-i Jahān Gushā*, 3 vols (Leiden and London, 1912, 1916, 1937).

Quatremère, E. (ed. and tr.) Raschid Eldin, *Histoire des Mongols de la Perse* (Paris, 1836).

Ratchnevsky, P. Šigi-qutuqu, ein mongolischer Gefolgsmann im 12.–13. Jahrhundert. *Central Asiatic Journal* 10 (1965), 88–120.

— Die Yasa (Ĵasaq) Činggis-khans und ihre Problematik. *Schriften zur Geschichte und Kultur des alten Orients 5: Sprache, Geschichte und Kultur der altaischen Völker* (Berlin, 1974), 471–87.

— *Činggis-Khan sein Leben und Wirken* (Wiesbaden, 1983).

Raverty, H. G. (tr.) Minhāj al-Dīn Jūzjānī, *Tabakāt-i-Nāṣirī*, 2 vols (London, 1881).

Reischauer, E. O. and Fairbank, J. K. *East Asia: the Great Tradition* (Boston, 1958).

Riasanovsky, V. A. *Fundamental Principles of Mongol Law* (The Hague, 1965).

Ricci, A. (tr.) *The Travels of Marco Polo* (London, 1931).

Richard, J. (ed.) Simon de Saint-Quentin, *Histoire des Tartares* (Paris, 1965).

— The Mongols and the Franks. *Journal of Asian History* 3 (1969), 45–57. Reprinted in Richard, *Orient et Occident au moyen âge*.

— Isol le Pisan: un aventurier franc gouverneur d'une province mongole? *Central Asiatic Journal* 14 (1970), 186–94. Reprinted in Richard, *Orient et Occident au moyen âge*.

— *Orient et Occident au moyen âge: contacts et relations (XIIe–XVe s.)* (London, 1976).

— *La Papauté et les missions d'Orient au moyen âge (XIII–XVe siècles)* (Rome, 1977).

— *Les relations entre l'Orient et l'Occident au moyen âge: études et documents* (London, 1977).

— Une ambassade mongole à Paris en 1262. *Journal des Savants* 1979, 295–303. Reprinted in Richard, *Croisés, missionaries et voyageurs*.

— *Croisés, missionaries et voyageurs* (London, 1983).

— *Saint-Louis, roi d'une France feodale, soutien de la Terre Sainte* (Paris, 1983).

Richards, D. S. Ibn al-Athīr and the later parts of the *Kāmil*: a study of aims and methods. In Morgan, D. O. (ed.) *Medieval Historical Writing in the Christian and Islamic Worlds* (London, 1982), 76–108.

Romaskevich, A. A., Khetagurov, L. A. and Alizade, A. A. (eds) Rashīd al-Dīn, *Jāmiʿ al-tawārīkh* vol. 1, part 1 (Moscow, 1965).

Ronay, G. *The Tartar Khan's Englishman* (London, 1978).

Rossabi, M. *China and Inner Asia from 1368 to the Present Day* (London, 1975).

— Khubilai Khan and the women in his family. In Bauer, W. (ed.) *Sino-Mongolica: Festschrift für Herbert Franke* (Wiesbaden, 1979), 153–80.

— The Muslims in the early Yüan Dynasty. In Langlois, *China under Mongol Rule* (1981), 257–95.

— (ed.) *China among Equals: the Middle Kingdom and its Neighbors, 10th–14th Centuries* (Berkeley, Los Angeles and London, 1983).

Runciman, S. On the writing of history. In *The Historical Association 1906–1956* (London, 1957), 112–22.

Saunders, J. J. Matthew Paris and the Mongols. In Sandquist, T. A. and Powicke, M. R. (eds) *Essays in Medieval History Presented to Bertie Wilkinson* (Toronto, 1968), 116–32.

— *The History of the Mongol Conquests* (London, 1971).

— The Mongol defeat at Ain Jalut and the restoration of the Greek Empire. In his *Muslims and Mongols* (Christchurch, NZ, 1977), 67–76.

Sauvaget, J. *La poste aux chevaux dans l'empire des Mamelouks* (Paris, 1941).

Schein, S. Gesta Dei per Mongolos 1300. The genesis of a non-event. *English Historical Review* 94 (1979), 805–19.

Schurmann, H. F. *Economic Structure of the Yüan Dynasty* (Cambridge, Mass., 1956).

— Mongolian tributary practices of the thirteenth century. *Harvard Journal of Asiatic Studies* 14 (1956), 304–89.

— Problems of political organization during the Yüan Dynasty. In *25th International Congress of Orientalists, Moscow 1960* (Moscow, 1963), 26–31.

Ṣiddīqi, M. Z. al- (ed.) Sayfī Harawī, *Ta'rīkh-nāma-i Harāt* (Calcatta, 1944).

Sinor, D. Un voyageur du treizième siècle: le Dominicain Julien de Hongrie. *Bulletin of the School of Oriental and African Studies* 14/3 (1952), 589–602. Reprinted in Sinor, *Inner Asia*.

— Horse and pasture in Inner Asian history. *Oriens Extremus* 19 (1972), 171–84. Reprinted in Sinor, *Inner Asia*.

— The Mongols and Western Europe. In Setton, K. M. (ed.) *A History of the Crusades* vol. 3 (Madison, 1975), 513–44. Reprinted in Sinor, *Inner Asia*.

— *Inner Asia and its Contacts with Medieval Europe* (London, 1977).

— The Inner Asian warriors. *Journal of the American Oriental Society* 101/2 (1981), 133–44.

Skelton, R. A., Marston, T. E. and Painter, G. D. (eds and trs) *The Vinland Map and the Tartar Relation* (New Haven and London, 1965).

Smith, J. M., Jr Mongol and nomadic taxation. *Harvard Journal of Asiatic Studies* 30 (1970), 46–85.

— Mongol manpower and Persian population. *Journal of the Economic and Social History of the Orient* 18/3 (1975), 271–99.

— 'Ayn Jālūt: Mamlūk success or Mongol failure? *Harvard Journal of Asiatic Studies* 44/2 (1984), 307–45.

Southern, R. W. *Western Views of Islam in the Middle Ages* (Cambridge, Mass., 1962).

Spuler, B. *The Muslim World: a Historical Survey. Part II: The Mongol Period* (Leiden, 1960).

— *Die Goldene Horde: die Mongolen in Russland 1233–1502*, 2nd edn (Wiesbaden, 1965).

— *Die Mongolen in Iran*, 3rd edn (Berlin, 1968).

— *The Mongols in History* (London, 1971).

— *History of the Mongols* (London, 1972).

Sutūda, M. (ed.) Awliyā Allāh Āmulī, *Ta'rīkh-i Rūyān* (Tehran, 1969).

Thorau, P. The battle of 'Ayn Jālūt; a re-examination. In Edbury, P. W. (ed.) *Crusade and Settlement* (Cardiff, 1985), 236–41.

Tornberg, C. J. (ed.) Ibn al-Athīr, *Al-kāmil fī'l ta'rīkh* vol. 12 (Leiden, 1853).

Trevor-Roper, H. R. History and imagination. In Lloyd-Jones, H., Pearl, V., and Worden, B. (eds) *History and Imagination: Essays in Honour of H. R. Trevor-Roper* (London, 1981), 356–69.

Van Den Wyngaert, A. (ed.) *Sinica Franciscana* vol. 1 (Quaracchi and Florence, 1929).

Van Ess, J. *Der Wesir und seine Gelehrten* (Wiesbaden, 1981).

Van Loon, J. B. (ed. and tr.) Abū Bakr al-Quṭbī al-Aharī *Ta'rīkh-i Shaikh Uwais* (The Hague, 1954).

Vernadsky, G. *The Mongols and Russia* (New Haven and London, 1953).

Vladimirtsov, B. Y. *The Life of Chingis-Khan*, tr. Mirsky, D. S. (London, 1930).

— *Le régime social des Mongols*, tr. Carsow, M. (Paris, 1948).

Voegelin, E, The Mongol orders of submission to European powers, 1245–1255. *Byzantion* 15 (1940–1), 378–413.

Waldron, A. N. The problem of the Great Wall of China. *Harvard Journal of Asiatic Studies* 43/2 (1983), 643–63.

Waley, A. (tr.) *The travels of an Alchemist* (London, 1931).

— *The Secret History of the Mongols and Other Pieces* (London, 1963).

Watson, A. M. A medieval green revolution: new crops and farming techniques in the early Islamic world. In Udovitch, A. L. (ed.) *The Islamic Middle East, 700–1900: Studies in Economic and Social History* (Princeton, 1981), 29–58.

Wittfogel, K. A. and Fêng, C. *History of Chinese Society: Liao 907–1125* (Philadelphia, 1949).

Yarshater, E. Mazdakism. In Yarshater, E. (ed.) *The Cambridge History of Iran* vol. 3, *The Seleucid, Parthian and Sasanian Periods* (Cambridge, 1983), part 2, 991–1024.

Yule, H. and Cordier, H. (trs) *Cathay and the Way Thither*, 4 vols, Hakluyt Society (London, 1913–16).

Supplementary Bibliography

This bibliography lists the items discussed in Chapter 9, as well as a number of other publications of interest or significance which have become available since 1985. It makes no claim to be at all comprehensive.

Aigle, D. *Le Fārs sous la domination mongole. Politique et fiscalité (XIIIe–XIVe S.)* (Paris, 2005).
— (ed.) *L'Iran face à la domination mongole* (Tehran, 1997).
Allsen, T. T. *Mongol Imperialism. The Policies of the Grand Qan Möngke in China, Russia and the Islamic Lands, 1251–1259* (Berkeley, 1987).
— The Princes of the Left Hand: an introduction to the history of the *ulus* of Orda in the thirteenth and early fourteenth centuries. *Archivum Eurasiae Medii Aevi* 5 (1985 [1987]), 5–40.
— Mongolian princes and their merchant partners, 1200–1260. *Asia Major* 3rd series 2/2 (1989), 83–126.
— Notes on Chinese titles in Mongol Iran. *Mongolian Studies* 14 (1991), 27–39.
— Changing forms of legitimation in Mongol Iran. In Seaman and Marks, *Rulers from the Steppe*, 223–41.
— Two cultural brokers of medieval Eurasia: Bolad Aqa and Marco Polo. In Gervers, M. and Schlepp, W. (eds) *Nomadic Diplomacy, Destruction and Religion from the Pacific to the Adriatic* (Toronto, 1994), 63–78.
— The rise of the Mongolian empire and Mongolian rule in north China. In *Cambridge History of China* vol. 6, 321–413.
— Biography of a cultural broker. Bolad Ch'eng-Hsiang in China and Iran. In Raby and Fitzherbert, *The Court of the Il-khans*, 7–22.
— Ever closer encounters: the appropriation of culture and the apportionment of peoples in the Mongol Empire. *Journal of Early Modern History* 1/1 (1997), 2–23.
— *Commodity and Exchange in the Mongol Empire* (Cambridge, 1997).
— *Culture and Conquest in Mongol Eurasia* (Cambridge, 2001).
— *Technician Transfers in the Mongolian Empire* (Bloomington, 2002).

— The circulation of military technology in the Mongolian Empire. In Di Cosmo, *Warfare in Inner Asian History*, 265–93.

Amitai, R. Mongol raids into Palestine (A.D. 1260 and 1300). *Journal of the Royal Asiatic Society* (1987), 236–55.

— The conversion of Tegüder Ilkhan to Islam. *Jerusalem Studies in Arabic and Islam* 25 (2001), 15–43.

— Whither the Ilkhanid army? Ghazan's first campaign into Syria (1299–1300). In Di Cosmo, *Warfare in Inner Asian History*, 221–64.

— The resolution of the Mongol–Mamluk war. In Amitai and Biran, *Mongols, Turks and Others*, 359–90.

— and Biran, M. (eds) *Mongols, Turks and Others. Eurasian Nomads and the Sedentary World* (Leiden, 2005).

Amitai-Preiss, R. In the aftermath of 'Ayn Jālūt: the beginnings of the Mamlūk-Īlkhānid cold war. *Al-Masaq* 3 (1990), 1–21.

— An exchange of letters in Arabic between Abaγa Īlkhān and Sultan Baybars (A.H. 667/A.D. 1268–69). *Central Asiatic Journal* 38 (1994), 11–33.

— *Mongols and Mamluks. The Mamluk-Īlkhānid War, 1260–1281* (Cambridge, 1995).

— Ghazan, Islam and Mongol tradition. A view from the Mamlūk sultanate. *Bulletin of the School of Oriental and African Studies* 59 (1996), 1–10.

— New material from the Mamluk sources for the biography of Rashid al-Din. In Raby and Fitzherbert, *The Court of the Il-khans*, 23–37.

— Sufis and shamans: some remarks on the Islamization of the Mongols in the Ilkhanate. *Journal of the Economic and Social History of the Orient* 42 (1999), 27–46.

— Mongol imperial ideology and the Ilkhanid war against the Mamluks. In Amitai-Preiss and Morgan, *The Mongol Empire and its Legacy*, 57–72.

— and Morgan, D. O. (eds) *The Mongol Empire and its Legacy* (Leiden, 1999).

Aubin, J. Le *Quriltai* de Sultan-Maydan (1336). *Journal asiatique* 279 (1991), 175–97.

— *Emirs Mongols et vizirs persans dans les remous de l'acculturation* (Paris, 1995).

Barfield, T. J. *The Perilous Frontier. Nomadic Empires and China 221 BC to AD 1757* (Oxford, 1989).

Bentley, J. H. *Old World Encounters. Cross-Cultural Contacts and Exchanges in Pre-Modern Times* (New York and Oxford, 1993).

Bira, Sh. Qubilai Qa'an and 'Phags-pa bLama. In Amitai-Preiss and Morgan, *The Mongol Empire and its Legacy*, 240–9.

Biran, M. *Qaidu and the Rise of the Independent Mongol State in Central Asia* (Richmond, 1997).

— 'Like a mighty wall': the armies of the Qara Khitai. *Jerusalem Studies in Arabic and Islam* 25 (2001), 44–91.

— The Chaghadaids and Islam: the conversion of Tarmashirin Khan (1331–34). *Journal of the American Oriental Society* 122/4 (2002), 742–52.

— The Battle of Herat (1270): a case of inter-Mongol warfare. In Di Cosmo, *Warfare in Inner Asian History*, 175–219.

— The Mongol transformation: from the steppe to Eurasian empire. In Arnason, J. P. and Wittrock, B., *Eurasian Transformations, Tenth to Thirteenth Centuries* (Leiden, 2004), 339–61.

— True to their ways. Why the Qara Khitai did not convert to Islam. In Amitai and Biran, *Mongols, Turks and Others*, 175–99.

— *The Empire of the Qara Khitai in Eurasian History. Between China and the Islamic World* (Cambridge, 2005).

Blair, S. S. The Mongol capital of Sulṭāniyya, 'the Imperial'. *Iran* 24 (1986), 139–51.

— *The Ilkhanid Shrine Complex at Natanz, Iran* (Cambridge, Mass., 1986).

— *A Compendium of Chronicles. Rashid al-Din's Illustrated History of the World* (London, 1995).

— and Bloom, J. *The Art and Architecture of Islam, 1250–1800* (New Haven and London, 1994).

— Patterns of patronage and production in Ilkhanid Iran. The case of Rashid al-Din. In Raby and Fitzherbert, *The Court of the Il-khans*, 39–62.

Bold, B-O. *Mongolian Nomadic Society. A Reconstruction of the 'Medieval' History of Mongolia* (Richmond, 2001).

Boyle, J. A. (tr.) 'Ata-Malik Juvaini, *Genghis Khan. The History of the World Conqueror*, reprint of 1958 edition, in one vol., with new introduction and bibliography by D. O. Morgan (Manchester, 1997).

Buell, P. D. Mongol Empire and Turkicization: the evidence of food and foodways. In Amitai-Preiss and Morgan (eds) *The Mongol Empire and its Legacy*, 200–23.

— *Historical Dictionary of the Mongol World Empire* (Lanham and Oxford, 2003).

Cahen, C., tr. Holt, P. M. *The Formation of Turkey. The Seljukid Sultanate of Rum: Eleventh to Fourteenth Century* (Harlow, 2001).

Chambers, J. *Genghis Khan* (London, 1999).

Christian, D. *A History of Russia, Central Asia and Mongolia I. Inner Asia from Prehistory to the Mongol Empire* (Oxford, 1998).

Collins, L. J. D. On the alleged 'destruction' of the Great Horde in 1502. In Bryer, A. and Ursinus, M. (eds) *Manzikert to Lepanto. The Byzantine World and the Turks 1071–1571*, special issue of *Byzantinische Forschungen*, 1991, 361–99.

Critchley, J. *Marco Polo's Book* (Aldershot, 1992).

Dardess, J. Shun-ti and the end of Yüan rule in China. In *Cambridge History of China* vol. 6, 561–86.

De Hartog, L. *Genghis Khan, Conqueror of the World* (London, 1989: reprinted 2005, with introduction by D. O. Morgan).

— *Russia and the Mongol Yoke. The History of the Russian Principalities and the Golden Horde, 1221–1502* (London, 1996).

Supplementary Bibliography 221

De Rachewiltz, I. The title Činggis Qan/Qaγan re-examined. In Heissig, W. and Sagaster, K., *Gedanke und Wirkung. Festschrift zum 90. Geburtstag von Nikolaus Poppe* (Wiesbaden, 1989), 281–98.

— Some reflections on Činggis Qan's *Ĵasaγ. East Asian History* 6 (December 1993), 91–104.

— Marco Polo went to China. *Zentralasiastische Studien* 27 (1997), 34–92.

— (ed. and tr.) *The Secret History of the Mongols. A Mongolian Epic Chronicle of the Thirteenth Century*, 2 vols (Leiden, 2004).

— et al. (eds) *In the Service of the Khan. Eminent Personalities of the Early Mongol–Yüan Period* (Wiesbaden, 1993).

DeWeese, D. *Islamization and Native Religion in the Golden Horde. Baba Tükles and Conversion to Islam in Historical and Epic Tradition* (Philadelphia, 1994).

Di Cosmo, N. Mongols and merchants on the Black Sea frontier in the thirteenth and fourteenth centuries: convergences and conflicts. In Amitai and Biran, *Mongols, Turks and Others*, 391–424.

— (ed.) *Warfare in Inner Asian History (500–1800)* (Leiden, 2002).

Dunn, R. E. *The Adventures of Ibn Battuta. A Muslim Traveler of the 14th Century*, 2nd ed. (Berkeley, 2005).

Dunnel, R. The Hsia Hsia. In *Cambridge History of China* vol. 6, 154–214.

Endicott-West, E. *Mongolian Rule in China. Local Administration in the Yuan Dynasty* (Cambridge, Mass. and London, 1989).

— Merchant associations in Yüan China: the Ortoγ. *Asia Major* 3rd series 2/2 (1989), 127–54.

— The Yüan government and society. In *Cambridge History of China* vol. 6, 587–615.

— Notes on shamans, fortune-tellers and *Yin-Yang* practitioners and civil administration in Yüan China. In Amitai-Preiss and Morgan, *The Mongol Empire and its Legacy*, 224–39.

Farquhar, D. *The Government of China under Mongolian Rule. A Reference Guide* (Stuttgart, 1990).

Fitzherbert, T. Portrait of a lost leader. Jalal al-Din Kharazmshah and Juvaini. In Raby and Fitzherbert, *The Court of the Il-khans*, 63–77.

Fletcher, J. F. The Mongols: ecological and social perspectives. *Harvard Journal of Asiatic Studies* 46/1 (1986), 11–50.

Fragner, B. Iran under Ilkhanid rule in a world history perspective. In Aigle, *L'Iran face à la domination mongole*, 121–31.

Franke, H. *China under Mongol Rule* (Aldershot, 1994).

— The Chin dynasty. In *Cambridge History of China* vol. 6, 215–320.

Franke, H. and Twitchett, D. (eds) *The Cambridge History of China* vol. 6, *Alien Regimes and Border States 907–1368* (Cambridge, 1994).

Gazagnadou, D. *La poste à relais. La diffusion d'une technique de pouvoir à travers l'Eurasie, Chine–Islam–Europe* (Paris, 1994).

Golden, P. B. *An Introduction to the History of the Turkic Peoples* (Wiesbaden, 1992).

— 'I will give the people unto thee': the Činggisid conquests and their aftermath in the Turkic world. *Journal of the Royal Asiatic Society* 3rd series 10 (2000), 21–41.

Grabar, O. and Blair, S. *Epic Images and Contemporary History. The Illustrations of the Great Mongol Shahnama* (Chicago, 1980).

Gumilev, L. N. *Searches for an Imaginary Kingdom. The Legend of the Kingdom of Prester John* (Cambridge, 1987).

Haining, T. N. Storm from the East. A review article. *Journal of the Royal Asiatic Society* 3rd series 4/2 (1994), 251–4.

Halperin, C. *Russia and the Golden Horde. The Mongol Impact on Medieval Russian History* (Bloomington, 1985).

— *The Tatar Yoke* (Columbus, 1986).

Hawting, G. R. (ed.) *Mamluks, Mongols and Crusaders* (London and New York, 2005).

Heywood, C. J. Filling the Black Hole: the emergence of the Bithynian Atamanates. In Çiçek, K., et al. (eds) *The Great Ottoman-Turkish Civilisation* vol. 1 (Istanbul, 2000), 107–15.

Hoffmann, B. The gates of piety and charity. Rašīd al-dīn Faḍl Allah as founder of pious endowments. In Aigle, *L'Iran face à la domination mongole*, 189–201.

— *Waqf im mongolischen Iran. Rašīduddīns Sorge um Nachrum und Seelenheil* (Stuttgart, 2000).

Holt, P. M. The Īlkhān Aḥmad's embassies to Qalāwūn: two contemporary accounts. *Bulletin of the School of Oriental and African Studies* 49 (1986), 128–32.

Hsiao, C. Mid-Yüan politics. In *Cambridge History of China* vol. 6, 490–560.

Huang, S. The Persian language in China during the Yuan dynasty. *Papers in Far Eastern History* 34 (1986), 83–95.

Irwin, R. G. What the partridge told the eagle: a neglected Arabic source on Chinggis Khan and the early history of the Mongols. In Amitai-Preiss and Morgan, *The Mongol Empire and its Legacy*, 5–11.

Jackson, P. The crusade against the Mongols (1241). *Journal of Ecclesiastical History* 42/1 (1991), 1–18.

— William of Rubruck in the Mongol Empire: perception and prejudices. In von Martels, Z. (ed.) *Travel Fact and Travel Fiction* (Leiden, 1994), 54–71.

— Marco Polo and his 'Travels'. *Bulletin of the School of Oriental and African Studies* 61/1 (1998), 82–101. Reprinted in Hawting, *Mamluks, Mongols and Crusaders*.

— From *Ulus* to Khanate: the making of the Mongol states, c.1220–c.1290. In Amitai-Preiss and Morgan, *The Mongol Empire and its Legacy*, 12–38.

— The Mongols and Europe. In Abulafia, D. (ed.) *The New Cambridge Medieval History* vol. V: *c.1198–1300* (1999), 703–19.

— The state of research: the Mongol Empire, 1986–1999. *Journal of Medieval History* 26/2 (2000), 189–210.

— Medieval Christendom's encounter with the alien. *Historical Research* 74 (2001), 347–69.

— The Mongols and the faith of the conquered. In Amitai and Biran, *Mongols, Turks and Others*, 245–90.

— *The Mongols and the West, 1221–1410* (Harlow, 2005).

Jackson, P. (tr., and ed. with Morgan, D. O.) *The Mission of Friar William of Rubruck. His Journey to the Court of the Great Khan Möngke, 1253–1255.* Hakluyt Society (London, 1990).

Jagchid, S. *Essays in Mongolian Studies* (Provo, 1988).

Jagchid, S. and Symons, V. J. *Peace, War and Trade along the Great Wall* (Bloomington, 1989).

Kahn, P. (tr.) *The Secret History of the Mongols. The Origin of Chingis Khan,* 2nd ed. (Boston, 1998).

Kappler, C. and R. (tr.) *Guillaume de Rubrouck. Voyage dans l'Empire Mongol (1253–1255)* (Paris, 1985).

Kennedy, H. *Mongols, Huns and Vikings* (London, 2002).

Khazanov, A. M. *Nomads and the Outside World,* 2nd ed. (Madison, 1994).

Khazanov, A. M. and Wink, A. (eds) *Nomads in the Sedentary World* (Richmond, 2001).

Kim, H. A reappraisal of Güyüg Khan. In Amitai and Biran, *Mongols, Turks and Others,* 309–38.

Klopprogge, A. *Ursprung und Ausprägung des abendländischen Mongolenbildes im 13. Jahrhundert* (Wiesbaden, 1993).

Kolbas, J. *The Mongols in Iran. Chingiz Khan to Uljaytu 1220–1309* (London and New York, 2006).

Komaroff, L. (ed.) *Beyond the Legacy of Genghis Khan* (Leiden, 2006).

Komaroff, L. and Carboni, S. (eds) *The Legacy of Genghis Khan. Courtly Art and Culture in Western Asia, 1256–1353* (New York, New Haven and London, 2002).

Lambton, A. K. S. Mongol fiscal administration in Persia, 2 parts. *Studia Islamica* 64–5 (1986–7), 79–99, 97–123.

— *Continuity and Change in Medieval Persia. Aspects of Administrative, Economic and Social History, 11th–14th Century* (New York and London, 1988).

— Changing concepts of justice and injustice from the 5th/11th century to the 8th/14th century in Persia: the Saljuq empire and the Ilkhanate. *Studia Islamica* 68 (1988), 27–60.

— *Awqāf* in Persia: 6th–8th/12th–14th centuries. *Islamic Law and Society* 4/3 (1997), 298–318.

— The *Āthār wa Aḥyā'* of Rashīd al-Dīn Faḍl Allāh Hamadānī and his contribution as an agronomist, arboriculturist and horticulturist. In Amitai-Preiss and Morgan (eds) *The Mongol Empire and its Legacy,* 126–54.

Lane, G. Arghun Aqa: Mongol bureaucrat. *Iranian Studies* 32/4 (1999), 459–82.

— *Early Mongol Rule in Thirteenth-Century Iran. A Persian Renaissance* (London and New York, 2003).

— *Genghis Khan and Mongol Rule* (Westport and London, 2004).

— *Daily Life in the Mongol Empire* (Westport and London, 2006).

Langdon, J. S. Byzantium's initial encounter with the Chinggisids: an introduction to the Byzantino-Mongolica. *Viator* 29 (1998), 95–140.

Larner, J. *Marco Polo and the Discovery of the World* (New Haven and London, 1999).

Lindner, R. P. How Mongol were the early Ottomans? In Amitai-Preiss and Morgan, *The Mongol Empire and its Legacy*, 282–9.

Lovell, J. *The Great Wall. China against the World 1000 BC–AD 2000* (New York, 2006).

Man, J. *Genghis Khan. Life, Death and Resurrection* (London, 2004).

Manz, B. F. *The Rise and Rule of Tamerlane* (Cambridge, 1989).

— Nomad and settled in the Timurid military. In Amitai and Biran, *Mongols, Turks and Others*, 425–57.

Martin, J. *Treasure of the Land of Darkness. The Fur Trade and its Significance for Medieval Russia* (Cambridge, 1986).

— *Medieval Russia 980–1584* (Cambridge, 1995).

May, T. M. The Mongol presence and impact in the lands of the eastern Mediterranean. In Kagay, D. J. and Villalon, L. J. A., *Crusaders, Condottieri and Cannon. Medieval Warfare in Societies around the Mediterranean* (Leiden, 2003), 133–56.

— A Mongol–Isma'īlī alliance? Thoughts on the Mongols and the Assassins. *Journal of the Royal Asiatic Society* 3rd series 14/3 (2004), 231–9.

Marshall, R. *Storm from the East. From Genghis Khan to Khubilai Khan* (London, 1993).

Melville, C. P. *Pādshāh-i Islām*: the conversion of Sultan Maḥmūd Ghāzān Khān. In Melville (ed.) *Pembroke Papers I. Persian and Islamic Studies in Honour of P.W. Avery* (Cambridge, 1990), 159–77.

— Wolf or shepherd? Amir Chupan's attitude to government. In Raby and Fitzherbert, *The Court of the Il-Khans*, 79–93.

— Abū Sa'īd and the revolt of the amirs in 1319. In Aigle, *L'Iran face à la domination mongole*, 89–120.

— The Īlkhān Öljeitü's conquest of Gīlān (1307): rumour and reality. In Amitai-Preiss and Morgan, *The Mongol Empire and its Legacy*, 73–125.

— *The Fall of Amir Chupan and the Decline of the Ilkhanate, 1327–37. A Decade of Discord in Mongol Iran* (Bloomington, 1999).

Morgan, D. O. The Mongols and the eastern Mediterranean. In Arbel, B. et al. (eds) *Latins and Greeks in the Eastern Mediterranean after 1204* (London, 1989), 198–211.

— The problems of writing Mongolian history. In Akiner, S. (ed.) *Mongolia Today* (London, 1991), 1–8.

— Persian perceptions of Mongols and Europeans. In Schwartz, S. B. (ed.) *Implicit Understandings. Observing, Reporting and Reflecting on the Encounters between Europeans and Other Peoples in the Early Modern Era* (Cambridge, 1994), 201–17.

— Marco Polo in China – or not. *Journal of the Royal Asiatic Society* 3rd Series 6 (1996), 221–5.

— Prester John and the Mongols. In Beckingham, C. F. and Hamilton, B., *Prester John, the Mongols and the Ten Lost Tribes* (Aldershot, 1996), 159–70.

— Mongol or Persian: the government of Ilkhanid Iran. *Harvard Middle Eastern and Islamic Review* 3, 1/2 (1996), 62–76.

— Rašīd al-dīn and Ġazan Khan. In Aigle, *L'Iran face à la domination mongole*, 179–88.

— Reflections on Mongol communications in the Ilkhanate. In C. Hillenbrand (ed.) *The Sultan's Turret* (Leiden, 1999), 375–85.

— Ibn Baṭṭūṭa and the Mongols. *Journal of the Royal Asiatic Society* 3rd series 11/1 (2001), 1–11.

— The Mongols in Iran: a reappraisal. *Iran* 42 (2004), 131–6.

— The 'Great *Yasa* of Chinggis Khan' revisited. In Amitai and Biran, *Mongols, Turks and Others*, 291–308.

— The decline and fall of the Mongol Empire. In Cummings, S. and Kennedy, H., *Empire and After* (forthcoming).

Morton, A. H. The Letters of Rashīd al-Dīn: Īlkhānid fact or Timurid fiction? In Amitai-Preiss and Morgan, *The Mongol Empire and its Legacy*, 155–99.

Mote, F. W. Chinese society under Mongol rule, 1215–1368. In *Cambridge History of China* vol. 6, 616–64.

— *Imperial China 900–1800* (Cambridge, Mass. and London, 1999).

Onon, U. (tr.) *The History and the Life of Chinggis Khan* (Leiden, 1990).

—- (tr.) *The Secret History of the Mongols. The Life and Times of Chinggis Khan* (London, 2001).

Ostrowski, D. *Muscovy and the Mongols. Cross-Cultural Influences on the Steppe Frontier, 1304–1589* (Cambridge, 1998).

Paviot, J. Les marchands italiens dans l'Iran mongol. In Aigle, *L'Iran face à la domination mongole*, 71–86.

— England and the Mongols (c.1260–1330). *Journal of the Royal Asiatic Society* 3rd series 10/3 (2000), 305–18.

Petech, L. *Central Tibet and the Mongols. The Yüan–Sa-skya Period of Tibetan History* (Rome, 1990).

Pfeiffer, J. Conversion versions: Sultan Öljeytü's conversion to Shi'ism (709/1309) in Muslim narrative sources. *Mongolian Studies* 22 (1999), 35–67.

Phillips, J. R. S. *The Medieval Expansion of Europe*, 2nd ed. (Oxford, 1998).

Potter, L. G. Sufis and Sultans in post-Mongol Iran. *Iranian Studies* 27/1–4 (1994), 77–102.

Raby, J. and Fitzherbert, T. (eds) *The Court of the Il-khans 1290–1340*. Oxford Studies in Islamic Art, XII (Oxford, 1996).

Ratchnevsky, P., tr. and ed. Haining, T. N. *Genghis Khan. His Life and Legacy* (Oxford, 1991).

Richard, J. D'Älgigidäi à Ġazan: la continuité d'une politique franque chez les Mongols d'Iran. In Aigle, *L'Iran face à la domination mongole*, 57–69.

— *Au-delà de la Perse et de l'Armenie. L'Orient latin et la découverte de l'Asie Intérieure* (Turnhout, 2005).

Rossabi, M. *Khubilai Khan. His Life and Times* (Berkeley, 1988). Reprinted with revisions (London, 2005).

— *Voyager from Xanadu. Rabban Sauma and the First Journey from China to the West* (Tokyo, New York and London, 1992).

— The reign of Khubilai khan. In *Cambridge History of China* vol. 6, 414–89.

Roux, J-P. *Genghis Khan and the Mongol Empire* (London, 2003).

Ruotsala, A. *Europeans and Mongols in the Middle of the Thirteenth Century. Encountering the Other* (Helsinki, 2001).

Ryan, J. D. Christian wives of Mongol khans: Tartar queens and missionary expectations in Asia. *Journal of the Royal Asiatic Society* 3rd series 8/3 (1998), 411–21.

Schmieder, F. *Europa und die Fremden. Die Mongolen im Urteil des Abendlandes vom 13. bis in das 15. Jahrhundert* (Sigmaringen, 1994).

Seaman, G. and Marks, D. (eds) *Rulers from the Steppe. State Formation on the Eurasian Periphery* (Los Angeles, 1991).

Sinclair, T. The economy of Armenia under the Il-Khans. *Journal of the Society for Armenian Studies* 11 (2000), 39–52.

Sinor, D. Notes on Inner Asian bibliography IV: history of the Mongols in the 13th century. *Journal of Asian History* 23/1 (1989), 26–79.

— The Mongols in the West. *Journal of Asian History* 33/1 (1991), 1–44.

Smith, J. M., Jr Demographic considerations in Mongol siege warfare. *Archivum Ottomanicum* 13 (1993/4), 329–34.

— The Mongols and world-conquest. *Mongolica* 5(26) (1994), 206–14.

— Mongol society and military in the Middle East: antecedents and adaptations. In Lev, Y. (ed.) *War and Society in the Eastern Mediterranean, 7th–15th Centuries* (Leiden, 1997), 249–66.

— Nomads on ponies *vs.* slaves on horses (a review article of Amitai-Preiss, *Mongols and Mamluks*). *Journal of the American Oriental Society* 118/1 (1998), 54–62.

— Mongol nomadism and Middle Eastern geography: qīshlāqs and tümens. In Amitai-Preiss and Morgan, *The Mongol Empire and its Legacy*, 39–56.

— Dietary decadence and dynastic decline in the Mongol Empire. *Journal of Asian History* 34 (2000), 35–52.

Sotoodeh, M. and Afshar, I. (eds) Rashīd al-Dīn, *Āthār wa Aḥyā'* (Tehran, 1989).

Soudavar, A. The Saga of Abu-Sa'id Bahador Khan. In Raby and Fitzherbert, *The Court of the Il-khans*, 95–218.

— In defense of Rašīd-od-dīn and his Letters. *Studia Iranica* 32 (2003), 77–122.

Thackston, W. (tr.) Rashiduddin Fazlullah's *Jami'u't-tawarikh. Compendium of Chronicles*, 3 vols (Cambridge, Mass., 1998–9).

Togan, A. Z. V., tr. Leiser, G. Economic conditions in Anatolia in the Mongol period. *Annales Islamologiques* 25 (1991), 203–40.

Togan, I. *Flexibility and Limitation in Steppe Formations. The Kerait Khanate and Chinggis Khan* (Leiden, 1998).

Tyler-Smith, C., et al. The genetic legacy of the Mongols. *American Journal of Human Genetics* 72 (17 January 2003).

Waldron, A. N. *The Great Wall of China. From History to Myth* (Cambridge, 1990).

Weatherford, J. *Genghis Khan and the Making of the Modern World* (New York, 2004).

Weiers, M. (ed.) *Die Mongolen. Beiträge zu ihrer Geschichte und Kultur* (Darmstadt, 1986).

Wood, F. *Did Marco Polo go to China?* (London, 1995).

Yinsheng, L. War and peace between the Yuan dynasty and the Chaghadaid Khanate (1312–1323). In Amitai and Biran, *Mongols, Turks and Others*, 339–58.

Chronology of Events

1253–5	Journey of William of Rubruck to Mongolia
1253	Hülegü's forces set off for Persia
1255	Death of Batu, first Khān of Golden Horde
1256	Hülegü takes Assassin castles in north Persia
1257	Accession of Berke, Khān of Golden Horde
1258	Fall of Baghdad to Hülegü. Death of last 'Abbasid Caliph'
1259	Death of Möngke
1260	Hülegü invades Syria, then withdraws. Battle of 'Ayn Jālūt. Rival *quriltais* elect Qubilai and Ariq-böke as Great Khān: civil war ensues
1261/2	Outbreak of warfare between Hülegü and Berke
1264	Qubilai victorious over Ariq-böke
1265	Death of Hülegü, first Ilkhān. Accession of Abaqa
1266	Building begins at new Mongol capital of China, Ta-tu (Peking)
1267	Death of Berke, Khān of Golden Horde
1271	Marco Polo, with his father and uncle, sets off for China (arrives 1275)
1272	Qubilai adopts Chinese dynastic title, Yüan
1274	First Mongol expedition against Japan
1276	Hang-chou, capital of Sung Empire, falls to Mongols
1279	End of Sung resistance to Mongols
1281	Second Mongol expedition against Japan
1287	Rabban Ṣaumā sent to Europe by Īlkhān Arghun
1294	Death of Qubilai. Arrival of John of Monte Corvino in China
1295	Accession of Ghazan as Īlkhān. Mongols in Persia become Muslim
1299–1300	Major Mongol invasion of Syria: briefly occupied by Ilkhanid forces
1304	Death of Īlkhān Ghazan. Accession of Ōljeitü
1313	Accession of Özbeg, under whose rule Golden Horde becomes Muslim
1335	Death of Abū Sa'īd, last Īlkhān of line of Hülegü
1346	Outbreak of Black Death in Mongol force besieging Kaffa, in the Crimea: from there it spreads to Europe
1353–4	Major outbreak of disease in China
1368	Mongols driven from China by Ming forces
1370	Death in Qaraqorum of Toghon Temür, last Yüan emperor

Dynastic Tables

The Great Khāns

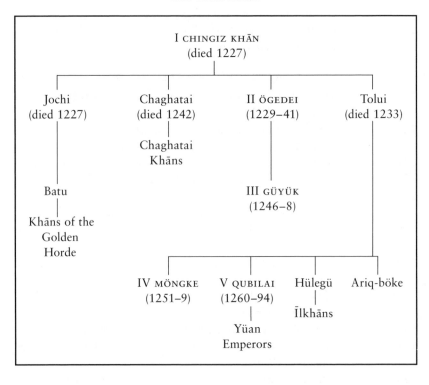

Yüan Emperors of China

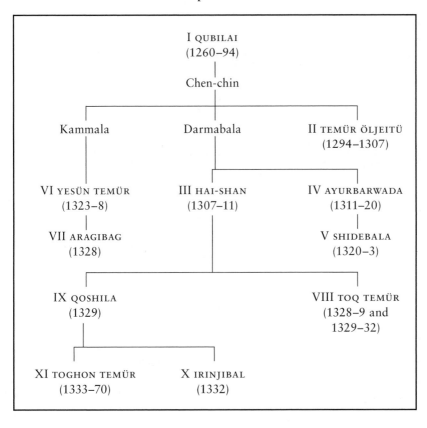

Khāns of the Golden Horde

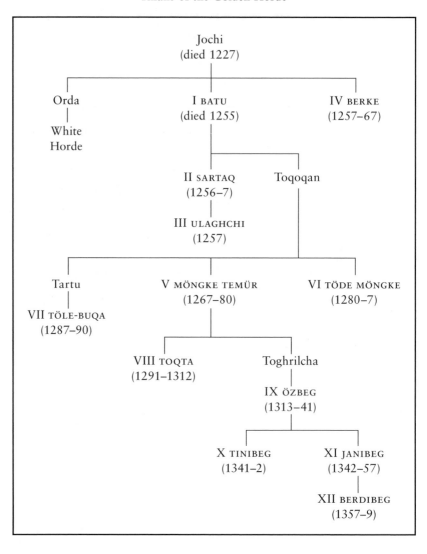

Jochi
(died 1227)

Orda

White
Horde

I BATU
(died 1255)

IV BERKE
(1257–67)

II SARTAQ
(1256–7)

Toqoqan

III ULAGHCHI
(1257)

Tartu

VII TÖLE-BUQA
(1287–90)

V MÖNGKE TEMÜR
(1267–80)

VI TÖDE MÖNGKE
(1280–7)

VIII TOQTA
(1291–1312)

Toghrilcha

IX ÖZBEG
(1313–41)

X TINIBEG
(1341–2)

XI JANIBEG
(1342–57)

XII BERDIBEG
(1357–9)

Īlkhāns of Persia

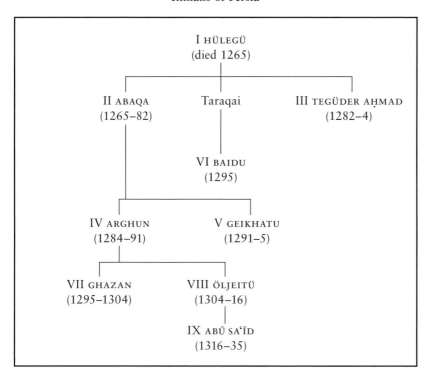

I HÜLEGÜ
(died 1265)

II ABAQA
(1265–82)

Taraqai

III TEGÜDER AḤMAD
(1282–4)

VI BAIDU
(1295)

IV ARGHUN
(1284–91)

V GEIKHATU
(1291–5)

VII GHAZAN
(1295–1304)

VIII ÖLJEITÜ
(1304–16)

IX ABŪ SAʿĪD
(1316–35)

Index